Architectural Design with SketchUp

Architectural Design with SketchUp

3D Modeling, Extensions, BIM, Rendering, Making, and Scripting

Second Edition

Alexander C. Schreyer

Cover image: Alexander C. Schreyer
Cover design: Wiley

This book is printed on acid-free paper. ∞

Copyright © 2016 by John Wiley & Sons, Inc. All rights reserved.

Published by John Wiley & Sons, Inc., Hoboken, New Jersey.

Published simultaneously in Canada.

For general information about our other products and services, please contact our Customer Care Department within the United States at (800) 762-2974, outside the United States at (317) 572-3993 or fax (317) 572-4002.

Wiley publishes in a variety of print and electronic formats and by print-on-demand. Some material included with standard print versions of this book may not be included in e-books or in print-on-demand. If this book refers to media such as a CD or DVD that is not included in the version you purchased, you may download this material at http://booksupport.wiley.com. For more information about Wiley products, visit www.wiley.com.

ISBN 978-1-118-97881-8 (paperback)—ISBN 978-1-118-97884-9 (pdf)—ISBN 978-1-118-97883-2 (epub)

Printed in the United States of America

10 9 8 7 6 5 4 3 2 1

For my father, Gerhard
(First Edition)
For my mother, Rosemarie
(Second Edition)

Contents

Preface

What a difference a few years make! In the time since the first edition of this book was conceived, SketchUp and everyone who makes it left Google and joined Trimble, a company until then mostly known for GPS technology for construction (and other related fields), and Tekla, a steel-design software from Finland. In the meantime, Trimble has integrated SketchUp into many of its work areas and is actively pursuing a broadening of its software offerings. Case in point being the acquisition of Gehry Technologies and its software products.

All of this came along with significant performance increases for SketchUp and the integration of substantial BIM-elements into the software. SketchUp also received an online Extension Warehouse as an easy means for users to find and acquire extensions that add capabilities to SketchUp. 3D Warehouse, an online repository for SketchUp models, has also received a major upgrade, and it now features a WebGL online 3D file viewer.

In the same timeframe, the maker-movement has gone into overdrive, leading to many "maker spaces" where people combine advanced yet cost-efficient fabrication techniques with electronics and programming to create fully functional prototypes of technology-based objects in a much shorter time and at a lower cost than was heretofore possible. 3D modeling has become an essential part of this process during digital prototyping and prefabrication steps (e.g., for 3D printing).

This second edition of *Architectural Design with SketchUp* pays heed to these developments. SketchUp's new capabilities have been highlighted mainly in chapters 2, 3, and 4. Where applicable, the updated Ruby scripting environment is reflected in chapter 7. While the title of this book retains its architecture focus, much of the content is now also applicable to many of the construction uses that come along with Trimble's application of this software.

An entirely new chapter 6, on making with SketchUp, has also been introduced. It covers the most common fabrication techniques in use with SketchUp (3D printing, laser cutting, CNC routing, and fabrication planning) to give the reader step-by-step instructions on using these in his or her work.

This edition, in other words, incorporates the many "faces" of SketchUp to an even greater degree than the previous edition. It provides an essential desk reference for any SketchUp user and a thorough and well-organized learning sourcebook for those that seek to enhance their knowledge of this software.

Acknowledgments

Having taught SketchUp to varied audiences of eager students, I should start my acknowledgments with exactly those students whose many questions and creative ideas have inspired me not only to look deeper into the software but also to put this text down on paper. To them I say: *Keep pushing the boundaries of the third dimension in your work!*

An amazing product can often be judged by the community that develops around it. SketchUp has always been a small, yet transformative piece of software, whose simplicity and power have enthralled users for many years. This has created a large user community, which in forums, in blogs, at user meetings, and at other venues has—often passionately—taken to using it to design whatever comes to their creative minds and educating others in how to use it to realize their ideas. I would like to acknowledge that community for its devotion, support, and inventiveness, and I am with this book paying forward any support they ever gave me.

Among the makers of SketchUp, I would like to foremost thank SketchUp product manager John Bacus, former product evangelist Aidan Chopra, marketing lead Mark Harrison, and education manager Allyson McDuffie for their feedback whenever I had a request—*and of course for the great time I had at Basecamp.*

This book would not have been possible without the support and feedback from acquisitions editor Paul Drougas and editor Seth Schwartz at John Wiley & Sons. This being my first book endeavor, I am still in awe of the amount of work that the editorial team puts into a publication like this. In particular, I would like to acknowledge production editor David Sassian's tireless suggestions of edits and revisions as well as copyeditor Kathy Grider-Carlyle's and editorial assistant Mike New's help in this process (as well as Nancy Cintron and Ginny Carroll, for the first edition). Judging by the editing initials in the manuscript, it passed through many more hands whose anonymous work I hereby gratefully acknowledge.

Finally—and most importantly—I would like to thank the love of my life, my wonderful wife Peggi, for her tremendous encouragement and constant support, and our two girls, Sophia and Mackenzie, for their patience with me while I was preparing the manuscript. I couldn't have done it without them! They are, together with my mother and my brother, the source of all my strength and joy.

Chapter 1
Introduction

During my years of teaching SketchUp, as well as other Computer-Aided Design (CAD) and Building Information Modeling (BIM) software, I have seen many very proficient users of this software. Students and professionals take easily to SketchUp, and, before long, most of them produce very detailed building models and professional-grade renderings. But I have also found that too many people don't go beyond the basics and believe that some of the advanced modeling (or good-quality photorealistic rendering) needs to be done using other software. Very often, they painstakingly pick up that other software only to find that it is too complex, which likewise leaves them unable to do what they wanted.

Sometimes even advanced users of SketchUp master one aspect of the software (photorealistic rendering, for example) but are completely unaware of the power that SketchUp holds in other areas—Dynamic Components and Ruby scripting are good examples. As you will find out in this book, SketchUp is a very powerful design and 3D modeling tool. Some of its core features—for example, its extendibility with *extensions* (these are sometimes also called *plugins*)—make it flexible enough to be useful for a variety of disciplines. The large number of high-quality extensions that are currently available for SketchUp bears powerful witness to this.

This book attempts to help the basic to intermediate user make the leap from simply creating "something" in SketchUp to using it as a powerful design tool. It also contains some more advanced topics (such as photorealistic rendering, Dynamic Components, BIM, and Ruby scripting) and provides a clear learning path that takes the reader through easy-to-follow examples to a thorough understanding of the core topics. **Figure 1.1** shows an example of how you could use Ruby scripting to create geometry, then render the scene using photorealistic rendering software, and finally "dress up" the image as a watercolor painting.

About This Book

Each chapter in this book presents a different SketchUp use in sufficient detail to get you started and working quickly. Interspersed with the text are many step-by-step examples, tips, and in-depth articles. At the end of each chapter, you will also find a collection of activities that you can undertake to try out new skills that you just learned.

Figure 1.1: Digital watercolor of a rendering of script-generated panels

Chapter 2, which follows this introductory chapter, brings every reader up to speed. Its purpose as a "SketchUp Refresher" is to review most of the basic modeling techniques and teach good practices for 3D modeling and software use. While many readers will already have some knowledge of SketchUp through introductory books or video tutorials, this chapter encompasses enough variety to be useful for everyone, independent of their skill level. In addition to modeling, this chapter covers materials, program setup and user interface, custom templates, geo-based modeling, and plan-based modeling.

Chapter 3 uses SketchUp not only as a modeling tool but also as a tool to inform your designs. In this chapter, you will learn more ways to efficiently work with SketchUp and add data and design intelligence to your models. Examples of this are creating hierarchical, component-based models (e.g., for virtual construction), using Dynamic Components and parametric design, and working with SketchUp's Classifier system. This chapter also lays out how SketchUp can fit into a BIM-based architectural design process.

Chapter 4 leads you into the wide field of SketchUp extensions and their uses. After an introductory section on finding and installing extensions, many individual extensions are discussed. Those small software add-ons to SketchUp provide tools for general modeling, such as drawing splines and lofting curves; tools for architectural design, such as stair making and wood framing; and tools for digital fabrication that will help you prepare your model for 2D and 3D digital printing and assembly. (See **Figure 1.2** for an example of a fabricated SketchUp model.) Furthermore, there are extensions for data integration that can import or export data such as Laser Imaging, Detection and Ranging (LIDAR) laser-scan points; extensions for animation and presentation that add object animation or serve as helpers for creating animations and walk-throughs using SketchUp; and, finally, extensions for analysis, which provide analytical tools—mainly from the field of building energy analysis and green building.

Chapter 5 introduces photorealistic rendering and covers all aspects of rendering in detail (see **Figure 1.3** and **Figure 1.4**). This chapter was written to be as independent of your actual choice of rendering software as possible, thereby providing a useful resource no matter which software you end up getting. As part of this chapter, you will learn about modeling for rendering, lighting, sky environment, materials, and objects, as well as how to edit and modify renderings for final presentation using image-editing software.

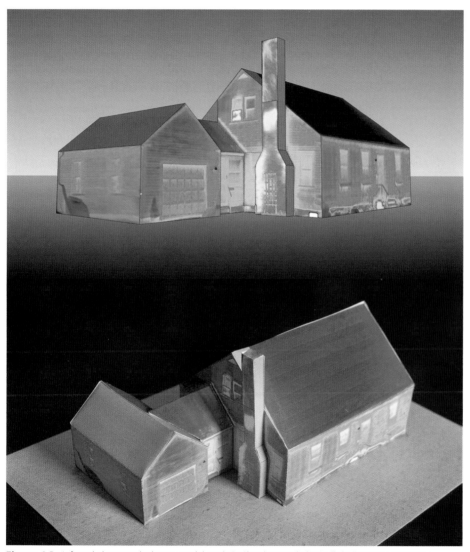

Figure 1.2: Infrared photography house model made in SketchUp and physically built using extensions

Figure 1.3: A night rendering of the cover scene

Figure 1.4: A grassy hill modeled and rendered in SketchUp

Chapter 6 lays out how SketchUp can be used for digital fabrication. While SketchUp has always been used to fabricate buildings, this was typically accomplished with a manual process (employing workers) and analog intermediaries (construction documents). Digital fabrication (as employed in cut preparation, 3D printing, laser cutting, CNC routing, etc.) uses the full precision that the computer provides from concept to final product. This approach offers many new and exciting possibilities (see **Figure 1.5** for an example), and this chapter provides you with step-by-step instructions on how to use these techniques with SketchUp.

Figure 1.5: SketchUp's CNC-cut WikiHouse pavilion for the 2013 New York Maker Faire *(Used by permission of Trimble Navigation Ltd.)*

The final chapter in this book (Chapter 7) introduces you to the exciting field of computational geometry in SketchUp. This chapter presents Ruby script examples that create undulating brick walls, solar-responsive facades, attractor-based colorful building designs, and other fun ways to create geometry in SketchUp without excessive use of the mouse (see **Figure 1.1** or the paneling on the title cover for examples). Most of the script examples accomplish their tasks in just a few lines of code, and all are good introductions to both the Ruby scripting language and the general field of computational geometry.

Chapter 7 can also serve as a "learn to code" curriculum for young or adult readers. It introduces basic programming concepts and applies them in a way that yields 3D models. It should be quite exciting for the learner that the results from this approach can even be 3D printed and, therefore, turned into physical objects.

As you will see in the chapters that follow, this book is intended to serve as a textbook as well as a desk reference. It was written to convey the presented material in a thorough yet easy-to-follow manner. It also covers common tasks using a cookbook approach, which allows you to simply copy the procedure to get a satisfactory result or modify it according to your individual needs.

In addition to reading this book, keep checking its companion website, which features news, tutorials, links, videos, and downloads related to this book. You can also interact there with the author and other SketchUp users and discuss any issues you may run into. Web links will be frequently updated there, and new ones added as new software is released.

This book's companion sites can be found here:

www.sketchupfordesign.com—Author's interactive companion site.

www.wiley.com/go/schreyer2e—Companion site for classroom use.

3D for All

Because SketchUp is not domain-specific, it has found a following with professionals and enthusiasts from many disciplines. This is why you will find SketchUp mentioned in discussions not only by architects, landscape architects, urban planners, engineers, construction professionals, woodworkers, and timber framers but also by robot builders, artists, sculptors, model-plane builders, paper-plane builders, mapmakers, historians, 3D game developers, and movie set designers (just to mention a few).

The techniques in this book are applicable to a variety of disciplines. Although many examples come from architecture or construction, some are from other disciplines (e.g., landscape design and interior design). Whatever your background is, feel free to take the examples that are presented here and adapt them to your discipline. (See **Figure 1.6** for a nontraditional use of SketchUp). The techniques you learn will be equally useful.

Taking this one step further, I can even say that I can't think of anyone who should *not* be using SketchUp. Living in a three-dimensional world and dealing with three-dimensional objects, everyone has the need at some point to model and visualize virtually in three-dimensional space.

Consider this hypothetical situation: You want to build a deck in your backyard and need to explain to the builder how it should look. Another example is a scientist who needs to explain a lab setup in a presentation. Far too often we resort to 2D representations of our thoughts (the classic floor plan, for example), which leaves too much unknown and unexplorable.

Admittedly, many people are not trained in hand-sketching in 3D, which often leads to poor visualizations of things that can actually be quite interesting when presented properly. *That* is where SketchUp shines. Its 3D modeling capabilities and its ease of use make it a simple yet very powerful tool for anyone to give shape to their thoughts.

Figure 1.6: Rendered 3D QR-code model

How Does SketchUp Fit into the Designer's Toolbox?

As a professional or student, you likely already have assembled a sizable software "tool chest" by now. Depending on your discipline, this might include office software, CAD software, image-editing software, print layout software, analysis software (for energy or structural analysis, for example), coordination tools, and many others.

SketchUp fits into this collection very well. While the free SketchUp Make provides a complete 3D modeling tool set for the hobbyist, the commercial SketchUp Pro broadens this further by adding layout and documentation abilities and other professional-oriented tools, such as multiformat import/export and BIM capabilities.

Depending on your needs and knowledge of the software, you can use it as an early design tool—after all, as its name indicates, it was developed for 3D sketching. In that capacity, it shines by providing easy editing and immediate 3D visualization (see **Figure 1.7**)—something that can be very useful during quick design iterations.

You can also use it for the complete design process from initial stages to a finished product (whatever that may be—buildings, gadgets, etc.). For that case, it provides the capability to create precise, organized models that can contain any level of data. Those models can then be used as the basis for construction or production documents (with SketchUp Pro's LayOut software) and/or be exported for digital-process-based fabrication, such as CNC routing.

Figure 1.7: Architectural design visualization model *(Image used with permission of Leers Weinzapfel Associates)*

SketchUp also works well with other software. 3D models from SketchUp can often be opened directly in those programs, making data exchange easy. Even if that isn't available, SketchUp's built-in file exchange options allow you to export a 3D model in a variety of formats. As shown in **Figure 1.8**, built-in services and extensions exist that connect SketchUp to online collaboration platforms where you can share your models with only a few clicks.

Figure 1.8: Trimble's Connect platform for construction collaboration and file exchange *(Used by permission of Trimble Navigation Ltd.)*

If SketchUp is already part of your tool set, then the best use of your time will be to expand on the skills you have developed already and deepen your knowledge of this software. This book provides you many avenues to do so.

Windows or Mac, Pro or Make?

SketchUp comes in a variety of flavors: While SketchUp Pro is the core commercial product, Trimble maintains (and has expressed its ongoing commitment to) a free "Make" version. Both are multiplatform software, which means they are available for both Windows and Mac computers. In addition, SketchUp has viewers for computers (both platforms), and Apple and Android tablets and phones.

The free version, SketchUp Make, is geared toward hobbyists, makers, and private 3D modelers. While it comes with a significant subset of the 3D modeling functionality included in the Pro version, its license limits it to noncommercial uses, and it does not include the LayOut presentation software. It is, however, capable of COLLADA and KMZ import/export, which is useful for makers, and it allows for installation of (most) extensions, including rendering applications.

The commercial version, SketchUp Pro, adds a variety of professional-oriented features:

- LayOut software for drawing-preparation and presentations
- Style Builder software for creating custom sketchy lines
- DWG/DXF import/export
- PDF, EPS, 3DS, IFC, FBX, OBJ, XSI, VRML export
- BIM classifier
- IFC import/export
- Component-based report-generation
- Dynamic Component authoring
- Solid Tools for Boolean modeling

Many of these features allow the professional SketchUp user to integrate it into their workflow by making it easier to exchange data with CAD software (such as Autodesk AutoCAD), BIM software (like Autodesk Revit), online collaboration platforms (like Trimble Connect), and presentation software (e.g., Adobe Illustrator). Modeling and workflow enhancements (such as the ability to create Dynamic Components) also provide the professional user with the capability to create and disseminate product-model databases that facilitate planning and estimating tasks.

LayOut, which comes with SketchUp Pro, has the ability to replace other drawing- and presentation-creation software, enabling you to keep that aspect of your workflow tightly aligned with SketchUp. 3D models created in SketchUp are always live-linked in LayOut so that updates propagate through the entire drawing set.

While the free Make version just requires a download, at the time of writing, the Pro version was priced at $590 (in the United States), which includes one year of upgrades and costs $95 per year thereafter. Both versions are currently available in a multitude of languages, which gives this software global reach. At this point, qualified students can get a time-limited license to use SketchUp Pro for $49 (also U.S. pricing). You can find out more about these purchase options on their website: www.sketchup.com.

Depending on your needs, you have to decide which version is right for you. If you use SketchUp only for noncommercial projects or for training and you have no need for any of the aforementioned Pro features, then the Make version should suffice—the majority of this book's content, such as photorealistic rendering, many extensions, and scripting, will work well with it. This book then offers a cost-efficient entry into relevant and current topics (such as 3D modeling, rendering, and computational geometry). If you, however, need the more advanced features and are planning on using SketchUp professionally, then your best approach is to get the Pro version right away.

This book was written to be applicable to both versions. However, when tools are discussed that are available only in the Pro version (e.g., creating a Dynamic Component or using Solid Tools), they are visually presented as a "Pro Only" section.

PRO ONLY   Pro Only sections look like this.

While all of this book's illustrations have been created using the Windows version of SketchUp, the tasks and tutorials are similarly usable with the Mac version. Menus and dialogs generally look the same and are in the same location on both platforms. There are minor user-interface differences, but they are easy to figure out. Consult SketchUp's help system if you run into trouble.

It is also a good idea to stay up to date with SketchUp. In addition to this book's companion website, bookmark the following sites to help you with this:

www.sketchup.com—The official home of SketchUp. You can get the latest Make or Pro version here.

http://blog.sketchup.com—The official SketchUp blog—a great source for updates, tutorials, and tips.

http://help.sketchup.com—SketchUp's knowledge center. If you get stuck, go here first!

http://forums.sketchup.com—SketchUp's user forums. Another great place to discuss problems and get help.

www.alexschreyer.net—My personal blog where I frequently post about SketchUp and other AEC software.

@alexschreyer—My Twitter handle under which I post news and links about SketchUp and AEC software.

How This Book Works

One way to use this book is linearly as a learning tool by moving from chapter to chapter. This method builds your skill set gradually and allows you to logically approach each subject.

You may also want to use it as a desk reference, or you might be interested only in individual chapters. In these cases, make use of the index and the appendices.

Some conventions in this book:

- Whenever I mention a *window* (e.g., the Materials window), this means the dialog window that can be accessed from SketchUp's Window menu.

- Other dialogs that open when the user clicks on something are commonly called *dialogs* in the text.

- Menu locations are typically presented in this format: **File** → **Open**....

- Whenever a tool from the context menu is mentioned, remember that you need to position the mouse cursor above something to get the menu options that relate to this object's context when you right-click.

- Any toolbars mentioned in the text can be opened from the **View** → **Toolbars** menu in SketchUp (or by right-clicking on any open toolbar). Extensions often install their own toolbars. They will, of course, not be available until a plugin has been installed.

- Many examples in this book use US-customary construction units such as the inch (") or foot ('). If you don't use these units, read the "Setting Units and Fonts" section in Chapter 2 and adjust the use of units in the examples to your unit system. SketchUp works well with any unit system.

- Following are some Mac-specific differences:

  - SketchUp's preferences cannot be found under the **Window** menu item, but instead are under the **SketchUp** menu.

  - Toolbars are called *tool palettes*.

  - Instead of right-clicking to bring up the context menu, you can left-click the mouse while holding the Control key.

Let's Go!

It's time to explore the world in the third dimension. Enjoy your modeling endeavors!

Chapter 2
A SketchUp Refresher

This chapter reviews some of SketchUp's basic techniques. You'll also learn about customizing the software environment and adjusting settings to help you with your daily tasks.

Key Topics:

- Where to get help with SketchUp
- Program interface and workspace customization
- Program and model preferences
- Working with templates
- Navigating SketchUp's 3D workspace
- Aids for accurate modeling
- Groups and components
- Applying materials and using other common tools
- Modeling from images
- Geo-based modeling
- Best practices for working with SketchUp

Let's Get Started!

Before we look at any of the more advanced SketchUp techniques such as extensions, rendering, and scripting, it would be helpful for any user to review some of the basic modeling techniques. This chapter presents in a condensed fashion an overview of the interface and the modeling and editing tools, as well as best practices and usability hints.

If you have no prior experience with SketchUp or would like to learn more about any of the basic topics, then my best recommendation is to get a copy of Aidan Chopra's excellent SketchUp primer *SketchUp 2014 for Dummies* (Wiley Publishing). It is a cost-efficient and thorough reference not only for modeling with SketchUp but also for presenting your models.

Two further sources for help are built right into SketchUp. One is the official help documentation. You can access it through the **Help** menu item, which simply opens a browser window at the following URL (if you end up using it frequently, it might be a good idea to bookmark it in your browser):

http://help.sketchup.com—SketchUp's online help system.

Alternatively, you can turn on the Instructor feature by selecting Instructor from the **Window** menu. This opens (and keeps open) a window that displays help for the tool that is currently in use. For example, if you start using the Circle tool (by clicking the Circle toolbar button, selecting Circle in the **Draw** menu, or simply pressing the C key on the keyboard), the Instructor shows the appropriate help, complete with a small animation. (See **Figure 2.1**)

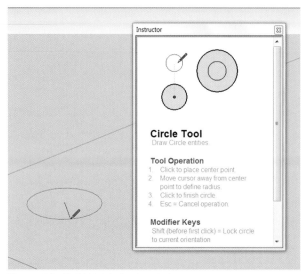

Figure 2.1: SketchUp's Instructor window

I also encourage you to visit this book's companion website www.sketchupfordesign.com for additional tutorials, forums, videos, and an updated list of links to online resources. In addition, many discussion forums, wikis, and online video sites are available that offer help for both beginners and advanced users. The most popular ones include:

www.sketchup.com/learn—SketchUp's own tutorials and training videos.

www.youtube.com/user/SketchUpVideo—SketchUp's YouTube channel.

http://forums.sketchup.com—SketchUp's official help forum.

http://sketchucation.com/forums—The SketchUcation forums, a user-based worldwide community.

www.mastersketchup.com—Matt Donley's tutorial site.

www.aidanchopra.com—Aidan's companion site to his book, which contains many YouTube instructional videos.

www.sketchupschool.com/sketchup-tutorials—A large collection of SketchUp video tutorials (subscription-based).

http://danieltal.com—Daniel Tal's SketchUp tutorials (subscription-based).

Interface and Program Setup

Once installed, SketchUp has a clean and rather empty appearance. The main portion of the screen is taken up by a large 3D-space work area in which only the ground plane or background (shown in green or gray), sky (blue gradient), the three main axes, and a modeled 2D person (included as a size reference) are visible.

TIP

The person in SketchUp's default template has historically been either an employee from the SketchUp team or someone close to them. For version 2015, this person is Steve. Earlier versions featured Sophie, Derek, Susan, Sang, and Brad.

Above the work area, the main toolbar buttons are nicely arranged on a toolbar called Getting Started. **Figure 2.2** shows the initial workspace on Windows; **Figure 2.3** shows the Mac equivalent. Both use the Architectural Design template that ships with SketchUp.

Figure 2.2: SketchUp's workspace on Windows

SketchUp's numerous features can be accessed either through the screen menu, by clicking a button on the toolbars, or with keyboard shortcuts. As with many other programs, any toolbars that are not currently activated and visible can be displayed by selecting them in the

Toolbars dialog. Open it either by going to the **View → Toolbars**… menu or by right-clicking on any toolbar area and selecting Toolbars… from the context menu. This right-click menu also lets you directly turn toolbars on or off.

Figure 2.3: SketchUp's workspace on the Mac

Figure 2.4 shows a modified toolbar setup where the very useful Large Tool Set toolbar has been activated and placed on the left side of the screen (in addition to the Standard, Styles, and Views toolbars on the top). It is always a good idea to have at least this one opened—even if no others are needed. In addition to the features in the standard Getting Started toolbar, Large Tool Set gives direct access to more navigation tools. However, it does not contain any of the 3D Warehouse, Extension Warehouse, or Google Earth buttons. If you need those, make sure you activate the Warehouse or Google toolbars, respectively.

It is a good idea to develop a well-organized workspace in any software. In SketchUp, this means that if you find yourself using the same tools over and over (and you can't access them using keyboard shortcuts, or you prefer toolbars), then you might want to display the appropriate toolbar and dock it on the screen in a convenient position.

A very useful feature of SketchUp's user interface is keyboard shortcuts. Even with the default settings, many tools can be accessed by pressing single keys. For example, the L key brings up the Line tool, R the Rectangle tool, and the spacebar the Select tool (and cancels any

Figure 2.4: Working with SketchUp's tools

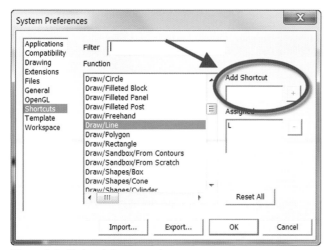

Figure 2.5: Keyboard shortcut preferences

other currently active tool). An overview of the default keyboard shortcuts (and most tools) is given in Appendix A. As you can see in **Figure 2.5**, you can, in addition, assign keyboard shortcuts to any tool that is available in the menu structure. Just remember to export your keyboard settings (from within the Preferences dialog) so that you have a backup available in case you need to reinstall SketchUp.

You can even assign a keyboard shortcut to plugin-supplied tools (as long as those tools have created their own menu items).

Although not absolutely necessary at this point, it might be a good idea to already be logged in with your Google account. Look for the person icon at the bottom of your SketchUp screen. This will be necessary later when you interact with the 3D Warehouse and the Extension Warehouse. Always being logged in has the benefit that SketchUp will tell you when any updates become available for installed extensions.

Adjusting SketchUp's Preferences

It is a good idea to spend some time tweaking all the options in SketchUp's Preferences to your liking, especially if you are a frequent user (access the dialog under **Window → Preferences**). The following is a list of the main options, along with some tips:

- **Applications**—Select the path to your default image editor here (e.g., Adobe Photoshop). This makes it possible, for example, to tweak textures using that editor by opening images in the external editor directly from within SketchUp.

- **Compatibility**—You can change your highlighting and mouse wheel preferences here.

- **Drawing**—You can select your click preferences here. For example, you have the choice of whether you want to draw a line by clicking and dragging or by clicking two points. Another useful feature is Display Crosshairs, which always gives you an axis reference when you have a tool activated.

■ **Extensions**—This shows a list of installed extensions (sometimes called *plugins*). The default installation should display the Sandbox Tools together with a handful of others. You can install extensions here manually using the Install Extension… button. Although the functionality of this tab has been largely replaced by the Extension Warehouse window, it is also possible to disable and enable installed extensions here by simply unchecking or checking the box next to the extension's name (a restart is often required). This sometimes becomes necessary when an extension leads to crashes but you don't want to uninstall it (by removing its files). You can learn more about finding, installing, using, and uninstalling extensions in Chapter 4.

■ **Files**—You can select locations on your hard disk for models, components, materials, and so on. These files are set up by default in the main SketchUp installation directory, but sometimes it is quite convenient to also have a separate location where custom components are stored. A use case for this is a company in which several SketchUp installations need to access models located in central network storage (for tips, see the note that follows this list).

■ **General**—These are some miscellaneous settings, of which the most important ones are Create Backup (make sure this is checked in order to have an *SKB* backup file of your model in case of a crash), Auto-Save (set this to a short interval, such as every five minutes), and Automatically Check For Updates (to be reminded when an update for SketchUp is available).

TIP

If you set up SketchUp to save backups, an SK<u>B</u> backup file will be saved in the same location where your SK<u>P</u> SketchUp file is saved. In case your main file becomes unusable, you can open the backup file directly with SketchUp. Just make sure you can see all files in the Open dialog by selecting All Files (*.*) at the bottom of the dialog.

■ **OpenGL**—These settings determine how the application graphics are being processed, which in turn determines how responsive SketchUp will be when you work with it. Unless you have a basic graphics card, make sure Use Hardware Acceleration is checked. This lets the graphics card do most of the display rendering and results in a responsive 3D work environment. Also check the Capabilities table below these settings. It shows which capabilities of your graphics card have been found by SketchUp. It is always a good idea to select one of the rows where the anti-alias number is larger than zero so that lines onscreen don't appear jagged. Experiment with these settings until you find the combination that works best for you.

■ **Shortcuts**—This allows you to add your own keyboard shortcuts. You can also export and reimport those settings here (e.g., when using multiple computers).

■ **Template**—You can select your default template here. Those that ship with SketchUp offer specialized settings for the various design disciplines plus 3D printing. To efficiently use a template in SketchUp, modify an empty file to your liking (including all settings in **Window → Model Info**, since they will be stored in the SketchUp file). You can even preload components and materials. Then save the file as a template (choose Save As Template… under the **File** menu) and preselect the file in this preference tab.

■ **Workspace**—This allows you to change the size of the toolbar buttons and to reset the workspace.

Using SketchUp on Multiple Computers

If you use SketchUp on more than one computer, it might make sense to work from the same set of components, materials, textures, and so on. You can then, for example, create a collection of your own (or your company's) custom components and materials that is synchronized across all the computers on which SketchUp is installed.

To accomplish this, there are two options:

- **Work with a central repository.** This option requires that you set up central data storage (e.g., network-attached storage or a server), where all relevant files can be stored. Then all you need to do is go into SketchUp's Preferences dialog and set all file locations to the appropriate folders on the network location. A drawback to this approach is that in order to access the stored data you need network access. Depending on your network connection and the size of your models, loading and saving might be slow.

- **Work with a synchronized repository.** This option is faster and safer because the repository is synchronized across all computers. It also ensures that the repository is available even when there is no network connection—for example, when you take your laptop on the road. The easiest way to make this option work is to sign up with Dropbox (**www.dropbox.com**) or a similar service. Then download the client application for your system from Dropbox and set up a dedicated folder on your computer to hold all synchronized data (you may use it for more than just CAD files, of course). After you do this on all your computers that run SketchUp, go to SketchUp's preferences and add the local (on your computer!) synchronized folder to the Files options. Thereafter, whenever you save, for example, a new component, Dropbox will synchronize it across all linked computers and, therefore, it will be available wherever you work with SketchUp.

With any of these methods, make sure you set up a good check-in/checkout system or use your network's document storage provider's history features so that a user can't inadvertently overwrite somebody else's files.

You might also want to try out Rich O'Brien's CloudUp extension in the Extension Warehouse, which lets you synchronize your model with various cloud-storage services.

Working with Templates

Beyond the program's core settings, quite a few other settings, data, and even 3D items are stored within a SketchUp SKP file and can therefore also be added to a template. Such a file is then opened as the default empty file each time SketchUp starts; it includes the following:

- All settings in the Model Info dialog, including dimension styles, text styles, and units
- Any entity placed in the 3D workspace (e.g., the person reference in the default template)
- The model's geo-location
- Model credits

- Animation tabs and their views with all settings, such as View styles
- In-model components, materials, styles, layers, and so on
- Component attributes
- Classifications such as the Industry Foundation Classes (IFC) schema
- Extension data if an extension stores data within the file

As you can see from this list, many options might warrant tweaking and saving in a template. Also, because the template settings can't be applied retroactively to an already existing file, it makes sense to preset template options before starting to work in a file. Let's look at setting some of the most useful options.

Setting Units and Fonts

Figure 2.6 shows the Units settings. Depending on your profession or where you are in the world, you may want to select architectural units (e.g., 6′ 5-1/2″), decimal units (inches or feet or a metric unit—e.g., 2.5′ or 3.2 m), engineering units (e.g., 100.623′), or, simply, fractional inches (e.g., 250-5/8″).

Depending on the resolution of your work (are you using SketchUp for woodworking or to design houses?), make sure you preset both the length snapping and the angle snapping to values that make sense for you. Finally, set the precision to display a number of digits or a fraction that is appropriate for your work. Whatever you set here, rest assured that the software internally stores all numbers at a much higher degree of precision.

Figure 2.6: Units settings in the Model Info dialog

A great way to personalize your SketchUp output is by using a custom font for in-model text as well as leaders and dimensions. You can do that in the respective settings (see **Figure 2.7** for text setting options and **Figure 2.8** for dimension settings).

Figure 2.9 shows a sample of various fonts: Windows' standard Tahoma font as well as some custom technical fonts and a handwritten font. You can even create your own font using your own handwriting. Some web resources are mentioned as follows.

Figure 2.7: Text settings in the Model Info dialog

Figure 2.8: Dimension settings in the Model Info dialog

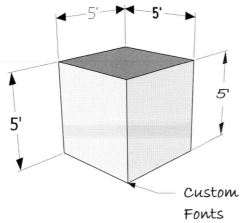

Figure 2.9: Using custom fonts in SketchUp

You can make your own font from your handwriting using several web services. Just search online for "create handwriting font" and follow the instructions to turn a handwriting sample into a standard font file that you can download. Alternatively, if you use a tablet device, look for software that allows you to do this by simply sketching the letters.

www.google.com/fonts and **www.dafont.com**—These are two of many websites that offer free or for-sale fonts. To install fonts, first download the desired font file (which can have any of these formats: TTF, OTF, or FON). Then, depending on your computer setup, either double-click the file and select Install or drop the file into the operating system's Font folder (usually under Preferences or Control Panel).

Adding Components

Think carefully about which components you want to add to your SketchUp model because each one will increase the SketchUp file size (especially if they contain photo textures). Having said that, it is always possible to purge unused file-space-heavy components and materials by using the options in the respective windows (see **Figure 2.10** for the Components window); therefore, it might be a good idea to start with a larger file and then simply get rid of unused components later.

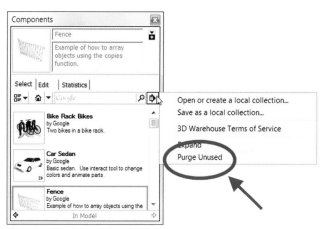

Figure 2.10: Purging unused components

　　Samples for preloaded components in architecture are people cutouts, a minimal set of trees and shrubbery, as well as any annotation elements that you might want to add to your model (e.g., a north arrow). While SketchUp's default components are easily accessible through the Components window or the 3D Warehouse dialog and, therefore, should not need to be loaded into a template, it's a good idea to do this if you have created your own set of these components to give your models a more personal touch.

One good example for this is your own person cutout (akin to the person shown in **Figure 2.2**). One of SketchUp's common criticisms is that its output can easily be identified as coming from SketchUp because this person is very often left in the view. So why not make your own?

To create a new person cutout, load a photo that you like into the view, scale it to the correct size, and then trace the shape of the person (and delete the outside faces). Then just apply color to all faces to your liking and make it a component. Make sure you select Always Face Camera in the Create Component dialog. Instructions for creating components appear later in this chapter, and a similar example (creating a cutout tree) is included in Chapter 5.

Views

If you often switch between working in perspective mode and in parallel projection views (top view, front view, etc.), it might make sense for you to preset the most important views as animation tabs. To do this, create new tabs through the **View** menu by clicking on **Animation → Add Scene** once you change all view settings to your liking (you can also update a tab's settings by right-clicking on it and selecting Update). You can switch between parallel and perspective views and select standard views from the **Camera** menu.

In **Figure 2.11**, the tab names have been changed in the Scenes window and Include In Animation has been unchecked so that these views will be excluded from any animations that you might create using the tabbed animation feature.

Figure 2.11: Several preset view tabs

Completed Template

Figure 2.12 shows a cleaner version of SketchUp's default template with several customizations. Feel free to create either a subtle or a bold template for your own work. Either way, visual consistency goes a long way when you use SketchUp professionally.

SketchUp's Tool Set

This section reviews most of SketchUp's tools. You will also practice them by modeling a garden trellis.

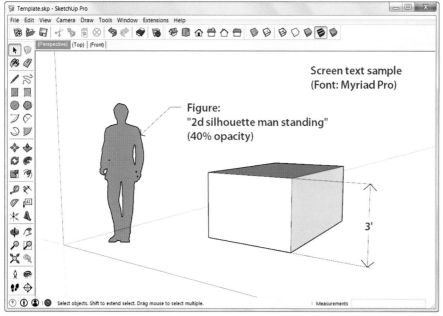

Figure 2.12: Custom template complete with premade tabs, custom fonts, custom dimensions, adjusted styles, and architectural units

Navigating the 3D Model

SketchUp provides various means to move around 3D space while you are working on your model. Analogous to many other CAD software programs, there are tools for zooming, panning, and orbiting the view. You can access these using the buttons on the main toolbar. If you are using a wheel mouse, however, you can do this much faster by rotating the wheel (to zoom in or out), pressing the wheel and dragging the mouse (to orbit), or holding the Shift key while you press the wheel (to pan sideways).

Two further tools of interest in this context are the Walk and Look Around tools:

- **Walk**—This tool allows you to explore 3D space interactively by walking back and forth through space as if you were walking through a building, for example. To use the tool, click on the icon that shows the two footsteps, which is found on the Large Tool Set toolbar. Then use your mouse (click and drag) to navigate.

It is a good idea to increase the field of view to one that is more similar to our own spatial perception (a quite narrow 35 degrees is the default setting). To do that, select the Zoom tool (the magnifying glass) and enter a larger value into the Measurements box at the bottom of the screen (e.g., *60* for 60 degrees). Also make sure eye height is at human level. To change it, select the Look Around tool (the single eye) or the Walk tool and type in a reasonable value (e.g., *6'*).

- **Look Around**—As the name implies, the way this tool works is similar to the way you move your head around a stationary position to explore a space.

IN-DEPTH

Alternatives for Controlling SketchUp's View

The aforementioned built-in methods are not the only tools that you can use to orbit, move, or walk around. Here are some suggestions for alternatives.

One method is a 3D mouse (e.g., the SpaceNavigator made by 3Dconnexion), which behaves more like a joystick and allows you to move more intuitively through 3D space because it combines the zoom, pan, and orbit motions into one tool. A common use case for this tool is to position it at the left hand (if you are right-handed) and use it in combination with the regular mouse at the right hand. (See **Figure 2.13**.)

Another option is to use a device that can be operated in 3D space similar to the actual motion in SketchUp. This offers the possibility of experiencing SketchUp's 3D space in a more immersive fashion. An example is a Wiimote controller (taken from a Wii video game console). This tool is very inexpensive ($40 is a current retail price), and its sensors (an accelerometer and others) can be set up to control any software using the freely available GlovePIE software or any similar game controller. (See **Figure 2.14**.) If you want to try this out for yourself, follow the instructions on my website: **www.alexschreyer.net/cad/when-wii-met-sketchup**.

Figure 2.13: Workspace with 3D mouse

Both of these tools might be better suited to exploring 3D space and models rather than being part of actual 3D modeling. Therefore, they are very useful for presentations, client walk-throughs, and the like. Feel free to experiment with them (and others) and see where they might fit into your workflow.

Another approach to viewing a SketchUp model is the immersive 3D experience that a virtual reality headset provides. Many commercial options are available these days (e.g., the Oculus Rift), but a cost-efficient approach is the cardboard viewer shown here (e.g., by Google or Sketchfab) that simply uses your smartphone as the display.

Figure 2.14: Using a Wii remote to move around in SketchUp

Accurate Modeling

The often-voiced notion that SketchUp is capable of merely rough and sketchy work is quickly dispelled when we look at how the program stores numbers internally. For example, querying the value of the mathematical constant pi using the internal scripting tools (covered in detail in Chapter 7) gives us the number 3.14159265358979. As you can see, this number is stored internally with precision to 14 decimal places. Any length or position value in SketchUp's 3D space is, therefore, internally stored with the same degree of precision.

Independent of where you use SketchUp in the world and what your unit settings are, length and coordinates are always stored internally as inches. These values are then conveniently converted into your local unit format before they are displayed in the Measurements box (the box that is displayed at the bottom of your screen by default in Windows) or anywhere else in the program.

To take advantage of this level of precision, use any of these tools when you are modeling:

- **Object snapping**—Like other CAD software, SketchUp offers a complete set of object snaps. This allows you to snap to endpoints, midpoints, edges, circle centers, and other locations. (See **Figure 2.15**.)

Figure 2.15: Object snapping while drawing a line on a box

- **Length snapping**—When modeling a line, for example, the mouse cursor snaps in increments of length that you have preset in the Preferences window (e.g., at every 1/8"). You can then simply click once the correct value has been reached, and the line will have the exact length. (See **Figure 2.16**.)

Figure 2.16: Line length snaps with preset 1/8" increments

■ **Inferences**—One of SketchUp's main strengths is a very intuitive inferencing system. This means that you can reference a point in 3D and model relative to it. To use this feature, start a tool (e.g., a line) and then move around 3D space. Especially if you move parallel to one of the axes (your "rubber band" line will change to the color of the axis), you will occasionally see a dashed line and a temporary reference point shown as a dot to indicate that you have acquired a reference point. The temporary tooltip will also display "From Point" to indicate that this has happened. You can then simply click, and the click position will have been determined by the referenced point's position.

TIP

It sometimes helps to constrain the direction of the temporary line. This is done by moving along the intended direction (e.g., parallel to an axis) and then holding down the Shift key. The rubber band line will increase in width to indicate that a temporary constraint has been activated. (See **Figure 2.17**.)

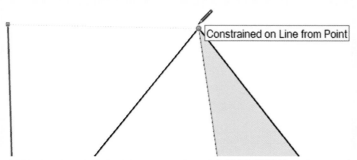

Figure 2.17: Using a constraint on the blue axis together with inferencing to acquire the pyramid's height as the top point for a vertical line

---

■ **Direct value entry**—Many tools provide the option to enter values directly into the Measurements box—even without the need to activate it by clicking. For example, you can start creating a line with a click, and then reference one of the axes and just type the intended length for the line (e.g., 10′).

TIP

SketchUp makes it easy to work with multiple unit systems. You can enter any unit into the Measurements box (e.g., 30cm), and SketchUp will internally convert it into your pre-set unit system and use the accurate values. You can even enter mixed units (e.g., 30cm, 3′ for the dimensions of a rectangle; see **Figure 2.18**).

Measurements	
Dimensions	2',4'

Figure 2.18: Direct value entry for a rectangle

Example 2.1: Starting a Trellis

Let's review and practice these techniques with a simple exercise: Let's build a garden trellis. As a first step in our trellis-building exercise, you need to create two vertical 8-feet-tall 6 × 6 posts.

1. Create a 5.5" × 5.5" square (using the Rectangle tool) on the ground plane (orbit your view if necessary so that you are looking "down" onto the ground). Use direct value entry into the Measurements box for this:

Measurements	
Dimensions	5.5,5.5

2. Then use the Push/Pull tool to pull this rectangle up to an 8' height (enter the distance again):

Measurements	
Distance	8'

3. Now use point inference on the front corner of the newly created post to position the new rectangle a distance along the red axis relative to the first post. Create the base square as you did in step 1.

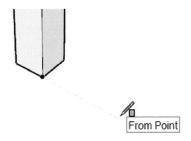

4. Use Push/Pull again, but this time don't enter a length value; rather, use inference with the top of the first post to make the second post exactly as tall as the first.

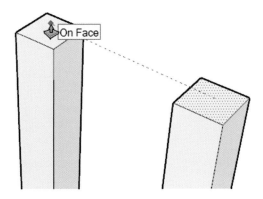

Temporary References

Beyond the aforementioned capabilities, SketchUp offers temporary lines and reference points for accurate modeling. They are created using the Measure and Protractor tools. Let's review their functions by continuing with our trellis model.

Example 2.2: Creating Beams for the Trellis

To create the beams, follow these steps.

1. Start by aligning your view with a vertical plane similar to the image shown here. This allows you to create a vertical rectangle that you will take as the basis for a 2 × 6 beam. Then draw the rectangle using the accurate dimensions (1.5″ × 5.5″).

Measurements	
Dimensions	5.5,1.5

2. Now use the Push/Pull tool to extrude it horizontally to 8'.

Measurements	
Distance	8'

3. It is a good idea to align your view with the side of the beam—either orbit and zoom or right-click on the side of the beam and select Align View from the context menu.

4. Start sketching temporary lines on the side of the beam. Using the Tape Measure tool, click on the top edge (make sure it snaps to the edge and not a point like the endpoint) and move the mouse downward. You should see a horizontal (dashed) guideline. Click when you reach 2" (this is possible because you preset length snapping earlier), or enter **2** into the Measurements box.

5. Now click at the point where the guideline intersects the right edge. Because you picked a point and not an edge as the start, you will not create a parallel guideline but rather a guide point. Move left along the guideline and click at 3" to place the point.

6. Use the guide point as the starting point for an angled guideline, which can be created with the Protractor tool. After starting the Protractor tool, you first need to place the center of the tool gizmo (the round protractor icon). Click on the temporary guide point for this. Next, you select a zero reference (click on the horizontal guideline). Finally, move down to the left until the protractor snaps at 30 degrees. Then click to place the angled guideline.

7. You can use the guidelines to "score" the front face by drawing lines onto them (make sure you snap to endpoints and intersections) and using the Push/Pull tool to remove the bottom corner of the beam (push all the way to the other side of the beam to completely remove the bottom corner).

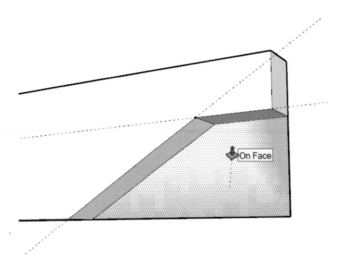

8. You can now erase the guidelines either in the same way as you would any other object using the Eraser tool, or by going to the **Edit** menu and selecting Delete Guides (this will erase all guidelines and guide points in the entire model, though).

Groups and Components

Groups and components are at the heart of modeling with SketchUp. Although both have one thing in common—they combine edges and faces into one object and thereby provide organization for the entire model—they work differently and are being used for different purposes. In essence, these are the differences:

- **Group**—When geometry becomes grouped, all selected entities (edges, faces, and other groups or components) are combined and are then selectable as one object. Any geometry that is drawn on top of a group does not "stick" to the group. You can also apply modifications such as scaling, moving, or copying to the entire group. It is important to note, though, that copying a group copies all of its contents and, therefore, doubles the storage space required in the SketchUp file.

- **Component**—A component is also a collection of geometry and other groups/components. Unlike a group, a component that is placed in the model is always just an insertion (an *instance*) of a component definition. A good way to imagine this might be that the geometry that makes up a component gets stored in a hidden part of the SketchUp file. When a component is placed into the model, a representation of it is inserted at the point you click. Multiple insertions (or copies) of the same component need only one insertion point per copy. While any of these insertions can have a different location, rotation, or scale, the underlying geometry is safely stored in that hidden location in the file. As a result, the file space required for a component is simply a single copy of the geometry plus a single insertion point for each copy. This makes components very efficient in terms of storage. In addition to this, components have their own (local) coordinate system that is stored within the component. They can also be set up so that they always stick to the horizontal or vertical plane or any face.

Furthermore, they can have a property whereby they will always face the viewer (this is the case with the 2D person cutout that comes with the default template). As in the case of a window component, they can also be set up to cut a hole in the underlying geometry (albeit through only a single face).

Beyond these differences, components can be shared in the 3D Warehouse, SketchUp's online 3D model storage service. They can also be set up to have interactive behaviors and may contain data when they are set up as Dynamic Components (we explore these in more detail in Chapter 3). This makes components very flexible and allows them to be used in a multitude of ways, for example, as parametric objects.

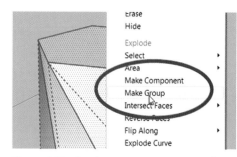

Figure 2.19: Creating a group or component using the context menu

So how are groups or components created? After you've selected the edges, faces, and groups/components that will make up a new group/component, one option is to right-click and select the appropriate item from the context menu (see **Figure 2.19**). Another is to use the menu items in the **Edit** menu. The fastest method may be a keyboard shortcut—typing **G** by default combines all selected objects into a component. See **Figure 2.20** and **Figure 2.21** for examples of groups and components, respectively.

TIP

Unfortunately, the Make Group function has no assigned default keyboard shortcut. However, this can easily be remedied in the Preferences window, where any convenient shortcut (e.g., Ctrl+G) can be assigned to the function.

Groups

Figure 2.20: Groups are best used when there are objects of many different sizes and configurations (especially if their texture does not tile).

Chairs are Components

Figure 2.21: Components are best used when there are many identical objects.

After inserting copies of components into your model, you can do this:

- **Edit the component definition.** (Double-click one insertion to get into edit mode.) All copies of the same component will automatically be modified when you edit something in one of them.

- **Make a component instance unique.** After inserting many copies of a component, all insertions (*instances*) are representations of that component. If you need one of them to be different, you can right-click on it and select Make Unique in the context menu. This creates a copy of the component definition and replaces the selection with it. This component will then behave differently from the original definition.

- **Replace all copies of a component.** This is useful if you want to use a placeholder (*proxy*) component in your model and replace it later or if clients change their minds and you need to replace one set of objects with another. This is accomplished by going into the Component window and displaying all of the components in the current model (click on the house symbol for this). You can then right-click on the to-be-replaced components and pick Select Instances. Then browse to the component with which you want to replace these, right-click on the component again, and select Replace Selected.

Example 2.3: Using Components for the Trellis

Let's practice working with components by continuing with our trellis exercise:

1. Because the trellis beams will have the same cuts applied to both ends, it is useful to create a nested component (two half-beams will make up the full beam). To do this, let's first reduce the beam length from 8′ to 4′. Use the Push/Pull tool on the unmodified end for this.

2. Now highlight the beam by either triple-clicking one of its sides or selecting it with a window selection. Then press the G key on the keyboard. A dialog will come up that allows you to give the new component a name. Keep all other settings as the default.

3. Use the Move tool to create a copy (click but don't hold the Control key after activating the Move tool to turn on copying—this tool combines both functions). After creating the copy (and still with the Move/Copy tool active), hover over one of the rotation icons (they look like small crosses) on the top of the beam to rotate the copy about the vertical axis.

4. Move the half-beams back together, highlight both, and create a new combined component from this.

5. Because four identical posts will be holding up the beams, it is a good idea to go back to the posts you modeled in the earlier exercise, delete the second one, and turn one of them into a component that you will name **Post**.

6. At this point, you can start moving the trellis beams into position. You need two support beams that will need to be attached 5-1/2" from the top of the posts.

When you move the beams into position using the Move tool, use object snapping (mostly on endpoints) and direct-distance entry to your advantage to place the beams exactly where they need to be. Pick up objects at a snap location and drop them at another. Never just "eyeball" pick points.

7. After the two beams have been placed, make a copy of the entire portal, which you will use later for the other side.

8. You can now take one of the beams and place a copy perpendicular to the portals.

Adjust overlaps as necessary

9. Let's use the divide option of the Copy function in this step to evenly distribute the cross-beams over the trellis top. To do this, select the last beam you placed, start the Copy function (Move tool + Ctrl key toggle), and use inference to acquire the point in the next graphic as the base point for the copy. Then copy it over to the other post.

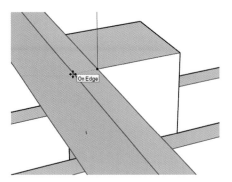

10. Without exiting the Move tool, type **/5** on the keyboard (which will then appear in the Measurements box). This evenly divides the space between the two copies into five segments and places copies of the beams at even distances. You can experiment with other spacings until you exit the Move tool—at that point, the array copy operation is final.

11. At this point, the trellis is complete. Let's use it, however, to see a benefit of having all beams be components, by applying an adjustment to the beams. To do this, double-click on one of the top beams—this gets you into component-editing mode (the rest of the model will be grayed out).

12. As you remember, this only got us into the beam component; you now have to double-click one of the half-beams to get into the underlying component.

13. This is where you can make your modifications. Because all of the half-beams are instances of this component, all of them will be updated. To illustrate this, you will change the sloped edge into an arc edge (just draw the arc on the side of the beam face). As before, use the Push/Pull tool to cut away the material at the bottom.

14. You can do further adjustments here—for example, you can stretch the beams to an overall length of 10′ (and thereby give them more overhang) by highlighting the entire end section and using the Move tool to move that geometry along the axis of the beam.

15. Finally, you don't want to see the edge at the center of the beams. Remember: You have this edge because you have two adjoining components at that point. Fortunately, SketchUp has an easy way to hide edges. Simply start the Eraser tool. If you hold the Shift key while you "erase" these edges, you are hiding them instead.

(Also hold the Shift key!)

Do not delete these edges. When edges that bound a face are erased in SketchUp, all the adjoining faces are also erased (because they need edges to exist).

16. Now click twice outside the actual model to get out of the component-editing mode, and enjoy your work! This is what you should see:

17. As a final step, take a look at the Components window. After opening it, click on the house symbol to see which components are loaded into your file. If you did everything right, you should see the three custom components in there: Post, Trellis Beam, and Trellis Beam Half (as well as the default person, of course).

In this exercise, you practiced various techniques:

- Creating components
- Working with nested components
- Moving, copying, and rotating objects
- Accurate positioning using inferencing, object snap, and direct distance entry
- Divide-copy
- Editing components

You should practice these techniques as much as possible. As you will see in the next chapters, a well-organized component-based model is essential to getting the most out of SketchUp.

Applying Materials

SketchUp has a very good and intuitive support for applying materials to faces. This is useful for a variety of activities, from a simple presentation to preparing a model for photorealistic rendering or modeling buildings from photos. Although SketchUp ships with a variety of good-looking materials (in the form of seamlessly repeating textures), it is important to note that you can always create a new material from your own textures (more on this in Chapter 5). To illustrate this, let's apply a wood material to the trellis.

Example 2.4: Applying Materials to the Trellis

To make the trellis beams look realistic, follow these steps.

1. Open the Materials window and browse to the Wood materials. This gives you a choice of the materials that ship with SketchUp. Before you apply a material to entire components, though, it is good practice to apply the material to faces inside the component.

2. Although there is no plywood in the model, we'll use the Wood_Plywood_Knots material for the wood. Feel free to modify its appearance size on the Edit tab of the Materials window.

3. As when you previously edited the components, when you start applying materials inside the component editor, all instances of that component will be updated. Therefore, after you finish applying the wood material to one half-beam, all of the beams are completed!

4. The next logical step is to go into editing mode for the posts and apply the same texture there. When you do that, though, you'll see that the material is oriented horizontally, which is not correct, as the wood grain runs along the posts and, therefore, vertically.

5. To correct this, we must rotate the texture. Fortunately, SketchUp has an easy-to-use built-in system to modify a texture's orientation. To access it, right-click on the textured face and select the context menu option **Texture** → **Position**. The screen will change to show the entire texture on a vertical plane along with four adjustment handles:

6. Now simply click and drag the scale/rotate handle (on the bottom right) and adjust the orientation of the texture. You can also experiment with the other handles to adjust position and skewness. Once you are done, right-click on the texture and click on Done.

7. To apply this corrected texture to all the other sides of the post, use the eyedropper in the Materials window to sample this texture from the front face of the post. Then simply apply it using the paint bucket on the other faces—they will retain the corrected orientation.

8. Now click outside of the editing area to get out of component-editing mode. At this point, all faces of the trellis should have correctly oriented textures. Your trellis should now look very realistic:

In this exercise, we reviewed some basic concepts for placing materials on faces. This will again be useful in a later chapter when we look at photorealistic rendering of SketchUp models.

Example 2.5: Modeling a Trellis Cap

Let's finish off the trellis exercise by adding a cap to the posts and practice using the Circle, Arc, and Follow Me tools.

1. Start by double-clicking one of the posts in the model. This gets you into editing mode for the "post" component definition. As discussed before, any changes that you apply here will propagate to all the other posts.

Zoom in on the top face and use the Push/Pull tool to extrude this face 1" upward. Before you do this, click the Ctrl key to start the extrusion with a new face. This gives you the extra line you see in the following graphic (textures are hidden for clarity in this exercise).

2. Next, draw a 4" circle centered on the top face. Start the Circle tool and hover over the midpoint of one of the side edges (don't click yet!) until you see the midpoint tooltip. Then hover over the midpoint of a non-opposing edge until you see that tooltip. Only then move the mouse to the center of the top face where you will see that SketchUp now snaps easily to that center point, inferenced from the two midpoints. Finally, click to place the center of the new circle there. Type **2** afterward (for a 2" radius) to give the circle exact dimensions and press Enter to finish the tool.

Because SketchUp is polygon-modeling software (it can work only with polygonal faces and edges), circles and arcs are always made up of line segments. Therefore, when starting the Circle or Arc tools, remember to set the number of segments in the Measurements box to an appropriate value—few segments make for "edgy" circles and many segments create rounder circles but increase file size.

3. Now you need a 4-inch-tall line at the center of the circle. Start the Line tool and hover over the circle's edge (again, don't click!). When you then move the mouse to the center, it will snap to the exact center of the circle, where you can click to start the line.

4. To be able to easily draw the outline of the rotated shape, it helps to have a plane on which you can construct it. Use the axis inference and, starting with the vertical line, draw three more lines parallel to a pair of axes that create that rectangle as shown in the following graphic.

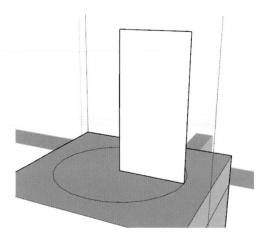

Starting with the 2015 version of SketchUp, you can use the Rotated Rectangle tool instead to do this even more easily. Start that tool, and then click both line endpoints and one point on the circle to place the rectangle.

5. Now use any of the Arc tools to create a half-outline of the lathed post cap shape on this rectangle. In the following graphic, I used a half-circle arc at top and a roughly drawn connecting arc at the bottom.

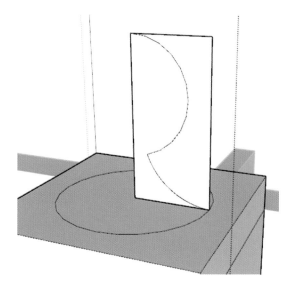

6. Now clean up any extra geometry on the rectangle using the Eraser tool so that only the outline of the rotated half-shape is left.

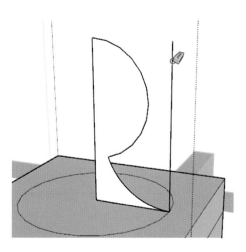

7. Given the outline and the circle at its base, you can now use the Follow Me tool to turn this into a rotated shape. As shown next, start the tool (#1), select the base circle edge as a guiding line (#2), and then click the outline face (#3) to finish the tool.

8. SketchUp will then create the rotated shape for you and clean up all of its edges. Your post cap is now finished, and you can texture it like the rest of the model.

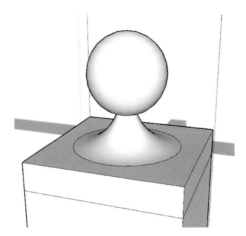

This example showed you some more inferencing tricks as well as a method to create rotated shapes with the Follow Me tool. You can use the same method if you need to create a sphere in SketchUp. However, because this tool is basically a sweep tool with which a face can be extruded along any set of edges (they do not need to be circular), this tool can be used to quickly make building foundations, roofs, and road curbs as well. Experiment with it to understand its functionality.

Using References for Modeling: Images and Location

The trellis example assumed that you could model from scratch and without reference simply based on material dimensions. Often, you'll need to use references instead, such as the geography of a site or a hand-drawn (or old) plan, and use those as starting points for our work. The two examples in this section explain SketchUp's tool set in those contexts.

Example 2.6: Modeling from an Imported Plan Image

If you have DWG/DXF or other plan (or site) data that you can import into SketchUp (at least in the Pro version), things are quite easy. But what if you don't? This example assumes you have a floor plan as a PDF and want to create a 3D model from it as precisely and quickly as you can. You will learn about scaling, axis positioning, and work organization through this example.

1. As a first step, you need to get the plan into SketchUp. Unfortunately, there is no native option to import PDF pages; however, you can take any image and place it into your SketchUp model. Using raster images as intermediaries is, of course, not as precise as if you used coordinates or imported vector data, but sometimes that will have to suffice.

Perform one of these steps to begin:

- Open the PDF in Adobe Acrobat (Reader) and take a screenshot either using your operating system's Screenshot function or using the **Edit → Take a Snapshot** menu item. Then save this image by pasting it into image-editing software from the Clipboard.

- Open the PDF in an image-editing software that can read PDFs (e.g., Adobe Photoshop). You can then select a size and DPI combination that will determine at which resolution the PDF will be rasterized. The following image shows how this looks in Photoshop.

2. Next, you need to get the image into SketchUp. You can do this by simply dragging and dropping it into the work area. Alternatively, you can go to **File → Import…** and make sure Use As Image is checked in the dialog box. At this point, don't worry about its scale in SketchUp. Just don't make it too small.

3. You can skip the next step if everything in the imported image is parallel to the axes in SketchUp. However, in my case that is not the case and I will need to rotate the axes before I can continue.

Right-click on any of SketchUp's axes and select Place from the context menu. This attaches the axes at the mouse cursor. Now you need to find a convenient spot in your drawing that you can use to place the origin and align the axes. In this example, I used a set of orthogonal structural grids. Place the origin at an intersection first and then place the red axis's direction along one of the lines. Finish off the operation with the green and then the blue axes (make sure blue points up, not down), and you will be good to go.

4. If you have set up any animation tabs beforehand (e.g., in your template), make sure you update them now so that the new axis orientation is saved with the tabs.

5. Next, you will scale the imported image. Find a (long) dimension in the image that is either shown or that you know some other way. Place a dimension in SketchUp right next to it. (You should change the unit system to decimal inches to make calculations easier)

6. As you can see, in this example, the scale factor is 2.395 (22 divided by 9.1875). Highlight the image and the dimension, start the Scale tool, and pick a yellow corner-scaling grip. Then type the scale factor into the Measurements box. You can verify that everything scaled correctly by checking the dimension that you placed earlier (it should also have updated now).

TIP

In group- or component-editing mode, you can scale even more easily: select all geometry and then measure a distance using the Tape Measure tool. Afterwards just type the new length and all geometry will be scaled accordingly.

---

7. Now you are ready to start modeling on top of your imported plan. You could either keep the plan as an image object and just model on top (which keeps your new geometry separate), or you could explode the image (which turns it into a rectangle with the plan as its texture) and model that way. If you choose the latter, the texture will be retained (as a *projected* texture) on all of the geometry that you extrude from the rectangle. In the example, I chose the second method and started by drawing a rectangle to outline the room.

8. Using the Offset tool, you can then offset the wall thicknesses from the rectangle. What results is an outline of the base of the enclosing walls, which you can push-pull up to the desired wall height. As you can see in the following image, I already started cutting out doors and replacing the projected texture on the wall with a simple white color.

9. If everything is modeled perfectly rectilinear, it is quite easy to fill in door lintels simply by drawing lines on wall openings and push-pulling the lintels across the openings.

TIP

Especially because you are not working with hard coordinates this time, it is imperative that you model as accurately as possible. Use inferences as much as you can. Also, when possible, draw lines that are parallel to the main axes (that you conveniently rotated earlier) and use any known dimensions (e.g., wall thicknesses). The more orthogonal and precise you are here, the easier it will be later when you need to clean up this model.

It is also a good idea to clean up the model as you go. If a push-pull operation created a superfluous line, get out the eraser immediately and get rid of it.

If you need to assign the plan texture to any new surface in your model, use the Material window's eyedropper feature to sample that texture and then paint it to the new surface. Because it is already a projected texture, it will always be applied in the correct plan orientation. (This only works if you exploded the image earlier, of course.)

10. Finally, once you have some geometry that you don't want to modify accidentally later (e.g., the existing part of your model or a building's structure), it is a good idea to group that geometry and lock it (using the command on the context menu). You can always unlock it as needed.

You have now easily turned a 2D plan into a rough 3D model, and you can use this as the basis for further design work.

Example 2.7: Geo-Based Modeling

Whenever you work on a project that is physically located anywhere on Earth (it can even be deep in the ocean!), you will likely benefit from SketchUp's abilities to add that location to your model (as a pair of Latitude/Longitude coordinates). Once you have your model accurately geo-referenced, you are able to use this information for anything from terrain-based designs to date-based shading analysis. Both of these can inform your designs in a variety of ways. Specifically, a geo-referenced model can use these three items:

- ■ **Ortho-photographs** (mostly satellite photography) that you know from Google Maps or Google Earth. The geo-locating process in SketchUp automatically adds a sufficient-sized base image on which you can begin tracing (e.g., building outlines).

- ■ **Terrain model** (at varying detail levels) for the entire globe. In addition to the flat ortho-photographs, geo-locating adds a textured terrain snapshot. Use the Toggle Terrain button on the Google toolbar to show it.

  Chapter 4 includes an example using SketchUp's terrain information to create a layered terrain model.

- ■ **Street View imagery.** These are car-top-height panoramic images of almost every accessible street in many cities. You can include them in your model using the Photo Textures window (for example, to texture the sides of a building).

A model's geo-location settings can be accessed through the Model Info window. Alternatively, you can click on the small pin symbol at the bottom of SketchUp's screen.

You can then either click on Add Location... in the dialog that follows to pick a location from the map or click on Set Manual Location... to enter a location based on coordinates. Note that the terrain snapshot is added only when you pick the location on a map.

Let's look at a few examples where geo-location was used for modeling.

In **Figure 2.22**, it was not necessary to model an entire building. Of interest here was interior light distribution for various window shading devices. Having modeled the single office in a geo-referenced SketchUp file gave enough information to compare them. As you can guess from the background in this figure, the office was simply created on top of the snapshot image that came into SketchUp through the Add Location tool.

Another example is the design of a gardener's clock (basically a sundial), as shown in **Figure 2.23**.

As you can see in **Figure 2.24**, the placement of the square stones was determined by adding a location to the SketchUp model and then setting SketchUp's shadows to the accurate time and date. The inner circle represents the spring equinox (3/21), and the outer ring is accurate at the summer solstice (6/21). Changing time to each full hour on those dates produced the locations of the hourly stone markers.

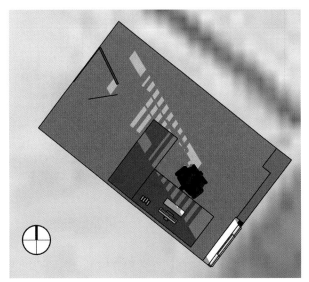

Figure 2.22: Using location information for accurate shading studies for an office

Figure 2.23: A gardener's clock, designed using SketchUp's shadows feature

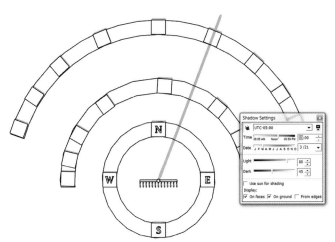

Figure 2.24: Plan view of the sundial with the Shadow Settings window

If desired, you can export geo-located, textured SketchUp models as KMZ files, which can then be imported into Google Earth and many other geo-based software packages (e.g., ESRI ArcGIS). The last image in Chapter 1 shows several buildings at the University of Massachusetts that were created and distributed this way.

Other Tools

SketchUp has many more tools than could be covered in a one-chapter review. The following list gives an overview of the tools not reviewed in this chapter. Consult the help topics for further instructions on these.

- **More Drawing tools: Polygon, Freehand, Pie**—These are best explored by experimentation. In each tool, keep an eye on the status bar and on the Measurements box to see which options are available.

- **More Edit tools: Rotate, Scale, Offset**—In many ways, the Rotate tool works similar to the Move tool. It allows you to rotate objects and make rotational copies (a good example is positioning chairs around a circular table). The Scale tool allows scaling of any object either graphically or by entering a scale factor. The Offset tool creates offset copies of edges on a face.

- **The Sandbox Tools**—This set of tools resides on the Sandbox toolbar and is not activated by default (activate via the **View → Toolbars** menu). These tools allow you to work with terrain objects (i.e., triangulated surfaces). You can use these tools to create terrain, modify it, and add building footprints and roads.

- **Intersect and Solid Tools**—The Intersect tool (which you can access from the context menu) is useful for easily finding intersections (intersecting faces and edges) between two objects in 3D. While it is not a true Boolean tool (due to the nature of SketchUp not using actual solids), it permits you to find intersecting volumes and perform manual cleanup of geometry.

PRO ONLY

SketchUp's Solid Tools

The Solid Tools (Intersect, Union, Subtract, Trim, Split, Outer Shell) offer a more convenient way to use Boolean operations for modeling than using the Intersect tool. They operate on grouped geometry that cleanly encloses a volume (often called *manifold* or *watertight* geometry). You can learn more about them in Chapters 3 and 4.

- **Shadows and Styles**—SketchUp has an accurate shadow generator that allows shadows to be displayed in a model at any time and date and at any given geographic location. This feature is useful for solar shading studies and for adding realism to model views. Styles affect the visual appearance of a SketchUp model and can be used to create presentation-ready views right inside the modeling environment without the need for an external application. Shadows and styles will be covered more extensively in Chapter 5.

■ **Photo match**—SketchUp can be used for modeling existing buildings for Google Earth and other software. Several methods exist to create an accurate representation of a 3D object. One is the "ground up" method of modeling a building and then texturing it (using the methods shown in Example 2.4). Another one is the Photo Match tool that uses one or more photographic views together with an adjustable axis to model a building by sketching and texturing right inside those photos.

Some of these tools will be covered in the following chapters.

TIP

If you are interested in more introductory or specialized SketchUp modeling tutorials, review SketchUp's help files and tutorial videos or refer to any of the excellent reference books mentioned on this page of the companion site:

http://sketchupfordesign.com/the-book/further-reading

SketchUp Best Practices

The following is a list of best practices that you should always keep in mind when you are working with SketchUp:

■ **Spend some time making your own template and adjusting the program's settings.** This was mentioned earlier in this chapter, and I can only reiterate how adjusting your workspace to your liking and comfort will help you when working with SketchUp (or any program, for that matter).

■ **Save early and save often.** It is generally best to press the Save button as soon as you start a new file and even before you start working on it. I have seen too many people lose hours of their work simply because they didn't do this. Once a file has been saved, SketchUp's Autosave function keeps saving the file and making backups.

■ **For computer-lab-based readers: Write your name on your USB stick.** It always amazes me how many USB memory sticks get left behind in computer labs or lost each semester. Therefore, if you work in a computer lab and you save your work to a USB stick, write your name and e-mail address on it; you might even put a file on it that lists your full contact information.

- **Group faces (or turn them into a component) as soon as they make up a logical object.** In SketchUp, all faces that touch each other become "sticky." This means that if you add a face on top of another face, you won't be able to remove the second face by simply moving it. A good practical example is that as soon as you have extruded a rectangle to form a 2 × 4 wood stud, turn it into a group or a component. That way, when you make a copy and place two of them side by side, they will behave like two physically separate objects.

- **Use components for repeating objects.** As soon as you have an object that will be copied multiple times in its current shape (e.g., floor joists or streetlights) or simply scaled, use components instead of groups. Components save file space and keep SketchUp working smoothly.

- **Model as precisely as possible.** Use SketchUp's precision modeling tools to create a model that is accurate and doesn't contain "crooked geometry" or gaps. A common problem occurs when one corner of an otherwise planar face moves out of plane. At that point, SketchUp needs to triangulate the face, which in turn breaks it up and makes texturing and other modeling tasks harder (e.g., using the Push/Pull tool or moving edges). Try to avoid this by modeling orthogonally where appropriate and using dimension entry and object snaps wherever possible.

- **Keep the polygon count low.** Because SketchUp is a polygon-based modeler, any curved shape must be approximated by a certain number of polygons (typically, triangles, rectangles, or polygons with more than four edges). The more polygons a model has, the more the graphics card will have to work to display the model and any shadows on it. This is true especially if you turn on edge display or even custom styles. A technique to reduce the polygon count is modeling circles or arcs with only the minimum number of edges needed. It is also beneficial to use components as much as possible, especially for curved objects that repeat.

TIP

Starting in 2015, SketchUp is now also available as a 64-bit version. If your operating system supports it, choose the 64-bit version to obtain the best program performance. Also newly introduced is the concept of *fast styles*. In the Styles window, look for a small icon on the available styles that will tell you that a particular style has a fast performance.

- **Use proxy components if needed.** If you need to work with high-polygon objects— for example, detailed trees for rendering—then insert *proxy components* (which can be as simple as a box with the rough outline size of a tree) into your model while you work on it. This keeps the polygon count low and lets you work well with SketchUp. You can then either replace these before you create renderings or—depending on your rendering software—replace them during the rendering process (outside of SketchUp).

Make sure the components' coordinate axes (the ones that you see in the component editor after you double-click a component) are at the same location—for example, at the center of the bottom of the objects. Otherwise, replacing the components will shift them.

- **Don't use textures that are too large.** If you use image-based textures, use only the image size that you need. Images can have very high resolutions, and several images with textures that are too large can slow down SketchUp significantly.

Your Turn!

The following tasks allow you to practice the topics in this chapter:

1. **Create your own template.**
   To customize SketchUp, start a new file and turn it into your own template by making various modifications (adjust fonts, colors, etc.). Activate it as the default template. Finally, create a new file using this template and model something with it. Add dimensions and text, and print a view to show off your style.

2. **Build your own trellis.**
   Take the examples in this chapter as a guide to model your very own garden trellis. Customize the end cuts of all beams, and add furniture, a few people, and whatever else you see as appropriate. Finally, print several views of the trellis (some perspective views and some orthographic views such as Front and Top). Add enough dimensions and detail so that a builder could actually construct it from your instructions.

3. **Model your house**.
   Use SketchUp's modeling tool set to model the exterior of your own house. Approximate the outside dimensions and the roof slopes, and create a model with an average level of detail (don't include details that are too small). If you like, read SketchUp's help files on adding photos to the walls as textures and follow those instructions. You can then upload the model to the 3D Warehouse if you like.

4. **Create a 3D model from a 2D plan.**
   Download a floor plan from the Internet or get a topography plan as an image. Then use the methods described in this chapter to turn it into a 3D model.

5. **Plan a local park.**
   Use SketchUp's location tools to locate your model and get satellite imagery as well as terrain data. Plan a small park (or plaza) and use location-based features for your design, which might include the terrain or shading effects.

Chapter 3
Component-Based 3D Modeling for Efficient and Data-Driven Designs

This chapter goes beyond using SketchUp as a simple 3D modeling tool. Although this software is excellent at that, 3D modeling in SketchUp can be about more than just *representing* your designs—you can use it very effectively to add design intelligence to your models through parametric objects or data and thereby *inform* your designs and/or create workflow efficiencies.The following sections cover group- and component-based modeling (for detailing, assembly planning, estimating, and other tasks), working with Dynamic Components, and using Building Information Modeling (BIM) principles.

Key Topics:

- Component-based modeling
- Reporting component attributes
- Assembly-based modeling
- Trimming and cutting in SketchUp
- Using and making Dynamic Components
- SketchUp and Building Information Modeling (BIM)
- Architectural space programming with SketchUp
- BIM classification and IFC (Industry Foundation Classes)

Group- and Component-Based Modeling

As you saw in Chapter 2, you can use groups and components to clean up your SketchUp model, keep it organized, create 3D geometry efficiently, and easily reuse modeling objects.

You also learned that *groups* in SketchUp are useful for logically grouping individual geometry (e.g., assembling six faces into a *brick*), while *components* are appropriate if you want to reuse the same component multiple times. In addition, components can attach (*glue*) themselves automatically to other geometry (any faces, horizontal faces only, etc.), or they can always face the camera (like the person model in SketchUp's default template). Groups and components can even contain other groups and components, which then become *nested.* You can also reuse components easily through SketchUp's Components window or SketchUp's 3D Warehouse online repository (which can be found at https://3dwarehouse. sketchup.com).

This section first explores groups and components a bit more in detail.

Effective Use of Groups and Components

Let's look at a mock-up of a stud wall assembly as an example of what you can do when you are consistent in using groups and components to organize your models. The following is a reasonably detailed model of a common part of house construction. This method is very applicable to construction and architecture (because of a building consisting of actual components like bricks and studs), but it should be mentioned that it is of equal value if you use SketchUp for woodworking, interior design, robot building, and many other tasks.

It is possible to model this construction detail in a variety of ways. If you wanted, you could start by drawing the base and use the Push/Pull tool to extrude the footing. You could then draw new outlines on it and extrude the foundation wall. After this, you could make your way upward simply by drawing outlines on surfaces and extruding them. This modeling approach is similar to modeling something out of a block of clay (by pinching, pulling, and pushing). You would finish your SketchUp model by adding appropriate textures to all faces and making the model look like **Figure 3.1**.

Figure 3.1: A detailed mock-up of a construction detail

Although this approach visibly gets you the result you want, it is not very flexible and—worst of all—it limits you in what you can do with this model later. As you can see in **Figure 3.2**, simply moving some faces distorts and ruins the entire model (after all, everything is attached if no part of the model has been grouped).

Because this example deals with many individual objects (the concrete foundation, the studs, the joists, etc.), it is much better and more efficient to approach modeling this detail by either grouping each object or turning it into a component while you construct it. In essence, you are creating an assembly in such a way that you could at any point take its components apart—as you can see in the exploded view shown in **Figure 3.3**.

In this detail (Figure 3.3), every logical object is separated from the others and is its own entity. What you can't see in this visible representation is which object is a group and which is a component. As discussed before, components work best if you need many similar copies (that are only different in scaling, rotation, and insertion location). Therefore, all of the wood pieces (joists, studs, plates, etc.) are components. Because there is only one copy of the foundation in the model, it was equally efficient to use it as a simple group, although a component would have worked, too.

Figure 3.2: Moving the parts of an ungrouped model can destroy it.

Figure 3.3: Exploded view of assembly made of groups and components

What you can do now is explore this model in the Outliner window (see **Figure 3.4**). This will give you more information on how this model has been organized. You can find the Outliner in the **Window** menu. As you will see, it is often a very useful helper to keep around in your workspace.

The Outliner reveals that there is actually a hierarchy of objects in this model: The joist components are part of a group called Floor, and the studs are part of a group called Wall. Outside of these two groups are the foundation and the sill. Everything is then contained in a group called *Mockup Detail 1*.

This hierarchy was created by *nesting* components, which means that all the joist components have been grouped and the resulting group has been given the name Floor. As you may already know, renaming an object can easily be done in the Entity Info window. That window is another good candidate to always have open in your workspace. It not only allows you to edit names but also lets you adjust shadow behavior on a per-object basis and modify the layer on which the object resides. (See **Figure 3.5**.)

You can use the Outliner window in a variety of ways. You could, for example, rearrange named objects and place them into groups simply by dragging and dropping them within the list to any position. You can also use this list in conjunction with the Entity Info window to select individual components and hide/unhide them and adjust their locked status. In any case, it is advantageous if you give objects (groups or components) in SketchUp recognizable names so that you can find them easily in the Outliner window.

Figure 3.4: The Outliner view of frame model

Figure 3.5: The Entity Info window for a group (top) and a component (bottom)

In a large model, the filter function of the Outliner window helps reduce the number of components and helps maintain focus on the object of your search. Just make sure you include useful text in your naming (e.g., **building1-floor3-window6**) so that you can search easily.

Generating Reports of Groups and Components

If you have the Pro version of SketchUp, you can reap another benefit from using groups and components: You can generate a report from your model. To do this, select the objects you want to have reported (the entire mock-up in this case) and go to File → Generate Report…. This opens the following dialog, where you can specify whether you want the report to be generated as an HTML file (a webpage for viewing in a browser or opening with Word) or a CSV (comma-separated values) file (for import into, for example, Excel). See **Figure 3.6**.

Figure 3.6: The Generate Report dialog

The report generated from the framing model then appears as shown in **Figure 3.7**.

PATH	DEFINITION NAME	ENTITY VOLUME	LENX	LENY	LENZ	MATERIAL
Mockup Detail 1	-		137	106.25	145	
Mockup Detail 1/Mockup Detail 1	Lumber_2x6	792	96	1.5	5.5	Wood - SPF
Mockup Detail 1/Foundation	-	46080	24	96	36	Concrete
Mockup Detail 1/Wall	-		3.5	96	97.5	
Mockup Detail 1/Wall/Lumber_2x4	Lumber_2x4	504	96	1.5	3.5	Wood - SPF
Mockup Detail 1/Wall/Lumber_2x4	Lumber_2x4	504	96	1.5	3.5	Wood - SPF
Mockup Detail 1/Wall/Lumber_2x4	Lumber_2x4	504	96	1.5	3.5	Wood - SPF
Mockup Detail 1/Wall/Lumber_2x4	Lumber_2x4	504	96	1.5	3.5	Wood - SPF
Mockup Detail 1/Wall/Lumber_2x4	Lumber_2x4	504	96	1.5	3.5	Wood - SPF
Mockup Detail 1/Wall/Lumber_2x4	Lumber_2x4	504	96	1.5	3.5	Wood - SPF
Mockup Detail 1/Wall/Lumber_2x4	Lumber_2x4	504	96	1.5	3.5	Wood - SPF
Mockup Detail 1/Floor	-		97.5	106.25	10	
Mockup Detail 1/Floor/Lumber_2x10	Lumber_2x10	1332	96	1.5	9.25	Wood - SPF
Mockup Detail 1/Floor/Lumber_2x10	Lumber_2x10	1332	96	1.5	9.25	Wood - SPF
Mockup Detail 1/Floor/Lumber_2x10	Lumber_2x10	1332	96	1.5	9.25	Wood - SPF
Mockup Detail 1/Floor/Lumber_2x10	Lumber_2x10	1332	96	1.5	9.25	Wood - SPF
Mockup Detail 1/Floor/Lumber_2x10	Lumber_2x10	1332	96	1.5	9.25	Wood - SPF
Mockup Detail 1/Floor/Lumber_2x10	Lumber_2x10	1332	96	1.5	9.25	Wood - SPF
Mockup Detail 1/Floor/OSB_4x8_Sheet	OSB_4x8_Sheet	3825	48	106.25	0.75	OSB
Mockup Detail 1/Floor/Lumber_2x10	Lumber_2x10	1332	96	1.5	9.25	Wood - SPF
TOTALS	-	63549	1750	533.25	384	-

Figure 3.7: Model data imported to Excel (some columns removed)

As you can see, not only does this report contain the objects, their hierarchy locations, and component definition names; it also includes their locations in space (not shown in **Figure 3.7**), their volumes, their materials, and their sizes (with LENX, LENY, and LENZ representing lengths in the three main directions—this information is useful when objects have been scaled).

You can now use this data to create various kinds of schedules: door/window schedules, material lists, concrete volume estimation, and more. As you will see soon, if you make a component *dynamic,* you can add any attribute to it and report those using this method, too.

Although not specifically mentioned here, adding layers (using the Layers window) gives you an additional method to organize objects. This could be useful, for example, if the floor group of components in the preceding situation consisted of existing and new joists and you wanted to be able to separate them visually.

In that case, you would add Existing and New layers to the list of available layers in your model and adjust entity properties by putting joists on the appropriate layers. You could then display the existing and remodeled construction situation simply by turning layers on and off.

The example in this section shows how beneficial it can be to assume a rigorous group- or component-based modeling workflow. This becomes even more useful when you include a good naming scheme. At that point, you will be starting to use *data* in SketchUp (in addition to plain geometry).

A good real-world example where this can be employed even on very large projects is the case of 4D (3D plus time) or 5D (4D plus cost) construction planning. Using those tools (one example is shown in **Figure 3.8**), construction models can be enriched with timeline data, and the construction process can be visualized (and scheduled), taking into consideration estimated component fabrication times. Commercial software packages that do this with or in SketchUp are Synchro, 4D Virtual Builder, and Envision.

Another example where groups and components can be useful to convey your message is the case of historic reconstruction. As **Figure 3.9** shows, timeline renderings can feature a model, which has been broken into components by construction dates, and then easily display it in the form of a timeline. In this case, you would use a combination of layers and the Outliner window to organize (and show/hide) buildings. This could even be animated using SketchUp's tabbed animation feature and saved as a video (see Example 3.2 for instructions).

Figure 3.8: Using a SketchUp component-based model in Synchro, a 4D construction scheduling software *(Image used by permission of Synchro Ltd.)*

Figure 3.9: Historic timeline renderings using components to separate buildings (original model from 3D Warehouse)

Modeling with Production Assembly in Mind

When working with components as shown in the preceding section, it might be tempting to ignore small modeling inaccuracies. This can be the case especially when there are oblique angles or overlaps. To illustrate this, consider two overlapped pieces of wood, as shown in **Figure 3.10**.

Figure 3.10: Overlapping components (left and middle: simple overlap; right: cutout)

Although the left image shows an overlap that looks appropriate, lifting the top piece reveals that it simply consists of two components overlapping without any resolution of the intersection. The third image then illustrates how an overlap should be resolved: exactly the way this example would actually be built—with a notch.

Fortunately, SketchUp is well equipped to help us model intersections like these. All you need to do is use the Intersect with Model tool (which requires some manual cleanup) or SketchUp Pro's Solid Tools. Once this notch is modeled in SketchUp, you have not only a proper component-based model but also one that can be built as modeled.

You can see a larger example in **Figure 3.11**, which is an assembly of four overlapping pieces of wood, where each one is angled 4 degrees off the horizontal. As shown in **Figure 3.11**, modeling this and including all proper cuts and notches immediately provides us with a buildable model. All I did to create **Figure 3.12** was copy one component and add dimensions in SketchUp.

Figure 3.11: Model of four overlapping wood beams

Figure 3.12: Dimensioned single beam, ready for manufacture

So, what is the benefit of using this modeling approach? By actually building (as in the sense of virtually constructing) the 3D models, you are incorporating something very useful into your design process: immediate design validation and error checking. For example, you can easily see if a cut didn't work in your 3D model and fix it, which—of course—is cheaper than physically building something and having to redo it.

In addition, virtually building assemblies in 3D allows you to conceptualize the construction process, making it much easier—and less error prone—when you actually have to build something in reality (see **Figure 3.13**). Especially when various layers are involved (in architecture this could consist of interior finishes—structure—building skin—exterior shading devices), this allows you to think through the process of matching and coordinating all those layers (and all of the subcontractors involved) at an early, conceptual stage.

Independent of your discipline, you can use this approach to test the feasibility of construction details on the job site, workflow processes (in plant layout), furniture assembly in the wood shop, modeling for 3D printing, and many more applications (see Chapter 6 for more on this). **Figure 3.14** shows how a large construction firm, Turner Construction Company, used SketchUp in its New York World Trade Center Transportation Hub project to visualize structural steel assemblies.

Figure 3.13: Finding an unprotected post top in your model lets you fix it before you build it.

Figure 3.14: Detailed model of box girder steel, precast smoke purge ducts, and temporary shoring *(Image used with permission of Turner Construction Company)*

Example 3.1: Trimming Groups Using Two Methods

This example uses two methods to trim groups: SketchUp's Intersect with Model tool (which is in both the Make and the Pro versions) and SketchUp Pro's Trim feature (from the Solid Tools). The task at hand is to miter two large steel beams at a corner. To begin, download a wide-flange cross-section component from the 3D Warehouse and turn it into two beams, using the Push/Pull tool.

Let's start with the Intersect with Model workflow:

1. To line up all necessary geometry, place the two beams in their final positions.

2. If you want to trim one of the beams at 45 degrees, you will need to have a plane that cuts it at exactly that location. This is easily accomplished by drawing diagonals and verticals into the corner using the Line tool to create a face. Extend this face a little bit vertically beyond the beam's edges (using the Move tool on its edges) so that you don't run into any problems when cutting.

3. SketchUp's Intersect tool creates edges at the interface of objects that are part of the intersection. As you can see in the right-click menu, SketchUp can intersect with the rest of the model, a selection, or the current context. In this case, you will simply use the Intersect with Model feature. It is important to understand that SketchUp will create these intersecting lines in the current context. This means that if you are intersecting the grouped beam and the face from outside the group, all lines will be created outside the group as well. You don't want that here because the intersecting lines need to *score* the beam sufficiently for you to be able to trim away the overlapping part. Therefore, before you use Intersect with Model, go into editing mode for the beam (double-click it) and select all of its faces. Only then right-click on them and use Intersect with Model.

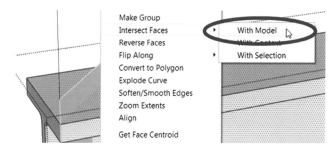

4. This creates scoring lines (#1 in the image shown here). You can now delete everything to the right of those lines (#2 in the same image) to cut away the mitered end.

5. At this point, you have a cleanly mitered end of this beam.

6. Copy and rotate this beam to create the mating part of the corner assembly.

The Trim Tool

If you own SketchUp Pro, you can perform this task much more easily using the Trim tool from the Solid Tools tool set. You can access this tool either from the Solid Tools toolbar or through the **Tools → Solid Tools** menu.

1. Start by creating a diagonal plane in the corner, similar to what you did previously. Because the Trim tool doesn't work with planes but with solids (closed or watertight groups and components), you need to extrude the plane using the Push/Pull tool. Do this so that it includes the entire end of the beam you need to cut away. Also, make sure you turn this box into a group.

2. You can now start the Trim tool. It will ask you to click two solids—first the box (that you want to cut against) and then the beam (the part you want to cut).

3. This creates the trimmed end of the beam in one step. Just delete the box, and your corner is done.

Example 3.2: Assembly Animation in SketchUp

A SketchUp feature that can be used to great effect with a component-based model is tabbed animation. Whenever you want to save a view in your model, you can add a tabbed *scene* (using the **View** → **Animation** menu). If you add more of these, you can even get SketchUp to animate through them. It is also possible to export this animation to a video file.

Of great benefit to us here is what is saved with each of these tabs. Not only is the camera location saved, but a tab also remembers which geometry or layers are hidden, where section planes were, which visual style the view had, and what the shadow settings were. For example, you can use these tabs effectively to illustrate shadow movements during a day.

In this example, you will add some scene tabs to the construction frame model from earlier in this chapter to create a small assembly animation.

1. Set up your model with all of the necessary objects. Make sure you group objects and use layers if needed. See **Figure 3.1** for the model used here.

2. Set up your basic view. This example keeps the view stationary, although you can just as well add different viewpoints in each scene tab. This would create more of a fly-around animation, of course.

3. Now click on the **View** → **Animation** → **Add Scene** menu item. This adds the first tab.

4. You will create the assembly animation backward (as a disassembly). Therefore, hide the first object(s) in your model (the wall studs, in my case). Then add another scene (you can do this now by right-clicking on the scene tab).

5. Hide the next object(s) and create another scene tab. Do this until you are at the end of your disassembly process. You should now see something like this:

6. The preceding image also displays the Scenes window. This window gives you a good visual overview of the animation tabs and lets you name the tabs. Name them, as shown, in reverse order.

7. Now use the Up and Down arrow keys in the Scenes window to reverse the order of the tabs. You should then see a properly organized animation layout like this:

8. Before playing the animation, it is always a good idea to adjust the animation settings (the length of time tabs are displayed or their transition duration). Do this in SketchUp's Model Info window:

9. You can now view the animation by right-clicking on one of the tabs and selecting Play Animation. A scene-by-scene breakdown for this example looks like this (one scene omitted here):

If you want to export this animation as a video, go to **File** → **Export** → **Animation** and save it. To create a good-quality video, shrink SketchUp's window to approximately the final video size (for example, use 1280 × 720 pixels for 720p HD resolution) and make sure everything looks good in the scenes before exporting. Export the video either as an Mp4, to get a small file size, or, for ultimate quality, uncompressed at a high frame rate (25 to 30 frames per second) and then edit and compress it later using video-editing software. Unless you want to create a looping animation, it is usually a good idea to uncheck the "Loop to starting scene" option that is enabled by default. You can adjust all of these export options in the video exporter dialog.

Whenever you want to remain longer on one scene during the animation, double up that scene by copying it in the Scenes window. This is usually a good idea, at least for the first and last scenes.

Using Dynamic Components to Your Advantage

Dynamic Components were introduced in SketchUp 7 and have in the meantime become a popular addition to SketchUp's core tool set. Their feature set has proven quite useful, especially for furniture and building component producers that need to add data to their 3D models—for schedules and other lists, for example.

How are Dynamic Components different from normal SketchUp components? As it turns out, a Dynamic Component's geometry is created exactly the same way a normal *static* component's would be. The dynamic feature gets added afterward, when the creator decides to add parameters and formulas to the component to embed data or make it responsive to something (e.g., a mouse click or the change of a parameter). **Figure 3.15** shows three Dynamic Components—all KraftMaid cabinetry—that were downloaded from the 3D Warehouse.

Figure 3.15: Dynamic Components in SketchUp

As you can see, highlighting a component brings up a description containing a part number and a link to the manufacturer's website. Because these are cabinets, it is also possible to click on doors and drawers and watch them swing or glide open. This is useful if you need to check clearances when planning kitchens.

Another way to use Dynamic Components is as parametric objects. **Figure 3.16** shows a bookshelf with geometry that can be changed by editing values such as height, material, and color in a dialog.

Figure 3.16: A parametric (Dynamic Component) bookshelf

Any user interaction with Dynamic Components is done using just a few tools. You can open the Dynamic Components toolbar in the **View → Toolbars...** menu to get access to them. As you can see in the graphic, this toolbar contains two or three icons (depending on whether you have the Pro or the Make version of SketchUp).

TIP

If this toolbar is not available, check that Dynamic Components are loaded and enabled. Open the Extension Warehouse window and go to My Extensions in the top-right menu (you may have to log in to see this). The list should show Dynamic Components as Enabled. If it doesn't, search for this extension in the same dialog and install it.

Figure 3.17: Interactive Dynamic Component behavior

In any version of SketchUp, you will see the hand icon on the left (the Interact tool). This tool permits interaction with a component by clicking, given that the component has that ability. For a good example, click on the person in SketchUp's default template—doing so will change some colors in the model (see **Figure 3.17**).

The tool next to it brings up the Component Options window, which is also available in both versions of SketchUp. Whenever you highlight a Dynamic Component (using the standard selection tool), this dialog shows all of the component's properties and attributes (which you can change right in this dialog). You can see this dialog in **Figure 3.16**.

Component Attributes Window

If you own SketchUp Pro, you will see another button. This one brings up the Component Attributes window (**Figure 3.18**).

Figure 3.18: The Component Attributes window

In this window you can create attributes and make a static component dynamic. You can always come back to this window and edit any of the parameters or formulas.

Example 3.3: Adding Dynamic Components to Your Model

This example allows you to start working with Dynamic Components by assembling a small kitchen. Feel free to use any manufacturer's cabinets that are in the 3D Warehouse. Just be consistent—otherwise, things might not fit. This example uses SketchUp's generic DC Cabinets, which you can find here: https://3dwarehouse.sketchup.com/collection.html?id=e89fe26ad13 04488de650492e45fb14f (short link: http://goo.gl/TmFudG).

1. Start by assembling the components you need. For this example, I downloaded two base cabinets and two tall cabinets. Although you can do this from the Component window in SketchUp, too, finding multiple components might be easier by browsing to the website in an external browser, downloading the component files, and then dragging them into SketchUp. They will then show up immediately at your mouse cursor, and you can place them anywhere in your model.

2. Now assemble the kitchen. If you like, add some walls and a floor and any other items, such as windows. In the following image, I also added a countertop and some spacer boards at the corner. You could color the cabinets by painting any material on them (I used a wood veneer here). As you can see, the components have been set up so that only the fronts are being painted.

3. Select the edge cabinets and open the Component Options window from the Dynamic Components toolbar. As you can see, you have several options available for these

components. Don't forget to make sure that the Finished Ends property is set appropriately. This adds color to the sides of the cabinets as well.

4. You can now use the Inspector tool to your advantage. Click on some drawers and doors. As you can see, they will slide out and swing open to their fully extended positions. This can give you some feedback on whether there are narrow spots and overlaps (especially in the corner). Because I added a filler strip in the corner (instead of just abutting the cabinets), everything fits well here.

This short example gives you a quick overview of how to use Dynamic Components in your designs. Feel free to browse some other Dynamic Component examples in the 3D Warehouse to see how they can be used for architecture, interior design, landscape design, manufacturing, construction, and other applications.

Next, let's look at how you can make your own Dynamic Components. Because quite a few functions are available for these, learning how to make them can become quite involved. Fortunately, the makers of SketchUp produced several sample components that convey this in more depth than can be covered here. You can find them at https://3dwarehouse.sketchup.com/collection.html?id=d86b819368a7afe98095ba2080357053 (short link: http://goo.gl/Cfp3lI). Also, please note that the ability to create Dynamic Components is included only in SketchUp Pro.

Making a Dynamic Component

In this example, you will create a 2 × 4 stud wall as a Dynamic Component and give it the capability of reporting material counts.

1. To start the wall, you need to begin with a basic amount of geometry. Draw a rectangle on the ground plane that measures 4" × 4'. This creates the base of the wall component. Because this is intended to be an interior wall, its width is 4" (3-1/2" for the studs plus a layer of 1/2" GWB drywall on each side).

2. Extrude this rectangle to the total wall height of 8' 3" (assuming a single top and bottom plate).

3. Use SketchUp's standard Make Component tool to turn this box into a component. In the Create Component dialog that opens, give it a name and select Glue To Horizontal (because you always want this to be a vertical wall).

4. At this point, the wall is a static component that you could use like any other in SketchUp. You need to turn it into a Dynamic Component, however. Therefore, open the Component Attributes dialog using the button on the Dynamic Components toolbar. It should look like this (when the wall component is selected):

5. As you can see, this dialog contains an Info tab that shows you all of the already defined attributes. It also has a Functions tab, which gives you an overview of all the functions that you can use with Dynamic Components. Let's add some attributes now. Click on Add Attribute to bring up a selection of common attributes. To begin, you will add the `LenX` and `LenZ` attributes.

6. These attributes will report the lengths along the component's (internal) red (X) and blue (Z) axes. At this point, they should show values of 48" and 99", respectively.

7. Let's add a calculated attribute now. Click on Add Attribute and type in a name (instead of picking one). Name it `GWB_Area` (you can't have spaces in names, hence, the underscore).

8. This attribute calculates the area of GWB drywall on both sides of the wall. Therefore, the formula for this attribute must be `=LenX*LenZ*2`. Enter this in the box to the right of `GWB_Area`. Instead of typing the attribute names, you can also click them. Doing so will insert them at the current cursor location and has the benefit of saving you from needing to check spelling.

9. The `GWB_Area` field should now report a value of 9504 (square inches of GWB area). You can click on the button that reads "=fx" in the top-right corner of the dialog to toggle between value view and function view.

10. Add another calculated attribute; this one reports the number of 4 × 8 GWB sheets that are needed. Call it `GWB_Sheets` and give it the formula `=GWB_Area/4608`.

11. Now click on the arrow to the right of this formula to bring up the attribute's options. Make sure to select User Can See This Attribute, give it a readable name, and display it as a decimal number.

12. Finally, add another attribute, `Studs_Num` to the list. Give it the formula `=ROUND(LenX/16+1)`. As you may have guessed, this attribute reports the (rounded) number of studs for this section (assuming 16" on-center spacing). We also used one of SketchUp's built-in functions for this attribute (`ROUND`). Don't forget to change the attribute's options so that the user can see this one, too.

13. To finish this component, let's add one more built-in attribute from the drop-down list: `ScaleTool`. This attribute lets you define which scale handles are shown to the user. For the wall component, you only want the user to be able to stretch the wall using the Scale Along Red (X) handle. Uncheck everything else.

14. The finished Dynamic Component should look like the following image when you use the Scale tool. All you should see is the scale handle in the red direction (the x-axis).

You can now stretch this component to your liking and see the reported attributes update in the Component Attributes and the Component Options windows. If you distribute this

Dynamic Component to SketchUp Make users (e.g., by uploading it to the 3D Warehouse), they will be able to place it, stretch it, and read the values from the Component Options window. They will not be able to edit it, though.

After inserting several wall component instances into your model, it is possible to use the **File→Generate Report...** menu item to report stud number and drywall sheet requirements for the entire model (or any selection).

As a reference, you can find a complete list of available Dynamic Component functions and predefined attributes in Appendix E.

If you don't have SketchUp Pro, don't worry. You can still go to this book's companion website and download this wall component for use in your models. You just can't edit its definition.

TIP

Although using Dynamic Components is an excellent way to add data and dynamic (*parametric*) behavior to a SketchUp model, there are also various extensions that can accomplish similar tasks in your models. See Chapter 4 for more on this.

Where Does SketchUp Fit into the BIM Workflow?

SketchUp has been used for years by many architecture, engineering, and construction (AEC) and related professionals to solve various tasks over the course of many building projects. Some firms use it in the early, conceptual phases to study design options and maybe perform energy analysis. In later design phases, SketchUp has also found a wide following as a render-ing preprocessing tool. Geometry can easily be imported from other software, and various low-cost rendering software packages can be used to create highly professional renderings (see Chapter 5 for more on this). In addition—as you saw before—SketchUp can be used successfully in construction planning for constructability analysis using assembly mock-ups, 4D scheduling for project management, and site layout design.

On the other hand, a firm might decide to use SketchUp as its sole planning and docu-mentation tool and benefit from LayOut's ability to create production-ready construction documentation. LayOut is a drafting add-on that ships with SketchUp Pro.

With the recent surge in demand for virtual construction tools and Building Information Modeling (BIM) emerging as both a tool and a process in digital construction, the question validly arises as to where SketchUp fits into all of this. After all, BIM is all about 3D modeling and data integration. As you know by now, not only is SketchUp capable of 3D modeling, it also features ways to include data in your models.

While SketchUp, at its heart, is a *general* 3D modeling software program (and not tied to a particular discipline), it can offer the following avenues for use in architectural, engineer-ing, or construction planning:

- **As a massing-modeling tool**—You can easily do massing-modeling in SketchUp by importing existing 3D buildings from the 3D Warehouse and elsewhere and then blocking out new buildings using SketchUp's tool set. Many larger BIM applications (e.g., Autodesk Revit and Graphisoft ArchiCAD) are able to import SketchUp models and use them to generate more detailed building models. **Figure 3.19** illustrates this for Revit.

Figure 3.19: Importing a SketchUp model into Revit (front walls were created in Revit using the Wall by Face tool)

- **As a programming tool**—When you are laying out a building program, it is possible to easily block out areas and spaces and arrange them in SketchUp (see **Figure 3.20**). It is even possible to create these spaces based on data from external software—examples are the Onuma Planning System and Trelligence Affinity.

Reception
Meeting
Offices
Cafeteria

Figure 3.20: Space planning in SketchUp

- **As a building energy-analysis tool**—With a building's energy performance more frequently being included into early stages of design, it is possible to use SketchUp as a rough modeling tool (these models often need to consist only of simple faces to work well) and an analysis pre-processor. Some of the available software then exchanges the SketchUp-created energy model with an external energy-analysis program or with other BIM applications using the gbXML (green building XML) format.

A list of currently available plugins and an example are included in Chapter 4.

- **As a parametric BIM modeling tool**—As shown in Chapter 4, several extensions exist that allow you to create parametric buildings and their components in SketchUp. This includes any level of detail from wall layer setup to parametric roofs. Combined with the LayOut software, such models can then easily be used for complete construction documentation.

- **As an Industry Foundation Classes (IFC) modeling tool**—With the classification tagging system that was introduced with SketchUp Pro 2014 and IFC file import and export, SketchUp now supports the IFC file format, which makes it easy to exchange data-heavy files with other BIM software. This approach and SketchUp's capabilities will be discussed in the next section.

- **As a mock-up building and constructability analysis tool**—While BIM software is able to create 3D models of sometimes very complex buildings, these are often not executed at a level of detail that might include individual studs or bricks. If 3D assembly models are required to evaluate or explain details, it is sometimes more efficient to do them in SketchUp and later import them into the construction documentation set.

As shown in the preceding examples, SketchUp can be used very effectively to create mock-ups and test assemblies as long as a strict component-based modeling approach is followed.

- **As a geo-based modeling tool**—One of SketchUp's strengths is that it is tightly integrated with Google's geo-based data. This was described in Chapter 2 and allows you to use orthophotographs, terrain data, some existing building models, and location-accurate shadows in your model (see Example 2.7 and **Figure 3.21** for examples).

Figure 3.21: Photo-textured geo-located model

You can exchange data and building models from SketchUp with other software in a variety of ways. SketchUp Make allows you to export 2D images, 3D models (as COLLADA DAE or Google Earth KMZ files), and video animations. The Pro version adds to that Autodesk's DWG and DXF, as well as some common 3D formats such as 3DS, IFC, FBX, OBJ, XSI, and VRML. You also have access to PDF and EPS vector-based 2D export.

To import 3D models into SketchUp, you can use either 3DS, DEM, DAE, or KMZ file formats in either version. The Pro version adds to this DWG, DXF, and IFC import.

Beyond these formats, many 3D software packages now include direct SKP file import, which makes it even easier to use a SketchUp model in another program. If this is not available, then a good file format, which is universally accepted and supported by all versions of SketchUp, is the COLLADA DAE format. This is also the format Google Earth uses (in its KMZ files).

TIP	It is a common malaise of many CAD software importers (not just SketchUp's) that they are usually at least one version behind! Therefore, whenever you want to import a SketchUp SKP file, for example, into Autodesk Revit, save the file as last year's or even an older version (using the File → Save As... dialog and choosing from Save As Type) to save yourself some headaches.

Example 3.4: Program Planning with SketchUp's Dynamic Components

When laying out a space program for a building, a common approach is to use rectangular blocks to represent spaces (offices, auditoriums, etc.) and then arrange them visually to outline the total space requirement and relationships among them. In this example, you will use simple rectangular Dynamic Components to help with this task.

If you don't have SketchUp Pro, you can still use the component from this example. Simply download the space component from the companion website and insert it into a model. Skip to step 7 in that case.

Making a Space Dynamic Component

`PRO ONLY`

1. Create a rectangle on the ground plane. At this point, neither size nor location is important. Turn the rectangle into a component and call it **Space**.

2. Add all of the attributes as shown in **Figure 3.22**.

Figure 3.22: Attributes for the Space Dynamic Component

3. Add these formulas: for `Z` use `=(Story-1)*StoryHeightFt*12` and for `LenY` use `=AreaSqFt/LenX*144`. This determines the elevation of the component based on the story on which it is located. In addition, component size is always calculated based on the square-foot area provided by the user. This is helpful when the user stretches the component.

4. For the `Material` attribute, add several of SketchUp's color names that are to your liking. Users are able to color-code spaces this way. Alternatively, you could program into the component the ability to automatically select a color based on the chosen use.

5. In the settings for the `ScaleTool` attribute, deselect everything except Scale Along Red (X) and Scale Uniform (From Corners) (XYZ).

6. Set the visibility of all attributes that show a dialog icon on the right in **Figure 3.22** so that the user can see and edit them.

7. Open the Component Options dialog. It should show all of the accessible attributes such as color, use, story height, story number, and square footage (see **Figure 3.23**).

Figure 3.23: Options for the Space Dynamic Component

8. When you start the Scale tool, you will be able to see the handles that are available. Use them to stretch the space component in various directions. As you can see, its area is automatically limited by the Dynamic Component to the entered value: 160 square feet, in this case. (See **Figure 3.24**.)

Figure 3.24: Scaling the space component

9. To roughly lay out a building, I used SketchUp's Grid Tool extension to add several grids (with a spacing of 4') at the story heights. You can install it from the Extension Warehouse (see Chapter 4 for details).

   Having a grid is not absolutely necessary; however, it provides a good reference for snapping.

10. After you do this, add several of your newly created space components from the Component window into the model, add use and size data in the Component Options window, and copy and place them wherever you like in your model. You can very quickly and efficiently lay out a building program based on this. (See **Figure 3.25**.)

Figure 3.25: Using the component to plan building spaces

You can do a lot with this seemingly simple approach. Here are some ideas:

- Use the Generate Report tool to create schedules of these spaces and export them to Microsoft Excel. If you need to attach more data to each space, do this in the Component Attributes window, as previously shown.
- Use the BIM Classifier tool to assign it the IfcSpace *classification* and use the IFC file format to transfer the model to another BIM software.
- Export all of the spaces as a 3D DWG/DXF (or any of the other available file types) and import them into other CAD software to start adding walls and other features.
- Export your space model to Google Earth (using the KMZ file format) and view it in its urban context.
- Learn Ruby scripting (covered in Chapter 7) and create spaces automatically based on CSV data provided from another application (e.g., Microsoft Excel).
- Upload your SketchUp model to the 3D Warehouse to share it with your clients.

BIM Classifier and IFC in SketchUp

Most BIM software file formats (including SketchUp's own) are proprietary and do not lend themselves well to file and, therefore, data exchange. Often a generic file format (e.g., DWG) is used for file exchange, with the downside that it typically removes any data that is contained within a model (such as the component attributes data discussed previously). This then forces reentry of said data after file import in the other software. However, approaches and file formats exist that can be used for exchange of BIM models for any of these purposes:

- Further refinement of the model in other BIM software
- Import into analysis software (e.g., for structural or building energy analysis)
- Other database-exchange tasks (e.g., for estimating)

Although those approaches are often related to a particular file format (IFC, for example), the best way to think of these is as a classification system. Take a structural beam in a model, for example. This beam needs to be classified (*tagged*) as such (so that the analysis software knows it is a beam), and it needs to be categorized in some form of hierarchy that includes the floor level the beam is located on and the overall building as higher-level (*parent*) elements. It also needs to provide the various data fields that will be important for the analysis software: material, shape, connection types, etc. Of course, this classification system should not only contain structural data; it also should comprise architectural, construction, procurement, geospatial, and many other fields.

At present, there are several such classification systems (*schemas*) in use that relate to the AEC domain:

- **IFC (Industry Foundation Classes)**—This schema covers the entire building life cycle from inception to operation and maintenance (see www.buildingsmart-tech.org) and is used in conjunction with other data-exchange systems (e.g., COBie).

- **gbXML (Green Building XML)**—This format is for exchange of building analysis data (see www.gbxml.org).

- **OpenGIS**—This format pertains to geospatial data (see www.opengeospatial.org).

- **CityGML**—This format is for virtual 3D city and landscape models (see www.citygml.org).

TIP

For more background on these schemas and Building Information Modeling in general, consult the following book:

Chuck Eastman, Paul Teicholz, Rafael Sacks, Kathleen Liston, *BIM Handbook: A Guide to Building Information Modeling for Owners, Managers, Designers, Engineers and Contractors,* 2nd ed. (John Wiley & Sons).

Because it is widely applicable in the AEC field, IFC is the file exchange format that has been implemented in almost all BIM software. Starting with SketchUp 2015, this file format is also available for both import and export in this program, and the schema ships with SketchUp as you can see in **Figure 3.26**.

It should be noted that in its implementation, Trimble chose a generic and universally applicable approach. Any schema can be loaded into the software and then applied to any components. SketchUp itself does not impose a particular hierarchy or object logic, which makes this approach ultimately the most flexible. On the other hand, it leaves any verification and logic-based tasks (e.g., is what was tagged a "beam" actually a beam?) up to the user or specialized extensions.

If none of the classification schemas here are applicable to your work, you can use the instructions in Appendix F to create your own schema file for use in SketchUp. Modify this approach to best suit your workflow and data requirements.

Figure 3.26: IFC classes in the BIM Classifier toolbar

TIP

If you work a lot with any particular BIM schema, then a good shortcut is to load it into your template file. A schema is saved inside the model file like any of the other elements that were discussed in Chapter 2. This prevents you from having to reload it every time you need it. Also, when you share a model with someone else, the schema data will be available to them, independent of whether they have the schema definition available on their computer.

The following example shows how to work with IFC tagging in the BIM Classifier tool and how to exchange IFC files with other software. Please note that the BIM Classifier functionality is only available in SketchUp Pro.

Example 3.5: Using IFC Classifications in SketchUp

In this exercise, you will tag a steel frame model with the IFC 2×3 schema, export it using SketchUp's IFC exporter, and then view it in another BIM application.

1. To get started, first check that the classification schema has been loaded into the model. You can do this in the Model Info window. As you can see in the next image, you can load as many schemas as you need into your model. If the list does not show the IFC 2×3 schema, click on Import... and load it.

2. Because the Classifier tool works with components in SketchUp, you should make sure your model is well organized using components (as described previously in this chapter). As you can see in this frame model, all objects are components (the column is shown in the Entity Info dialog as an example).

3. Let's apply the column classification using the Entity Info window. Highlight a column component and then click the Type drop-down in the window. You should see a list of all the installed schemas (only IFC 2×3 in my case). When you expand that list, all the classifier elements that you can use will appear (you will need the IfcColumn class). Toggle the Simplify button to switch between a short and a long list of options. If you can't find the column item, type **column** into the search box; the list will shorten to items that contain that word in their name. Finally, click on IfcColumn to apply this classification to the column component.

4. For the beams, let's apply the classification using an alternative method: the toolbar. With nothing selected in the model, click on the Classifier toolbar's drop-down (the selection will be similar to what you saw in the Entity Info window). Select IfcBeam from the list and then click the Classifier tool button (it looks like a bunch of tags). This lets you quickly tag items in your model. Just click on one of the beams and you are done. Check the Entity Info window to verify that the proper type is now shown for the beam component.

5. Because the classification is applied to components, all copies of the same component are automatically classified as well. Just go ahead and classify (*tag*) all other elements in your model as needed.

6. You are now ready to export the IFC file. Go to **File** → **Export** → **3D Model...** and select IFC File from the file *Export type* drop-down. If desired, adjust the export options as shown here.

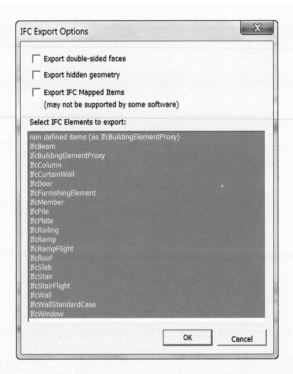

7. As a final step, import the IFC file (and thereby the model) into any software that accepts it (e.g., Autodesk Revit, Graphisoft ArchiCAD). **Figure 3.27** shows the model in the Solibri IFC Model Viewer software. As you can see, the beams and columns are classified correctly and show up in the building's IFC-based hierarchy.

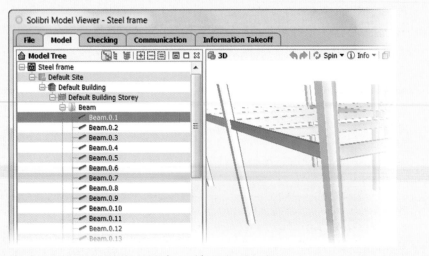

Figure 3.27: SketchUp's IFC model of a steel frame in a BIM viewer

It is important to keep some details in mind when you're working with the BIM Classifier and IFC. Please note that these are relevant to the 2015 version of SketchUp.

- You can access all of the attributes/properties of a classification (such as the IfcBeam's Name or Description) through SketchUp's Component Options dialog (similar to what was previously described for Dynamic Components).

- Those attributes/properties are stored with the component definition. Therefore, if you need to change only attributes/properties for an otherwise similar component, make the second component unique before editing.

- SketchUp's Generate Report tool will report the IFC class together with all applicable attributes/properties similar to what was shown previously for Dynamic Components.

- SketchUp allows you to reclassify a component without warning. While this makes it easy to apply classifications quickly to a model (using any of the methods described earlier), it also means that classification data (including attributes/properties) can easily be removed.

- While fairly reliable, IFC importers across the various BIM software platforms may work differently and use imported data in different ways. Consult the importing software's help file for details. Those importers also typically apply some mapping (of imported objects to internal objects) that can be edited. As an example, the next image shows Autodesk Revit 2014's dialog where IFC classes (shown in the left column) are matched to Revit's family categories (shown in the right column).

Import IFC Class Mapping

IFC Class Name	Category
IfcRailing	Railings
IfcRamp	Ramps
IfcRampFlight	Ramps
IfcReinforcingBar	Structural Rebar
IfcReinforcingMesh	Generic Models
IfcRoof	Roofs
IfcSanitaryTerminalType	Generic Models

As you can see, all main architectural components are correctly mapped. Others are mapped as a Generic Model, which is akin to an in-place Revit family. None of these are mapped to Revit's system families, which means that a wall's structure cannot be edited after import.

You can, however, edit this mapping file or look for a more specialized third-party importer that gives you more control over the import process.

When working with IFC, it is advisable to have a model viewer on hand to be able to check and troubleshoot IFC files. These are some examples:

- Solibri Model Viewer—**www.solibri.com/products/solibri-model-viewer**

- Tekla BIMsight—**www.teklabimsight.com**

If needed, you can look up the IFC support level for many BIM software applications on this buildingSMART Alliance website:

www.buildingsmart-tech.org/implementation

Your Turn!

The following tasks allow you to practice the topics in this chapter:

1. **Create an exploded view of an assembled object.**
   Similar to **Figure 3.3**, create an exploded view of an assembly or an object (e.g., a furniture item) in which all the parts are spaced slightly apart. This is a great way to explain how this object was produced, and it will teach you good component-based modeling along the way.

2. **Create an assembly animation.**
   Take any assembly or process you are interested in (e.g., a construction detail or a factory layout) and create an assembly animation. Use the technique from Example 3.2 to accomplish this. Also export your animation as a video (and share it

with the world by uploading to a video-sharing website). If you want to physically animate objects in SketchUp, look in Chapter 4 for plugins that can help you accomplish this task.

3. **Create a wooden puzzle toy.**

   In SketchUp, design a realistic 3D puzzle toy, which is produced using overlapping wooden blocks and cutting them at intersections. The toy must consist of more than three parts and needs to be able to be disassembled and reassembled. If you like, produce it physically afterward in the wood shop to see how well executed your design was.

4. **Make a Dynamic Component.**

   If you have access to SketchUp Pro, make a Dynamic Component that is relevant to your discipline. Add it to a model in SketchUp and then report its parameters in an Excel spreadsheet.

5. **Create a building space plan.**

   Use a fictitious building space program (several offices, meeting rooms, assembly areas, etc.) or a real building's space layout and create a 3D space plan using the technique shown in Example 3.4. Also add more attributes (`department`, `occupant`, etc.) to the space component.

6. **Export an IFC File to other BIM software.**

   Use one of your models in SketchUp (practice with the trellis model from the last chapter or use one from another project). Classify all of its components with the proper IFC classes and export it as an IFC file. Then open it in a different BIM application (e.g., Autodesk Revit) and see a) how you need to tweak the settings to correctly import the model, and b) what you can afterward use it for in that software.

Chapter 4
Using Extensions Effectively

In this chapter, you'll explore the many extensions (frequently also called *plugins*) that are available for SketchUp. They are used for tasks that can't (efficiently) be accomplished using SketchUp's built-in tool set alone. These extensions are often freely available, they are easy to install, most work in either version of SketchUp, they add a wide range of functionality, and you can use as many or as few as you need for a given task.

Some of the things that are possible with extensions are advanced creation/deformation of objects, organic modeling, fabrication preprocessing, physics simulation, building energy analysis, and—as you will see in Chapter 5—photorealistic rendering.

Key Topics:

- Where to find extensions and how to install and maintain them
- Extensions for:
  - General 3D modeling
  - Architectural modeling
  - Digital fabrication
  - Data integration
  - Animation
  - Analysis

What Does an Extension Do?

Arguably one of the most forward-looking and best features of SketchUp (and one that was implemented early in the software's development) was the inclusion of a scripting language called Ruby. Having many program functions available in this scripting language effectively made it possible to control every aspect in SketchUp using only a few lines of code. It was thereafter possible for any user to extend the functionality of SketchUp by writing some Ruby code, posting it on the Web, and letting other people use the tool they created, too. Typically, most available extensions can be used with any version of SketchUp (Make or Pro), which is a tremendous benefit for users on a budget who want to use powerful 3D modeling software.

Over the past years, extensions have expanded from small pieces of code that come in one file and add one tool in SketchUp to sometimes very complex software packages that provide an entire tool set and a visual user interface and that allow SketchUp to exchange data with external software such as a photorealistic rendering or a building energy analysis program.

The number of available extensions has increased, too. One of the oldest repositories, Didier Bur's Ruby Library Depot, at the time of this writing was listing almost 1,100 extensions—not even counting many commercial extensions that are available on other websites.

This chapter presents some of the more common extensions. Due to the large number of them (and the small space available here), you are encouraged to keep browsing repositories and following new extension announcements—especially when you run into a problem that SketchUp alone can't help you solve.

Getting and Using Extensions

Before you can use any extensions in SketchUp, you obviously have to acquire them. Fortunately, it is quite easy to do this within SketchUp by visiting the Extension Warehouse. This repository, built by Trimble and hosted on the Web at http://extensions.sketchup.com, is integrated closely with SketchUp, which makes finding, installing, and updating extensions very easy. In addition to the Extension Warehouse, there are also other community-based repositories, which I will introduce later.

You can get to the Warehouse by either opening the Extension Warehouse window or by clicking on the small "ruby in a box" icon on the Getting Started or Warehouse toolbars.

You should next see the main screen shown in **Figure 4.1**, where you can either search or browse for extensions. Make sure you sign in here (using your Google account) if you haven't already done so. Signing in allows you to directly install extensions and keep track of your list of extensions (for updating or when you need them on a different computer).

Once you have found an extension you want to install, just click the Install button and follow the installation instruction dialogs. (See **Figure 4.2**.)

Often, extensions can be used immediately. Sometimes, however, a restart of SketchUp is required. It should also be noted that while most extensions are free, some of them are commercial and will require you to complete a purchase process before you can install them.

Figure 4.1: The Extension Warehouse

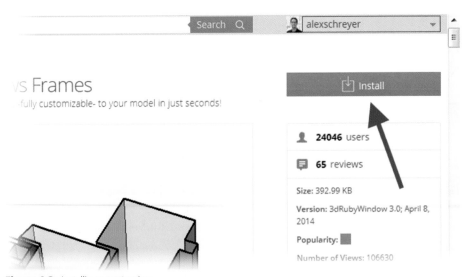

Figure 4.2: Installing an extension

After you assemble your collection of SketchUp extensions, you can use the My Extensions section of the Extension Warehouse window to update, disable, or uninstall current extensions and reinstall those that you may have uninstalled previously (or installed on a different computer). As you can see in **Figure 4.3**, you can even install or uninstall all of your extensions with just one command, which makes setting up computers or updating from one SketchUp version to another a breeze.

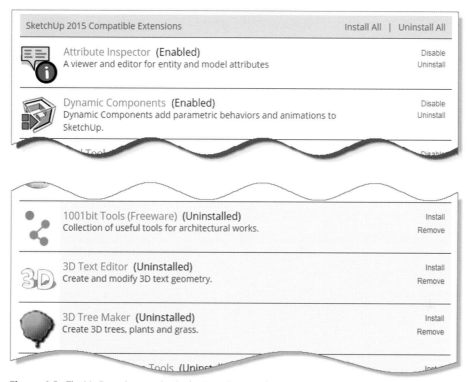

Figure 4.3: The My Extensions section in the Extension Warehouse window

TIP

As long as you are logged into your Google account in SketchUp, the availability of updates for extensions will be indicated with a small circle over the "ruby in the box" toolbar icon.

TIP

Although you can alternatively go to the Extension Warehouse website in any browser (outside of SketchUp) and download an extension (as an RBZ file), the installation method shown here is preferable for these extensions.

Beyond Trimble's Extension Warehouse (EW, for short), there are also other, community-based repositories and indexes. If you can't find an extension in the Extension Warehouse that satisfies your needs, look for it somewhere else. Each one of the following sites has its benefits and drawbacks. However, note that the extensions are usually not scrutinized as much for quality as they are on the Extension Warehouse (where Trimble even checks the underlying Ruby code).

- **SketchUcation Plugin Store (SP)**—This extension repository has many additional extensions that are not included in the EW. It also provides a store extension, which lets you find, install, update, and uninstall extensions right inside SketchUp. http://sketchucation.com/pluginstore

- **Ruby Library Depot (RL)**—This site has been collecting and indexing extensions for a long time now and might have the largest index of freely available community-supplied extensions. http://rhin.crai.archi.fr/rld

- **Smustard (SM)**—A site that provides many free or low-cost extensions for common tasks. www.smustard.com

- **SketchUp Plugin Index (PI)**—This site serves as an index (instead of a download repository) for commercial and freely available extensions. http://sketchupplugins.com

Please note: The abbreviations in parentheses in the preceding list serve as references as we examine extensions in the next few sections.

To make finding extensions a little easier for you, I created a Custom Google Search Engine that searches all of the sites mentioned here, which can sometimes help with hard-to-find extensions. If you would like to use it, follow this URL: http://goo.gl/yj7zaT

TIP

When looking for extensions, you may find that some are available only through the SketchUcation Plugin Store and not in the Extension Warehouse. Therefore, it is a good idea to install the Plugin Store extension as well. At this point, however, it is not available in the Extension Warehouse and must be installed manually. Follow these steps to install and use it:

1. Download the Plugin Store extension as an RBZ file from the following URL: **http://sketchucation.com/resources/plugin-store-download.**

2. In SketchUp, go to the Preferences window's Extensions tab and click on Install Extension…. Browse to the RBZ file that you downloaded and follow the dialog instructions to install it.

3. You should then be able to go to **Extensions → SketchUcation → SketchUcation Plugin Store** and access the Store dialog:

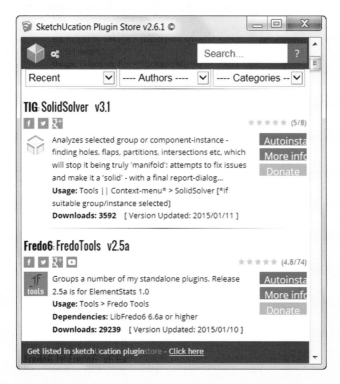

This Plugin Store extension provides functionality similar to the Extension Warehouse (installing, updating, organizing, and removing of extensions). Neither one acknowledges extensions installed through the other one, though. Therefore, use a consistent system when downloading—for example, try the EW first, the SP next, and only if you can't find a plugin there, try all other repositories.

How Exactly Do Extensions Work?

For most users, the previous instructions should be sufficient when working with extensions. However, when you need to manually install (or uninstall) an extension or troubleshoot an issue, it is helpful to know the following details as well.

Extensions come in four file types: RB, ZIP, RBZ, or an installable EXE or DMG file. There is even a fifth one, RBS, an encrypted version of an RB file. All of these file types require different installation methods. As a first step, it is important that you know *where* SketchUp extensions are installed.

The default location, which serves as a home for installed extensions, depends on your operating system. If you accepted SketchUp's suggested location on your hard disk during installation, you can locate this folder as follows.

On Windows:

C:\Users\<YOUR USERNAME>\AppData\Roaming\SketchUp\SketchUp 2015\SketchUp\Plugins

On Macs:

Open a new Finder window, press and hold the Option key on your keyboard, and then click **Go** (in the menu bar) → **Library** → **Application Support** → **SketchUp 2015** → **SketchUp** → **Plugins**.

Adjust the version numbers in these paths as appropriate. These locations are valid for the 2015 version. For older versions, consult this help article: http://help.sketchup.com/en/article/38583.

When you install an extension in SketchUp (using any of the methods described here), the extension files are copied into this folder. Every time SketchUp starts, it looks in this folder and automatically loads all of the extensions it finds.

TIP

If you use a lot of extensions, the Extensions folder can become quite crammed. You can free up some space there (and speed up SketchUp's start-up time) by removing some of the extension files and saving them somewhere else. You can always return them when you need them again.

If you used the Extension Warehouse or the SketchUcation Plugin Store, you can simply disable or uninstall them.

Let's look at how to install extensions, depending on the file type.

- **RB or RBS file**—This is simply a Ruby code text file that by itself will contain all the necessary instructions for the extension. Take this file and copy it into the Extensions folder. Then restart SketchUp and you can use the extension. If you have an RBS file, it is just an encrypted version of the extension. While you can't read its contents, SketchUp can. Install it exactly as you would an RB file.

- **ZIP file**—A ZIP (compressed) file contains not only the RB file(s) but often other necessary files (e.g., images) and folders. Unzip this file using any compression software you like and paste its content exactly as it is into the Extensions folder (this is sometimes called *extracting* the file contents). It is important to make sure you keep its internal folder structure intact. Usually your operating system will open a ZIP file if you just double-click it. If that doesn't work, look for compression software such as 7-ZIP (www.7-zip.org) to help you out. Note that you can also install a ZIP file extension using the method described for the RBZ file.

- **RBZ file**—To install an RBZ extension, all you need to do is go to the Extensions tab in the Preferences window (see **Figure 4.4**). There you will find a button labeled Install

Extension…. Click that button, browse to the RBZ file, and okay any confirmation dialogs that come up. SketchUp will install this extension for you, and you don't even have to browse to the Extensions folder. As mentioned before, this method also works with ZIP files (because an RBZ file is just a ZIP file with a different filename ending).

Figure 4.4: The Install Extension… button

TIP

In Windows, you should be able to simply copy the web URL of an RBZ or ZIP extension and paste it into the filename box of the dialog that opens when you click the Install Extension… button. Windows will download the file for you, and then SketchUp will install it—all in one step.

- **An installable EXE, MSI, or DMG file**—If an extension comes as this type of file, the extension author will have packaged it in a system-specific installation or setup file (an EXE or MSI file in Windows and a DMG file for use on Macs). You can install it as you would any other software on your computer. Usually this format is used with larger, commercial extensions. Most of them do not require you to do anything other than click a few Next buttons. You might be required to confirm SketchUp's installation location, though. Modify this only if you installed SketchUp in a custom location.

After installing your extension, you might be required to restart SketchUp. At that point, any new functionality will be available. Consult your extension's documentation (if any is available) to see how you can use it. Typically, extensions add a menu item to one of the main menus (often under the **Extensions** menu). You might also find new tools in the right-click menu.

It is possible that the extension added an entire toolbar. If you can't see the new toolbar, go to the **View** → **Toolbars…** menu and make sure you enable it (there should be a check mark next to the extension's toolbar).

At this point, you are ready to work with your new extension.

If you prefer *not* to have all of your extensions load when SketchUp starts and would rather load them on demand, use this method:

1. Install my Plugin Loader extension from this link: **www.alexschreyer.net/projects/plugin-loader-for-sketchup**.

2. Save your extension files (what is contained in an RBZ or ZIP file) wherever you like—you can even create a folder on a USB drive and save them there. Just make sure you save each extension with its folder structure intact (exactly as it would be in SketchUp's Extensions folder).

3. Using the **Plugin Loader** menu under the **Extensions** menu, browse to the main RB file of the extension you want to load and select it. After loading, your extension should be available in SketchUp.

Keep in mind that once you restart SketchUp, the extensions you load with this method are no longer available and must be reloaded.

Updating, Uninstalling, and Organizing Extensions

Updating, disabling, and deleting extensions is easy if you installed them using either the Extension Warehouse or the SketchUcation Plugin Store. Just go to the respective dialog (you might have to visit both) and work with the links there. Two of the main benefits of using these repositories are that they will alert you when an update is available and that disabling or uninstalling is easy.

If you manually installed an extension using any of the methods described previously, you will have to chase down any updates and use a similar installation process as initially required to update it. Often, files can just be overwritten and the new version is available after a restart of SketchUp.

What can you do, however, if you no longer want an extension in SketchUp? If the extension takes advantage of SketchUp's built-in Extension management system, then it is very easy to disable it and prevent it from loading. You do this in the Extensions tab of the Preferences window. As shown in **Figure 4.5**, just uncheck the box next to the extension's name, and it will not be loaded in the future (it remains installed, though). If you need it again, just check the box and restart SketchUp (if prompted).

If you can't find the extension you are looking for in that list, your only option is to remove its file(s) from the Extensions folder. This is a little more involved than the previous method because you have to delete or move the respective files from a folder that is buried reasonably deep on your hard disk.

To do this, browse to SketchUp's Plugins folder (as mentioned earlier). If you know which extension files you intend to remove, simply select all of them and press the Delete key. If you don't know, some detective work might be required. Just remember that extension files end in RB or RBS. Also, some extension authors add their initials at the beginning of the file. In addition, there is often an associated folder that contains more files that this extension uses (it is not necessary to remove this folder, though).

Figure 4.5: Disabling an extension in the Extensions tab

Once you have found the appropriate files, it might be a good idea to move them to a separate folder (you could create a folder called Inactive Extensions for exactly this purpose). The benefit of moving the files instead of deleting them is that if something goes wrong (or you want to have your extension back), you can always troubleshoot and move the files back. You also won't have to search for and download the extension again in the future.

TIP

If your extension came as an installable EXE, MSI, or DMG file, look in your operating system for the uninstall function and uninstall it this way instead.

Another related issue is the messiness of the **Extensions** menu in SketchUp once you have installed several extensions. Unfortunately, SketchUp does not give you a way to organize this menu (it simply loads extensions in alphanumeric order based on filenames). If you want to do any spring cleaning, you should disable or uninstall any unused extensions.

Extensions Overview

The following sections present a selection of the most commonly used and popular extensions. This list is by no means a complete reference. As I mentioned previously, hundreds of extensions are available currently. Use these extensions for your most common tasks, but feel free to search the sites mentioned previously if you have a special application that is not covered here.

TIP

Some of SketchUp's tools such as Advanced Camera Tools, Dynamic Components, Sandbox Tools, and Photo Textures are actually extensions that either come shipped with SketchUp or can be downloaded from the Extension Warehouse.

Unfortunately, the quality of documentation for these extensions varies widely. Commercial extensions and those by the more prolific creators (such as ThomThom, Fredo6, and TIG) are usually well documented. For others, read the accompanying text on the web pages where you downloaded them.

Whenever I mention an extension, the name (or alias) shown below its title is that of the author. I also mention the cost of the extension (if known) and where you can find it. The letters in brackets refer to the list of website(s) that appeared in the "Getting and Using Extensions" section earlier in this chapter.

A final note before you get going with extensions in SketchUp: Extension development and especially maintenance are quite involved tasks. Although many extensions have been provided for free to the community, consider donating to the authors if they offer a way to do so and you find their extensions useful. If you get inspired by what is possible in SketchUp and take to Ruby scripting yourself (especially after reading Chapter 7 in this book), then an alternative idea to pay back to the community might be to share your own code as extensions.

Extensions for General Modeling

Artisan Organic Toolset

By Whaat—$39 (EW, SP, www.artisan4sketchup.com)

This has been the organic-modeling extension of choice in SketchUp for a while now. What started as the SubdivideAndSmooth extension has become the expanded Artisan extension. While SketchUp may not be known specifically for polygon-based organic modeling, it is very

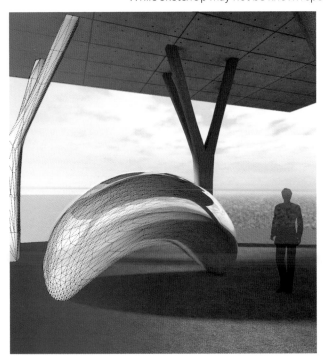

much capable of creating nonrectilinear shapes, as this extension shows.

With this extension, you can subdivide any object and then crease, push/pull, sculpt, paint, and otherwise deform and change polygons to your artistic liking.

Beyond using it for shaping humanoid and animal-shaped blobs, you can benefit from its capabilities to create landscapes, rocks, beanbags, jewelry, and much more.

Another extension that lets you freely deform any shape (based on an encircling grid of points) is the Sketchy FFD extension by C. Phillips. It is free, and you can get it from (SP).

Sculpt Tools by BTM also lets you modify meshes by sculpting. It is free, and you can download it from (SP).

Vertex Tools by ThomThom is another commercial extension ($20) that helps edit vertices on objects such as surfaces. You can select vertices smoothly and then modify them. You can get it from (EW, www.ThomThom.net/software/vertex_tools).

Bezier Spline

By Fredo6—Free (SP)

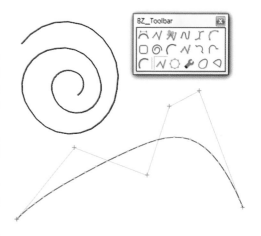

If you need a smooth curve (a spline) for a walkway or a kidney-shaped table, for example, use this extension to create curves that are determined by control points. You can edit created curves by moving control points and applying various parameters, such as the precision of the curve.

As always in SketchUp, once a curve closes, a face is created. Although edges appear as curves, they do consist of connected polyline segments just like any other curved shape in SketchUp.

Keep in mind that this extension is also excellent for smoothing "edgy" polylines, subdividing curves, and welding edges into polylines.

A simpler version of this is SketchUp's own Bezier Curve tool (EW).

BoolTools

By Whaat—$10 (SM)

If you don't have the Pro version of SketchUp and are therefore lacking the Solid Tools, then this extension offers a cost-efficient way to use Boolean operations such as subtract, add, or difference on components.

For 2D Booleans, look for the 2D Simplex Bool extension by Skelion in the (EW).

CleanUp³

By ThomThom—Free (EW, SP)

This extension provides various model cleanup tools. It erases duplicate faces or hidden geometry, repairs edges, merged materials, and much more.

Also look up ThomThom's Edge Tools to simplify edges, close gaps, etc. on EW and Fredo6's Curvizard to clean up curves on (SP).

Components onto Faces

By C. Fullmer—Free (EW, SP)

This extension copies components orthogonally onto all selected faces. The result is similar to what can be seen in the "Placing Components on Faces" example in Chapter 7.

Curviloft

By Fredo6—Free (SP)

This extension makes it easy to fit a surface (consisting of quadrilateral or triangular faces) between a set of controlling lines or curves. You can create either a lofted surface, a swept surface, or a surface bordered by edge curves.

Once you pick your controlling surfaces, the extension gives you many options for editing them before finally committing.

Driving Dimensions

By Menhirs NV—Free/EUR 145 (www.drivingdimensions.com)

This commercial extension allows you to parametrize your SketchUp model. Adding dimensions using this extension provides you with a dimensional constraint in your model. You can then modify these dimensions by updating their value rather than by moving objects or stretching them.

Extrusion Tools

By TIG—Free (SP)

This is a collection of several extrusion tools that are contained in a single toolbar. The individual tools allow extrusion of lines into faces, edges by edges (one is the shape and the other is the rail along which it extrudes), lofting, multiedge surface creation, a follow-me-type extrusion (e.g., for handrails), and many others.

As you can see in the image shown here, this tool is useful for creating curtains, piping, handrails, lofted shapes, edge-ruled shapes, structural lattices, and much more.

Fractal Terrain Eroder

By Eneroth3—Free (EW, SP)

When a model is just a bit too straight, use this extension to randomize (*erode*) edges and faces to give them a more natural look. As you can see in the image, it is a great tool for making rocks and other terrain elements!

FredoScale

By Fredo6—Free (SP)

This extension picks up where SketchUp's Scale tool leaves off. You can scale with this tool, too, but more options are available (specifically, *about* which point you want to use each tool). In addition, you can use it to shear, stretch, twist, rotate, and bend any geometry.

In the image shown here, the original shape was a square extrusion. Hidden lines are shown to illustrate how the shape's surfaces were modified.

Geometry Extensions

By Regular Polygon—Free (SP)

This collection of several extensions allows you to create various geometric shapes that wouldn't be possible using SketchUp. These shapes are Ellipse, Superellipse, Superellipsoid, Sphere, Torus, Loxodrome (Spherical Helix), and Spherical Spiral (Archimedes Spiral).

Another useful geometric tool for curves is Curve Maker by Terry R. It is also free, and you can download it from (EW).

Joint Push Pull Interactive

By Fredo6—Free (SP)

This extension is an excellent tool for "thickening" surfaces. It allows you to use a Push/Pull-like tool on the connected faces that make up a surface, yet keep everything joined during this process. Available functions include Joint Push Pull, Vector Push Pull (thicken all surfaces in the same direction), and Normal Push Pull.

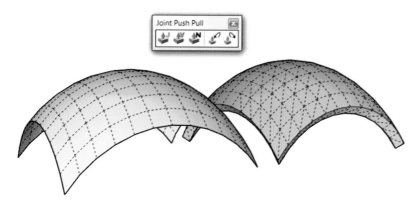

This extension is used mainly for (1) adding material thickness to surfaces (e.g., to create a concrete shell), (2) offsetting surfaces, and (3) adding thickness to a surface object to apply a subsurface-scattering material to it in your rendering software.

Layer Manager

By D. Bur—Free (EW, SP)

This extension provides many more tools to control layer states and arrangements than SketchUp's own Layers window.

If you prefer a graphical layer manager that looks similar to Photoshop's, get Layers Panel by jiminy-billy-bob (EW, SP).

Lines2Tubes

By D. Bur—Free (SP)

Whenever you need to take a set of lines or curves and turn them into tubes, use this extension. It is even possible to use it on branching lines as in, for example, a truss. You can specify parameters such as diameter, precision, and even material.

A similar extension that also allows for an inner diameter to be set is PipeAlongPath by TIG (SP). It won't work well with branching lines, though.

LSS Matrix

By Kirill B.—Free (EW)

This extension lets you make multiple 2D or 3D array copies in one step based on spacing, rotation, and scaling. It does this parametrically, so that you can even change settings after the original copies have been made.

For a simpler version, try Grow by TIG on (SP).

Make Fur

By tak2hata—Free (SP)

This is a fun and very useful extension. It allows you to place a large number of randomly scattered objects onto faces. These objects could be some of the default shapes (rectangles, grass blades, leaves) or any component in your model.

You have full control over the extension's options, such as how many to place per unit area, maximum objects per face, and their scattering (randomness of scale, rotation, etc.). You can also apply a *force* parameter that distorts each object similar to bending blades of grass or hair in wind.

This extension begs to be experimented with. Common usage includes placing grass on ground (as individual blades or PNG materials with transparency) and trees on hills, or creating any other "furry" object, such as a shaggy carpet.

Another extension that allows you to "spray" components onto any surface is Compo Spray by D. Bur. It is free, and you can get it from (SP).

MakeOrthoViews

By J. Folz—$5 (SM)

This extension allows you to take a 3D object (a group or a component) and create standard engineering views (front, right, and top) as additional 2D objects in your model. This is very useful if you want to export them into 2D CAD software for annotation.

Mirror

By TIG—Free (SP)

This extension does exactly what its name implies: It adds the missing Mirror tool to SketchUp. You can use it on 2D shapes or 3D objects.

PathCopy

By R. Wilson—Free (EW)

Whenever you need to copy objects along a path (rather than orthogonally), you need to use this extension. It places a component regularly along a curve either at its vertices (endpoints of line segments) or at specified distances. The image here shows streetlights copied along a spline at 10' increments.

Mirror Axis

117

Pen Tool +

By R. O'Brien—Free (SP)

This extension adds a toolbar from which you can use various pen-based functions. They help you modify meshes manually and add soft lines, hidden lines, guidelines, and others.

Place Shapes

By A. Schreyer—Free (EW, SP)

Instead of SketchUp's standard push-pull modeling, novices especially might prefer *solids modeling*, where you place uniformly sized geometric shapes (*primitives*), such as boxes and spheres, and then scale and combine them (e.g., using SketchUp's Solid Tools). This extension adds a toolbar that serves this purpose. Working with only added and subtracted primitives automatically leaves you with perfectly watertight objects that pose no problems for 3D printing, for example.

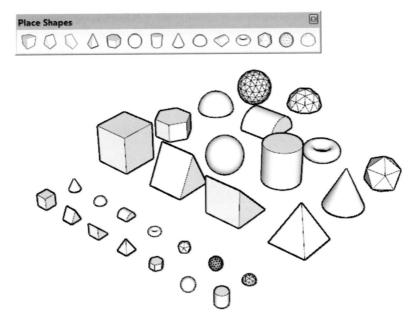

If you prefer to have control over shape sizes (via a dialog), try out SketchUp's Shapes extension (EW) or J. McClenahan's SU Draw Parametric Shapes on (SP).

Round Corner

By Fredo6—Free (SP)

The lack of classic CAD-type chamfer and fillet tools in SketchUp has spurred several extension creators into action.

While 2D versions are available that can operate on a face or polylines, this 3D version cleanly rounds (*fillets*) or breaks (*chamfers*) all the connected edges in your model. Use it to give materials a more realistic appearance for rendering (no edge in real life is as sharp as a computer-produced edge) or to connect pipes realistically.

Scale and Rotate Multiple

By C. Fullmer—Free (EW, SP)

This extension randomly rotates and scales a selection of components. This is especially helpful for making landscape objects such as trees look more natural, because when they are initially placed in SketchUp they all appear with the same size and orientation. The "Randomizing Everything" example in Chapter 7 creates a similar result.

Shape Bender

By C. Fullmer—Free (EW, SP)

When you do woodworking, you sometimes need to bend a shape based on a curve. This extension lets you do this virtually. When you select a group or a component, a reference line, and a curve (or a set of curves), everything is bent along the curve shape.

Selection Toys

By ThomThom—Free (EW, SP)

This extension adds a toolbar containing a multitude of tools to aid in selecting objects in SketchUp. It works very much as a selection filter and allows you to include or exclude certain categories (faces, edges, components, etc.) from the current selection. In addition, you can select connected edges or faces and similar components. This can even be done by layer.

As a bonus, this extension lets you customize the number of buttons that are shown—a very nice user interface feature.

Shapes

By SketchUp Team—Free (EW)

This extension adds an item to the **Draw** menu that lets you parametrically create eight different shapes, including prism, torus, pyramid, and dome.

An expanded version of this extension is SU Draw Parametric Shapes by J. McClenahan on (SP).

Soap Skin & Bubble

By J. Leibinger—Free (EW)

Based on the theory of tensile structures (fabric or canvas roofs), this extension takes a set of edges and stretches a surface between them. With this extension, it is quite easy to create hyperbolic paraboloids (*hypar shells*) as well as surfaces that are held up by internal pressure

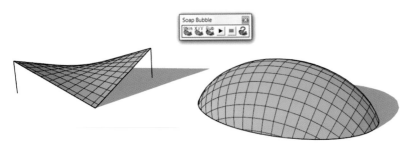

(as in air-supported structures). You can also use it well for landscape modeling tasks.

To use this extension, select a set of edges and fit a surface with the first tool on the toolbar. If you want to add pressure to the surface (to blow it outward or suck it inward), use the third tool on the toolbar.

Simplify Contours Tool

By SketchUp Team—Free (EW)

Survey contours (and similar data) can sometimes be quite detailed. This tool simplifies such line data and reduces edge count with minimal impact on the result.

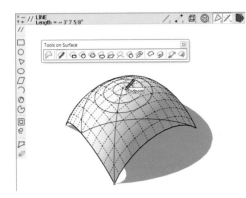

Tools on Surface

By Fredo6—Free (SP)

When you work with surfaces, at some point the need will arise to "draw" on them. One example is creating a line that needs to connect two points on the surface but can't leave the surface (on a sphere that would be a so-called geodesic line).

This extension allows many other geometric shapes to be drawn on a surface. The accompanying image illustrates this by showing two lines extending from edges of the surface on one side to the other side's midpoint. You can also see how easy it is to create circles on a surface.

You can use this tool to section a surface for application of different materials. You can also use it to help you construct shapes that are defined by the surface's geometry.

Unwrap and Flatten Faces

By A. Schreyer—Free (EW, SP)

Whenever you end up with one or more coplanar faces (e.g., from unwrapping geometry) that are arbitrarily oriented, use this extension to lay them flat on the ground plane. As of version 2, you can also use it to automatically unwrap connected, non-coplanar faces.

Weld

By R. Wilson—Free (EW, SM)

To be able to use some tools in SketchUp, you'll need to connect lines into a polyline. This will allow all of the lines to be selected and modified as one object. This extension adds the ability to *weld* many individual (but attached) lines into a polyline.

See TIG-Weld by TIG (SP) for similar functionality.

Table 4.1 lists some additional extensions for modeling with SketchUp.

Table 4.1 Some Other Useful Modeling Extensions

Name	Description
Align (D. Bur)	Aligns entities in 3D space (EW, SP)
Arcs Circles+ (D. Bur)	Adds more ways to create arcs and circles (EW, SP)
Arc Centerpoint Finder (C. Fullmer)	Draws a construction point at the center of an arc (EW, SP)
Fredo Tools (Fredo6)	Offers various smaller tools for editing (SP)
FilletTool (T. Track) / Chamfer Along Path (A. Joyce)	Adds the missing fillet and chamfer features (RL, SM)
S4u Make Faces (Suforyou) / MakeFaces (T. Burch)	Creates faces where possible (EW, SP, SM)
Nudge (T. Burch)	Uses arrow keys to move objects (SM)
RandomPushPull (TIG) / Greeble (C. Fullmer)	Randomly pushes/pulls faces (EW, SP)
Bezier Surface (ThomThom) / Bezier Patch (ngon)	Creates a Bezier surface/patch (EW, SP)
Guide Tools (ThomThom)	Places construction points easily (EW, SP)

Example 4.1: Creating Trusses

In this example, you'll create two trusses made of different materials: steel and wood. This will allow you to use the Lines2Tubes and Extrude Tools extensions as well as one of SketchUp's Solid Tools. Make sure you have both extensions installed before you proceed.

1. Set up a grid with your desired spacing using the **Tools** → **Grid** menu. You might need to install the Grid extension first—see Chapter 3 for instructions. In this example, I am using a 4′ grid to lay out the truss.

2. Draw lines at the centerlines of all members. SketchUp fills in the areas, but you can delete those faces (see the next step).

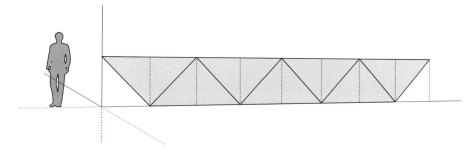

3. Highlight all of the created faces and delete them.

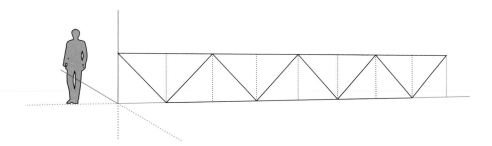

4. Select all of the lines (the axis centerlines in the truss). In the **Tools** menu, select the item Convert Arcs, Circles…, after which the dialog shown here will appear.

5. Set the parameters as shown in the image. As you can see, you can enter the diameter, the circle precision, and the material. Make sure the Each Tube Is A Group option is selected so that you can use those groups later. Then just click OK. The extension will give you a confirmation, and your truss should resemble the image shown here.

6. When you look more closely at the truss, you will see that it needs some cleaning. The ends don't extend (or at least don't clean up nicely) as would likely be the case in reality. Also, the internal ends overlap too much, creating a lot of internal geometry.

7. To clean up the ends, double-click the horizontal tubes to get into group-editing mode. Then extend each of them by a reasonable number (8″, in this case).

8. At this point, your truss looks better, but the geometry is still overlapping quite a bit. You can see this when you turn on X-ray mode.

Now you can do one of two things. The classic SketchUp method to clean up overlaps is to actually explode the entire truss and use the **Intersect with Model** right-click menu item on the entire truss. This creates lines where faces intersect, which would let you clean up overlapping faces easily.

For this example, you will instead use one of SketchUp's Solid Tools. Although most of them are reserved for the Pro version of SketchUp, the Outer Shell tool is included in the Make version, too. You can find it under the **Tools** menu (or on the Solid Tools toolbar).

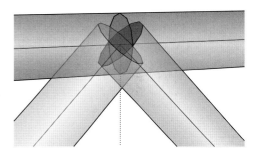

9. You can use the Outer Shell tool only on solid (or watertight objects without holes). Because you created separate groups for each tube, you actually have a model that consists only of those. Select the entire truss (select the groups that make up the members) and make SketchUp use the Outer Shell tool on it. Intersections will then resemble the image shown here.

As you can see, intersections are now cleanly mitered and all internal geometry has been removed. The steel tube truss is finished!

Now let's try this with a wood truss. Obviously, we won't be able to use circular cross sections this time; therefore, we'll use the Extrude Edges by Face tool from the Extrude Tools extension.

1. Start with the centerlines as before (you can move away the truss you just created; the centerlines will still be in their original position). Add a rectangle near them on the ground plane (the x-y plane). This rectangle must be aligned as shown and have the cross-sectional dimensions of the wood members you want to use.

2. Select the rectangle and all of the lines that make up the truss. Then click on Extrude Edges by Face on the Extrude Tools toolbar.

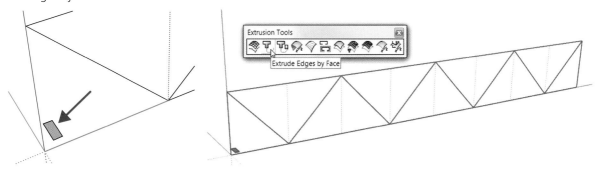

3. In the dialog that follows, say Yes to Process Extrusion In Pieces. As you can see in the accompanying image, the truss has again been created as a collection of individual members (as groups).

4. Now use the same process as before to clean up the truss and make it a solid piece. The final result should resemble the image shown here.

Example 4.2: Making Shells in Different Ways

In this example, we'll use the Extrude Tools and the Soap Skin & Bubble extensions to create various shapes of shells and fabric structures. Make sure you have both extensions installed before you proceed.

First, you'll create a domed shell:

1. Draw two vertical arches that are at a right angle to each other: one on the x-z plane (between the red and blue axes) and one on the y-z plane (between the green and blue axes).

2. Now turn each of them into a group by highlighting each separately and selecting Make Group from the **Edit** menu. The result should resemble the image shown here.

3. With both groups selected, click the Extrude Edges by Edges tool from the Extrusion Tools toolbar. In the set of dialogs that pops up, ask the extension to orient the faces, not reverse faces if white is up already, not intersect with self, erase coplanar edges, not triangulate any faces, and keep the original groups. The result should resemble the image shown here.

You could have done this in many other ways, too. If you had created four guiding arches, the Extrude Edges by Rails method would have worked. In addition, the Skinning tool from the Curviloft extension would lead to the same result.

Next, let's create a *hypar shell* (a hyperbolic paraboloid):

1. Draw a square (30′ × 30′, for this example) and delete the internal face so that you are left with only edges, as shown here.

2. Move a corner point upward (by 10′ along the blue axis) using the Move tool.

3. Repeat this with the corner point on the opposite side. You should now have two opposing edges "on the ground" and the other two "in the air."

4. Now select all four edges and click on Generate Soap Skin from the Soap Skin & Bubble toolbar. This adds a temporary set of faces into your edges.

5. You now have the option to modify the number of divisions in the Measurements box. The default is 10; enter a different value if you want a more detailed mesh. Then press the Return key and watch how the extension fits the surface between your edges.

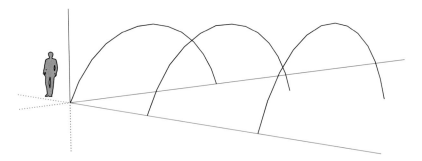

This third shell will be executed as a *lofted shape*. For this, you need to use the Curviloft or the Extrude Tools extension.

1. Create three parallel, vertical arches as shown here.

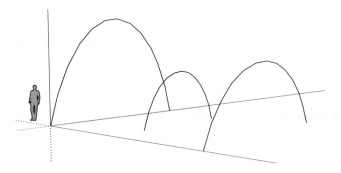

2. Now scale them so that they all have different heights and widths.

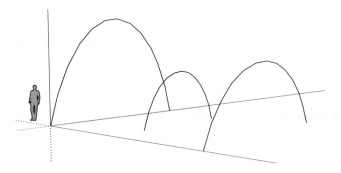

3. Highlight all three curves and select the first tool (the Loft tool) from the Curviloft extension's toolbar. This creates a temporary shell on which you can still make modifications (move vertices, for example).

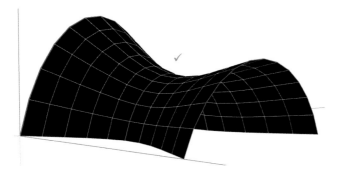

4. Once you are satisfied with the shell's shape, click the mouse to accept. You should now have a shell that is smoothly defined by the three guiding arches.

Interestingly, if you use the Extrude Edges by Loft tool from the Extrude Tools extension for this, you will get a different lofted shape, which resembles the image shown here.

Extensions for Architecture, Engineering, and Construction (AEC) Modeling

1001bit Tools

By Goh Chun Hee—Free/$48 (EW, SP, www.1001bit.com*)*
This is a large collection of architecture-related tools that will help you model those pesky details. It currently comes in both a free and a Pro version and even has a shadow-analysis

tool as an add-on. The tools vary from general modeling helpers (fillet, chamfer, arrays, etc.) to tools for creating walls, openings, stairs, floors, roofs (including rafters and purlins), and doors and windows.

3D Doors Windows Frames

By RubySoft— €49/€139 (EW, www.rubysoft.nl*)*

This is a very detailed window-and-door-creation tool, which parametrically creates windows and doors in your model—frames, glazing, and all.

3D Tree Maker

By 3DArcStudio— Free/€10 (EW, www.3darcstudio.com*)*

Adding vegetation such as grass, shrubs, and trees can be challenging (see Chapter 5 for some tips). This extension makes it easy by providing many species from which to choose. You can also switch between a fast "proxy" preview that lets you place and adjust items easily (and won't slow down your model) and a full-detail view that inserts the textured objects instead (e.g., when you are ready to start a rendering).

3skeng Tools

By SHK—Trial (EW, SP, www.3skeng.com*)*

This set of extensions contains parametric tools for piping and channels as well as steel design, giving an MEP contractor a full tool set to plan and specify pipe and ductwork layouts in 3D. Layouts can be created interactively and edited as needed.

For similar functionality, also try out The Engineering ToolBox by editor e on (EW).

Architect Tools

By ThomThom—Free (EW, SP)

A collection of small tools to make it easier to work with DWG imported data. You can, for example, use an imported file with building outlines to create the massing for an entire city in just a few clicks. Another tool moves all selected geometry to the ground (z = 0) or onto Layer0.

Also look for TIG's 2D Tools (SP).

BIMobject SketchUp App

By BIMobject Team—Free (EW, SP)

This extension connects SketchUp to the large product repository on the BIMobject website. You can insert many premade building objects directly into the model this way. In contrast to many Extension Warehouse objects, these are preconfigured with an extensive set of data and are live-linked back to the website, which helps in specifying.

BIMUp 5D

By BIMUp LTD—£149 (EW, www.bimup.co.uk*)*

An extensive set of estimating and scheduling tools that picks up where SketchUp's Generate Report tool leaves off. Counting parameters can be adjusted graphically, and reports can be exported in PDF and Microsoft Excel CSV formats.

BuildEdge Plan/Pro

By BuildEdge—$75 (SP, www.buildedge.com*)*

A complete BIM building design solution—with parametric walls, roofs, windows, doors, etc.—that takes advantage of SketchUp's simplicity.

BuildingStructureTools

By tak2hata—Free (SP)

This extension helps with creating beams, columns, slabs, and the like. You can customize the database of shapes that it ships with and add your own profiles.

Dibac for SketchUp

By Iscarnet—€69 (EW, www.dibac.com*)*

This is another parametric architectural extension for SketchUp. You can easily create walls and floors, and place windows and doors, which are even interactive and can be operated using the Dynamic Components tools.

Greeble

By Chris Fullmer—Free (EW, SP)

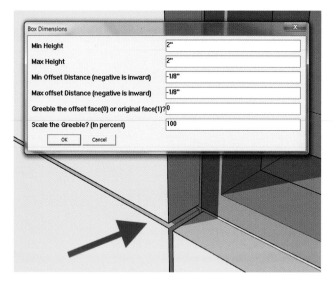

Chris' Greeble extension lets you extrude or recess faces while also applying an offset to all edges. It does so randomly, but for architectural uses, keeping values non-random allows you to create consistently thickened facade panels with gaps.

HouseBuilder

By S. Hurlbut, D. Bur—Free (RL)

If you want to model each stud, rafter, and joist in a light-framed house, then give this extension a try. It hasn't been updated in a while but may still prove useful. It comes in both metric and imperial versions and adds a toolbar that gives you easy access to all of its tools.

You can use the Wall tool to create a stud-framed wall based on two selected points. To add a window or a door, select the appropriate tool and pick a location along a wall. The extension places the opening and frames the wall around it. To add a roof (with evenly spaced rafters), select two points on the gable end and one point on the opposite side. The extension then creates rafters—complete with birdsmouth and eave cuts.

Instant Architecture

By C. Vali—$118 (EW, www.valiarchitects.com)

This set of extensions covers tools for quickly creating roofs, walls, site grading, terrain, roads, fencing, and railing. Many options and templates are available to cover most common tasks.

Land F/X

By Ecografx—Free (EW, www.landfx.com)

This extension links landscape plans created in Land F/X's AutoCAD application with SketchUp for visualization tasks. You can also create plans right in SketchUp using 3D plant material from a large database.

LSS Arch

By Kirill B.—Free (EW, SP)

Create building elements such as beams, walls, slabs, columns, and roofs parametrically using this extension.

MEP Designer

By Trimble MEP—$349 (EW)

Targeted at electrical contractors, this extension allows for creation of conduits and other electrical components right inside a SketchUp model of a building.

MODELUR

By Modelur Team—Free (EW)

This extension brings SketchUp into the realm of urban planning by providing parametric conceptual models at the city scale. You can also run calculations on the entire model and check if certain constraints (e.g., distances) have been satisfied.

Profile Builder

By Whaat—Free/$19.99 (EW, SP)

This extension picks up where the Follow Me tool leaves off. It allows you to create an extruded profile without having to create a guiding edge first. It can also apply extruded cross sections to existing edges in your model.

The current selection of cross-section shapes includes millwork, road curbs, concrete shapes, and an international collection of structural steel shapes. You can preview the shape and apply various parameters when placing them.

Roof

By TIG—Free (SP)

If you don't want to create a complex roof yourself using extrusions, intersections, and quite a bit of cleanup, then download this tool. It automatically creates clean hip, mansard, gable, and pyramid roofs for you. As you can see in the image shown here, even angled floor plans work with this extension.

For extended functionality, also see Instant Roof Nui by C. Vali on (EW), which will detail such a roof even further.

Skalp

By Skalp—$79 (EW, SP, www.skalp4sketchup.com)
Sections are a powerful tool in SketchUp especially when doing architectural modeling. By default, however, walls and other solid objects appear hollow in a section. This extension adds color fills and customizable standard patterns to sectioned walls.

Also see the following extensions for similar functionality: SectionCutFace by TIG (SP) and RichSection by pgarmyn (SP).

SketchThis Kitchen Design Extension

By Eric S.—Subscription (EW, SP, www.sketchthis.net)
This extension will let you quickly plan a kitchen using premade components, edit its various configurations (such as doors and drawer fronts and hardware), and specify it.

SketchUp Ivy

By Pierreden—Free (SP)

This is a great extension if you want to quickly add foliage to an architectural scene. By default, it creates an ivy stem that grows along a face or a set of faces. You can control branching, scattering, and direction parameters, but due to the random nature of the algorithm, you will get different results each time you run this extension.

This extension should work equally well for gnarly bushes and for vines—all you need to do is provide appropriate foliage. You can accomplish this by adding to the model leaf components that have "ivyleaf" in their names.

For good results, you need to edit the foliage materials that come with the extension. Export the leaf images to your image-editing software, remove the background (make it transparent), and then reimport it into SketchUp's materials as a transparent PNG.

Tools for Architects

By rubits—Free/various prices (www.rubits.com)
These tools help with massing, textures (materials), and selections. The Massing Box tool allows you to draw rectangular shapes with a defined (fixed) area, and the Area Scale tool lets you scale any shaped face to a defined area. Both of these tools are excellent help in the programming layout phase of planning.

Windowizer

By R. Wilson—Free/$10 (SM)

If you need "storefront" mullion-type windows in your model or want to panelize a surface, then this extension can create them for you based on a collection of selected faces. You can specify mullion width and a variety of other parameters. The extension then places mullions at each face edge and replaces the face's material with a transparent glass material.

To use this extension, select one or more faces and then right-click on one of them. The Windowize command is in the context menu.

Window Maker (EW) is another tool (by the SketchUp team) that parametrically creates double-hung and slider windows. For single windows or doors, this can be done with one of the 1001bit Tools, as well.

Example 4.3: Mullion Windows

In this example, you will use the Windowizer extension to create storefront windows for an otherwise quite plain concrete building. Make sure the extension is installed before you continue.

1. Start with a large box. In this example, I used a 30′ × 30′ square, which I pulled up by 15′, and to which I then applied a concrete texture.

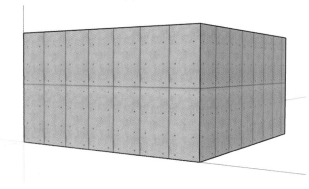

2. Create locations for the windows. For this example, offset the front facade by 2' and then push it inward by 1'.

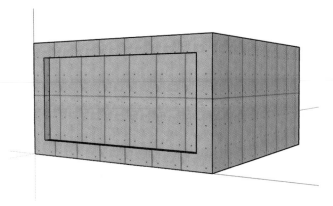

3. On the facade rectangle, draw lines wherever you want to have mullions. This will break the large face into many small ones.

4. Now highlight all of the faces that will be windowized and right-click on one of them. In the context menu, you will find the Windowizer tools. Click on the Windowizer tool menu item to get to the Settings dialog.

5. Adjust these settings to your liking. As you can see, you can even preselect the materials for the frame and the glass. When you click OK, your windows will be generated for you.

Extensions for Digital Fabrication

CADspan Tools

By CADspan—Free and Pro (EW, www.cadspan.com/software*)*

In addition to providing 3D printing services, this company has published a free extension for SketchUp that allows you to detect problems in a 3D model and provides a resurfacing tool that produces 3D-printable watertight meshes. You can then export your model as an STL file.

Center of Gravity

By TIG—Free (SP)

Given a solid volume, this extension finds the 3D center of gravity of a shape and marks it. If you do this for more than one shape, it can also calculate the combined center of gravity.

This extension can help with sculpture as well as mobile making.

CutList

By S. Racz—Free (EW)

This excellent extension is geared mainly toward woodworkers but may be useful to others as well. It takes a model that consists of parts (components such as individual wood pieces that make up a table) and produces materials lists as well as cut sheets (with layout optimization and efficiency reporting). The user can separate solid wood, sheet goods, and hardware simply by adding keywords to the components.

135

DrawMetal

By Draw Metal—Free (SP)

Geared toward metal fabricators, this set of three free SketchUp extensions (Curve Maker, Taper Maker, and Stock Maker) allows you to create intricate bent metal shapes for railings and other projects. Curve Maker was covered in the previous section; the other two can then create swept profiles based on those curves.

Face Centroid and Area Properties

By A. Schreyer—Free (EW, SP)

This extension finds the true centroid of any face (even if it contains holes) as long as it is drawn on the ground plane. The centroid is then marked, and several relevant properties such as Area, Moment of Inertia (in two main directions), and Radius of Gyration are reported.

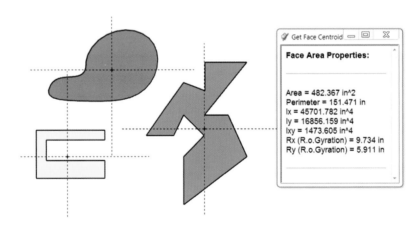

Flatten

By T. Burch—$10 (SM)

This extension allows you to flatten a 3D group or a component by arranging all faces on the ground plane.

For another automatic approach, try out the Unwrap and Flatten Faces extension by A. Schreyer (EW).

Flattery Papercraft Tools

By pumpkinpirate—Free (SP)

This extension lets you flatten objects similar to the Unfold extension. It has interactive features such as adjusting the unfolded shape and adding glue tabs.

Although not a SketchUp extension but rather an external software, Pepakura Designer should be mentioned here, too, because it can take a SketchUp model exported as a COLLADA DAE file and unfold it. *$38* (www.tamasoft.co.jp/pepakura-en)

Glue Tab

*By rschenk—Free (*https://github.com/rschenk/Sketchup-Glue-Tab-Plugin*)*
This extension makes a great companion tool to the Unfold tool. It allows you to select edges in an unfolded model and then adds glue tabs to them.

Poly Reducer

By Whaat—Free (SP)
Although the author claims that this extension is not perfect, it is a good tool to have if you need to reduce face count in any polyface mesh.

SketchUp STL

By SketchUp—Free (EW)
An absolute must-have for 3D printing with SketchUp, this extension lets you export and import geometry as an STL file. In the Export dialog, you can set the unit system and limit the export to selected geometry only.
I will discuss this extension in more detail in Chapter 6.

Slicer

By TIG—Free (SP)
When you have an object that encloses a volume (such as a blimp or a sculpture), one manufacturing method you might use is the egg-crate approach, whereby the object is sliced into evenly spaced thin sheets in two main directions. You can then cut the 2D sheets and reassemble them into the "core" of the original shape by sliding each one into overlapping slots.
This extension allows you to egg-crate any geometry. Its options let you specify dimensions and spacing of the slices as well as other parameters. After the slicing operation, all slices can be neatly arranged on the ground plane (for printing or exporting). If you have SketchUp Pro, a DXF export option is included. In the free version, use orthogonal view printing (or a free DXF exporter extension) to create scaled output.

Solid Inspector

By ThomThom—Free (EW, SP)

This useful extension checks groups and components to determine whether or not they are *solids* (watertight manifold geometry). If errors (e.g., holes or stray edges) are found, the extension circles them. This helps prepare geometry for 3D printing.

Solid Solver

By TIG—Free (SP)

This extension goes one step further than Solid Inspector and tries to fix geometry that is not a *solid*. It can't fix every case, but it's usually at least worth a try.

Timber Framing Extensions

By daiku (C. Bremer)—Free (EW)

Geared toward timber framers, this extension allows a frame designer to either use components (such as beams, posts, joists, and braces) from a library or make their own. Bents and entire building frames can be assembled quickly using these components (including all connections and cuts), and frame members can be individually exported for multiview cut sheets, as you can see in this image.

Company Name
Project: TF_Ruby Example
Timber: Girt III-IVA - 8.0 x 8.0 x 16
Created on: 01/24/2012

Unfold

By J. Folz—Free (http://sketchuptips.blogspot.com/2007/08/plugin-unfoldrb.html)

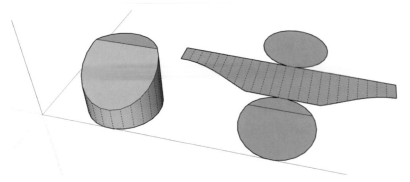

This extension is an excellent helper if you need to take 3D geometry from SketchUp and flatten it into 2D for cutting and manufacturing. This method works very well, especially for thinner materials like paper or sheet metal.

By itself, this extension does not add glue tabs to the flattened sheets; use the Glue Tab extension (previously discussed) for that.

Wudworx Tools

*By Wudworx—Various prices (*https://sites.google.com/site/wudworx*)*
Also geared toward woodworkers, this site currently offers three extensions: Board Maker, Mortise & Tenon, and Dovetails.

Example 4.4: Slicing Up a Volume

This example shows how you can use the Slicer extension to prepare a solid for egg-crate-type manufacturing. To make things easy, we'll use one of SketchUp's default spheres (get it with the Component window) for this. However, the extension will work on any solid group or component (it just must be watertight and without holes). Make sure you have the extension installed before you begin.

1. Highlight the sphere and select Slicer5 from the **Extensions** menu (you can also use the toolbar for this). This opens up a dialog with options.

2. For this model, you want to slice the sphere into vertical and horizontal planes. Therefore, select XZ as the axis combination. Also, set all other parameters as you see them in the dialog image.

3. Because we are slicing this sphere in two directions, the extension asks us for the second axis parameters in another dialog.

4. After you click OK, the extension gets to work. Be patient at this point because this could take some time. You can follow its progress at the bottom of the screen, if you like. When everything is done, you should see something that looks like the image shown here.

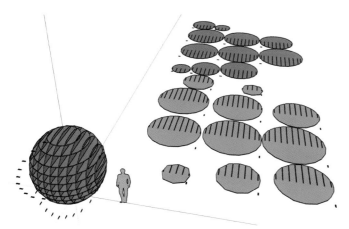

5. As you can see, the sphere has been sliced evenly into planes in both the horizontal and the vertical direction. In addition, copies of all of these planar elements have been placed onto the ground next to the sphere, ready to be printed or exported. Everything is color-coded and neatly labeled. The image here shows a close-up of one of the slices.

You can now export the slices as DXF shapes if you have the Pro version of SketchUp (or if you have a DXF exporter extension installed). If you instead want to print the shapes, switch the camera mode to Parallel Projection and go into top view before printing (you can do both in the **Camera** menu).

Example 4.5: Making a Terrain Model

A common task for architects and landscape designers is to create a 3D site model. This is frequently done by slicing up a site horizontally (at equally spaced elevations), fabricating contoured slices, and then assembling the terrain model. You'll use the Slicer extension again to accomplish this task.

1. A benefit of using SketchUp is that you can import any terrain into your model through SketchUp's location tools. Unless Google's terrain model is too coarse or inaccurate, there should be no need to find alternative data sources. To locate your model, click on the Add Location tool on the main toolbar.

2. This brings up a dialog where you can browse to your site. Once you have the location in view, use the Select Region button to select an appropriate region.

3. This process imports two items into SketchUp: a flat orthographic view of your site and a textured terrain model (both are correctly georeferenced and oriented). You can switch between them by toggling visibility for the appropriate layers, as shown here.

4. Turn on the terrain model visibility. Next, add a rectangular box where you want to acquire site data. Make sure they overlap, as shown here.

5. Select the terrain model. As you can see, it is highlighted by a red box, which means that it is locked. Right-click on it and choose the Unlock menu item. This makes the terrain editable (it will also get a blue outline).

6. Right-click on it again and choose Explode. This removes the terrain from its grouping.

7. Now *triple*-click the box you created earlier and select **Intersect Faces → With Model** from the right-click menu.

8. This intersects the two objects so that you just have to remove the top portion (simply erase the lines and faces). You will be left with a clean solid terrain model.

9. You could leave the terrain as is, but, ultimately, you won't need the thickness below the terrain. Therefore, push the underside up as far as it will go.

10. Group the site object first so that you can start the Slicer extension. Go with the settings shown here (we want to get horizontal slices at 4' intervals).

11. This slices up the site and creates flattened slices that you can again print/plot or export to a laser- or CNC-cutter, for example.

Example 4.6: Unfolding a Shape

In this example, you'll use the Unfold (or alternatively the Flattery) extension to manually unwrap a solid shape for manufacturing. The shape you use here is a circle extrusion that received an angled planar cut.

1. Start by creating a shape. This does not have to be a solid; surfaces also work well.

2. Because you will be unwrapping a circular shape, you need to see all the hidden lines during the process. Go to the **View** menu and make sure Hidden Geometry is turned on. You should now see the dashed lines, as shown here.

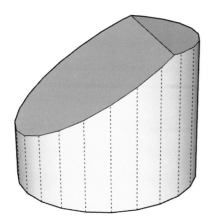

3. With nothing selected in your model, go to the **Extensions** menu and click on [JF] Unfold. To make the first unfolding, click first on the face you want to unfold and then on the face that has the orientation you want the first face to acquire. In the example shown here, do the clicks in the order shown to fold the angled face upward.

4. Now you need to fold both of those faces so that they are parallel with the center face on the rear of the object. First, click in white space to unselect the last face. Then Shift+click both top faces to select them. Finally, let go of the Shift key and click the back-side face.

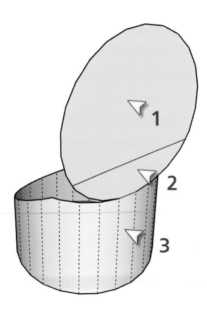

5. Again unselect everything by clicking in white space, and turn to the front of the object. Start in the center and unroll the sides by clicking on consecutive faces (stop when you match up with the back side).

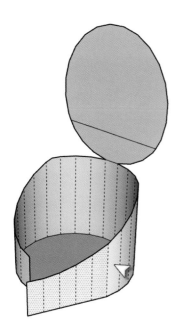

6. Your object should look like this after you unroll both sides.

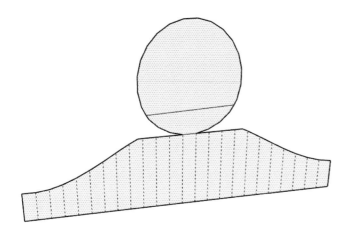

7. As a final step, flip the base backward, too. Then you can exit the tool.

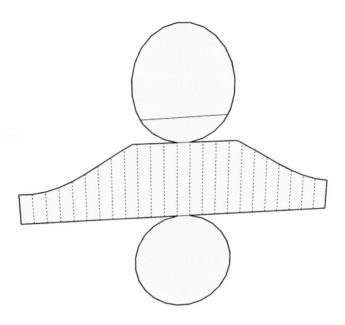

You can now rotate this shape onto the ground plane and switch your view to a parallel projection from the top. At this point, you are ready to print the unfolded shape scaled and use it as a template for cutting the shape out of, for example, sheet metal.

After you perform this process with different shaped surfaces, you will notice that some surfaces can be easily unrolled (as in our example) while some others cannot. A surface that is unrollable is generally called a *developable* surface. Examples are cylinders, cones, and any ruled surface that was derived using a line. Double-curved surfaces (like the shells shown earlier in this chapter) cannot easily be unrolled using this method. You may be able to unroll them in strips, though.

This manual process can get quite tedious. For a more automatic approach, try using the aforementioned Unwrap and Flatten Faces extension. It should be able to unwrap this shape automatically in one go.

TIP
See Chapter 6 for instructions on how to turn the results of these three examples into actual objects.

Extensions for Data Integration and Exchange

Attribute Inspector

By Aerilius—Free (EW, SP)

As discussed in Chapter 3, data can be added to components using attributes. This extension lets you explore and edit that data in tabular format in a dialog.

Attribute Editor by Eneroth3 on (EW, SP) provides similar functionality.

Cloud

By D. Bur—Free (SP, RL)

You can import x-, y-, and z-coordinates into SketchUp from a text file using this extension. Coordinates are added as construction points, and the resulting point cloud can be triangulated after import (to create a surface). This can be useful, for example, if you have LIDAR laser-scanned point data that you want to use as a basis for building modeling. Be careful with LIDAR data, though, as this extension slows down with too many data points.

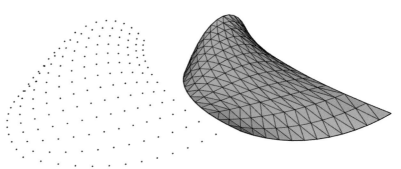

As a bonus, existing vertices (edge points) of any highlighted geometry can be exported to a CSV file.

Import/Export Extensions

By Various—Free (EW, SP, RL, SM)

Currently, many limited-feature import/export extensions are available for SketchUp. If you need one for a particular file type, search the extension repositories for the file extension (such as DXF). The most popular file formats for exchange are DXF (to exchange linework and other shapes with lots of other software, including Autodesk AutoCAD), OBJ (to exchange with 3D modeling software), and STL (to send files to 3D printers).

Here is a small sampling: Dxf_In, Dxf2Skp, PLY importer, FreeDXF Importer, DXF_export, Import OBJ with Materials, OBJexporter, OBJ Import, and su2stl.rb, jf_stl_importer.

Note that if you own SketchUp Pro, DXF and DWG import/export is included.

Product Connect

By Igloo Studios—Free (EW)

Using this extension, product-specific information (such as a piece of furniture's barcode number) can be stored in a model and then reported in spreadsheets. This extends SketchUp's own attribute system and provides a graphic interface for entering attributes that can be attached to any component. Many models in the 3D Warehouse have been prepared with this extension and work well with its reporting functions. Common uses are estimating, bills of materials, quantity takeoffs, and so on.

For similar functionality, also look up Render Plus's Space Design extension (EW).

Trimble Connect

By SketchUp—Free (EW)

Trimble Connect is a web-based collaboration platform for the AEC market where people can share 3D models, explore and analyze BIM model data, maintain a project file repository, and discuss project workflows. It is built on Gehry Technologies' GTeam platform and makes it easy especially for Trimble software products (e.g., Tekla, SketchUp) to interact, but it also supports other file formats (SKP, IFC, 3DM, DWG, DXF, DGN, OBJ, FBX, 3DS, STP, STEP, IGES, IGS, STL, SLDPRT, SLDASM, KMZ, DAE, X3D, and OFF).

This extension connects SketchUp directly with this web service, providing upload and download functions as well as file linking.

Trimble Scan Explorer

By Trimble—Free (EW)

This extension combines LIDAR laser-scanned data from Trimble's scanners with an import workflow into SketchUp, where it can then be used as basis for precision modeling. LIDAR data needs to be preprocessed outside of SketchUp but then can be used with this extension to extract points, lines, and planes that serve as basis for 3D modeling.

If you want to process raw LIDAR data files (that typically come in the native LAS format) for use with SketchUp (as x-, y-, z-formatted CSV files), then the freely available LAStools software might be of help:

www.lastools.org

Triangulate Points

By TIG—Free (SP)

This is a triangulation-only version of the Cloud extension. You can use it to triangulate point clouds (made with construction points) that you already have in SketchUp.

Extensions for Animation and Presentation

CubicPanoOut

By J. Wehby—Free (SM)

This tool takes your current viewpoint and exports a cubic panorama as a set of six JPGs. This is an easy way to create interactive 3D panoramas from SketchUp models. You can even create panoramas for models that have custom styles (e.g., in the blueprint style). See the companion website for a tutorial.

Depending on the 3D panorama format (e.g., WebGL, QuickTime), it is possible to embed such a panorama on a webpage and let visitors explore a space virtually.

For similar functionality, also look up Renderiza's PanoScene on (SP) or rami_lpm's Cubic Panorama on (SP). This last extension exports the panorama as a WebGL file that can then be viewed in the browser (see Example 4.7 for more details on WebGL).

FlightPath and FlightPath2

By R. Wilson—Free/$7 (SM)
Although SketchUp's tabbed animation feature is very useful for walk-throughs and fly-arounds, its results are not very smooth, and the path is controllable only through a tab's viewpoint. Use this extension to define a path and create walk-throughs based on this path.

Also try out Whaat's Smoothstep Animation extension on (SP) and R. Wilson's Page Utilities on (SM).

Keyframe Animation

By Regular Polygon—$24 (EW, SP)
This is an object animation extension. You use it by assigning animation tabs in SketchUp where you want keyframes to be. This extension saves object positions with animation tabs and animates objects (linearly and by rotation) when you switch tabs or play the scene animation. Animations can also be exported to a movie.

For similar functionality, look up SimFonIA's Animation Tools on (EW) and David W's SU Animate on (EW).

Mover

By Various—Free (SP)
This small extension lets you add object animation to SketchUp's tabs. Unfortunately, it is not well documented, but it works well.

Alternatively, look up morisdov's Proper Animation extension (on SP).

[Re]Scene

By Renderiza—Free (EW)
This extension can simplify your workflow with animation tabs by letting you update styles and reordering tabs easily.

SketchUp to Sketchfab.com Uploader

By A. Schreyer—Free (EW, SP)
If you want to share a SketchUp model with someone who doesn't have SketchUp installed, try out this extension. It uploads your model to the Sketchfab web service, where it can be shared and viewed right in the browser using the built-in WebGL format. See Example 4.7 for instructions and more details on this technology.

Of course, models uploaded to Trimble's own 3D Warehouse can be viewed using its built-in WebGL viewer as well.

SketchyPhysics

By C. Phillips—Free (SP)

SketchyPhysics has two amazing purposes: (1) simulating physically accurate motion behavior (including collisions) in SketchUp and (2) bowling or playing dominos right in SketchUp. This extension incorporates a physically accurate simulation engine into SketchUp that comes from game software. When it is running, it is capable of simulating gravity, bounces, drops, and even buoyancy—you can interact with the model, too, by simply dragging on objects. A good example is pulling a bowling ball toward some pins that fall over on impact (see the images that follow for examples).

One use for this extension is to create realistically piled-up objects for rendering. To do this, group each object separately and place them all above the ground plane that SketchyPhysics provides. Then run the simulation and watch your objects fall and tumble over each other. Save a copy of the SketchUp file to preserve the geometry before you exit SketchyPhysics.

Another extension, SketchyReplay, allows you to record this motion in SketchUp, which can later be used for rendering animations.

Zorro2

By Whaat—Free (SP)

When you need to cut a model at an arbitrary plane (e.g., to create section renderings for a house model), this extension facilitates the process.

Example 4.7: Sharing Interactive 3D Models from SketchUp

Until not too long ago, sharing 3D SketchUp models for interactive viewing meant that the receiver would have to install either the SketchUp viewer on their computer or a VRML-plugin in their browser. Or the 3D model would have had to be prepared to work with the Flash or Quicktime players. Modern web browsers (like Chrome, Firefox, Safari, or Internet Explorer), however, have built-in technology, called WebGL, that provides all the technical features needed for displaying 3D content and interacting with it right inside the browser window. This even works on mobile devices such as smartphones and tablets. As a result, a slew of web services take advantage of this and provide 3D model sharing, viewing, and, in some cases, editing. Some of these are CL3VER, Clara.io, p3d, Revizto, Sketchfab, and Verold.

Another example of a WebGL viewer is built right into Trimble's 3D Warehouse (http://3dwarehouse.sketchup.com). You can easily share your SketchUp models there using the *Share Model...* toolbar button (the "SketchUp logo in a box").

This button will bring up a dialog in SketchUp where you can add a title and other information (including setting the privacy level for the model). Once the model has been uploaded to the 3D Warehouse, open it in any browser and look for the WebGL viewer button to turn the model's picture view into a 3D viewer.

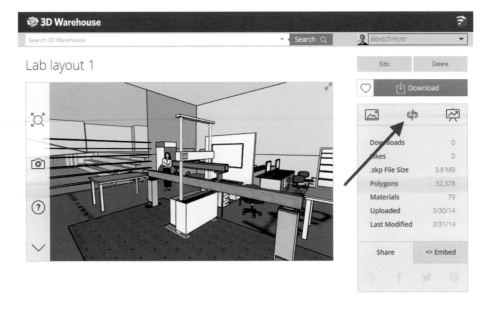

You can then make the viewer full-screen and even navigate all the original scenes in the model by using the provided camera tools. Access them from the small Up arrow in the bottom-left corner of the viewer.

Let's look at Sketchfab's service next as an alternative approach. To be able to use it, make sure you have the SketchUp to Sketchfab.com Uploader extension installed. Also, before you can use this extension, sign up for an account on www.sketchfab.com and browse to your account settings page. Once there, look for your API token (it is a long string of numbers and letters) and copy it.

1. Back in SketchUp, open the model you want to upload. If you only want to upload parts of a model, make sure you select only those parts before the next step.

2. Now go to **File** → **Upload to Sketchfab**, which will bring up the Uploader dialog as you can see in this image:

3. In the dialog, fill in all of the required information and adjust the options. Make sure you enter the API token you copied from the Sketchfab website here, too. Fortunately, you only have to do that once because it will be saved afterward. Then click on Submit Model and wait for the upload process to complete.

   Once the model has been uploaded, a dialog should appear asking whether you want to open it in your browser.

4. You can now view the model online, navigate it with your mouse, and share it with the world. Please note that SketchUp scenes don't get saved with this service, though.

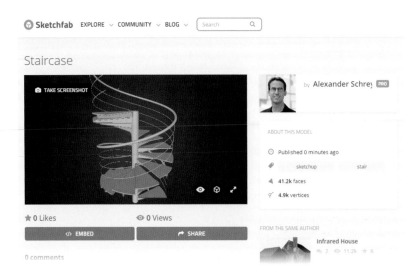

5. After you're done, you can go into the 3D Settings editing mode in Sketchfab and edit the background, lighting, all materials, and even annotate the model. You can also perform some postprocessing here, like a vignette or light bloom.

| TIP | On mobile devices (running iOS or Android), instead of viewing SketchUp models in a web browser, you can install apps that let you view those models even without an internet connection. Good examples are SketchUp's own Mobile Viewer, SightSpace, and Viso3D. |

Extensions for Analysis

Archelios PRO

By Cythelia—Free (EW)

If you want a way to estimate solar PV systems quickly in SketchUp, try out this tool. It uses SketchUp's geo-based modeling capabilities to quickly create a roof model on which you can place standard solar modules. From this, it calculates insolation and power-generation capacity and summarizes everything in a report.

ArchiWIZARD

By ArchiWIZARD—Free (EW)

This extension exports SketchUp models to the ArchiWIZARD service, where they can be analyzed for insolation. It provides exterior shading and interior daylighting analysis. You can also place solar PV systems and analyze them.

Color by Slope and Color by Z

By Chris Fullmer—Free (EW, SP)

These extensions color faces according to their slope or the z-value (height), respectively. You can specify minimum and maximum color values, and it interpolates based on what you've specified. This extension is quite useful for analyzing surface gradients. Just be aware that coloring is permanent (existing materials will be replaced), so make a copy of your model before you use this extension.

ecoScorecard

By SmartBIM—Free (EW, http://ecoscorecard.com*)*

This online service offers a SketchUp extension that integrates their data, consisting of green certification information for architectural and interior products, with 3D components that can be downloaded into SketchUp from the 3D Warehouse. Once a SketchUp model has been populated with these components, it is possible to run an environmental audit on the entire model and report certification criteria.

ecoScorecard
by ecoScorecard

The ecoScorecard channel contains ecoScorecard enabled projects and models which allow for product evaluation, decision-making and green documentation, at the point of design. This is green building for everyone. Download the free sketchup plug-in from http://ecoScorecard.com.

For more information, visit:
http://ecoscorecard.com

Collections

Stonecraft
by: ecoScorecard

Spaces
by: ecoScorecard

HBF Furniture
by: ecoScorecard

J+J INVISION
J+J Invision

Centiva
Centiva

GEIGER
Geiger

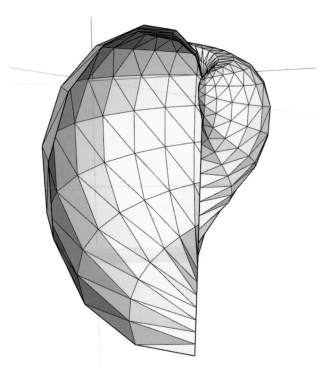

gModeller

By GreenspaceLive—Free (Subscription) (EW, http://greenspacelive.com*)*

This extension adds gbXML modeling capabilities to SketchUp (for architectural energy analysis using an analysis program of your choice). You can designate surfaces as walls, openings, and so forth, as well as add labeled spaces. It is even possible to use an autosurfacing function that will do most of this work for you. gbXML files can then be exported as well as imported.

Graphing Extensions

If you need to visualize mathematical functions in SketchUp either to serve as a basis for geometry creation or simply to get a 3D representation, these extensions will help you.

GraphIt

By R. Wilson—Free (SM)
   Draws 2D Cartesian equations.

k-tools

By K. Krusch—Free (RL)
   Draws 2D and 3D Cartesian, polar, and cylindrical functions. Creates faceted shells for 3D functions.

IES Virtual Environment

By IES—Free/Commercial (EW, www.iesve.com)
   IES provides a free building energy estimation and carbon analysis extension (VE-Ware) for SketchUp as well as a commercial extension (VE-Toolkit) that allows for quick, iterative, early-stage design analysis of a SketchUp energy model.
   The commercial extension analyzes climate, natural resources, building metrics, construction materials, energy, carbon, daylight, solar shading, water, low- and zero-carbon technologies, and ASHRAE/CIBSE heating and cooling loads. An additional module can also provide Leadership in Energy and Environmental Design (LEED) credit assessment.

OpenStudio

By NREL/USDOE—Free (EW, http://openstudio.nrel.gov)
   This extension is part of the U.S. National Renewable Energy Laboratory's free suite of building energy analysis tools that include building energy modeling using their EnergyPlus software and lighting analysis using their Radiance software.
   The SketchUp extension provides tools to add data to a coarse building model and to preprocess it for analysis. This includes designating surfaces (individual faces in SketchUp) as walls, openings, glazing, interior partitions, and so forth. Material properties can be added and adjusted for the analysis. In addition, the tool features a gbXML (green building XML) importer, which facilitates data exchange with other BIM software.
   This extension has extensive capabilities for the architect or engineer interested in evaluating a building's energy performance. It is even possible to use Ruby scripting (discussed in Chapter 7) to modify this tool's features and adapt it for new uses.

Sefaira

By Sefaira—Subscription (EW, http://sefaira.com)
   While other building energy and daylighting analysis tools need to be *run* at some point during the design process, this tool can always be "on" while you are working on conceptual models. This has the main benefit of immediate feedback, which can instantly inform the design process.

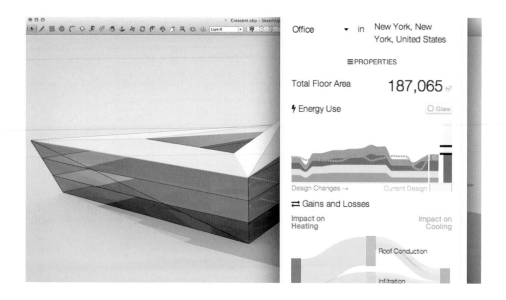

Skelion

By Skelion—Free/$200 (EW, http://skelion.com*)*

This extension, which comes in a free and a Pro version, lets you design residential, commercial, and ground mounted solar PV systems. It uses SketchUp's geo-based modeling tools together with PVWATTS meteorological data to create energy reports.

Example 4.8: Creating an Energy Analysis Building Model with OpenStudio

In this example, using the OpenStudio extension, you'll create a small building (only a single room, actually), which could serve as a model for use in EnergyPlus building energy analysis. This is just a very basic example model. For more details and to learn about running and interpreting the analysis, consult the OpenStudio documentation. To enable the OpenStudio functionality, make sure you have the extension installed before you begin.

When you create building models for energy analysis, keep in mind that you usually don't need to model actual material thicknesses. Walls, for example, are just single quadrilateral faces in SketchUp. Too much geometry is often counterproductive (and increases analysis time); therefore, you can usually ignore small wall recesses or protrusions.

1. Before you can add any walls, you need to designate a space (a zone) that will contain the area. Use the New Space tool on the OpenStudio Tools toolbar for this.

2. Click at the origin and place the new Space group. It appears as a blue outlined box.

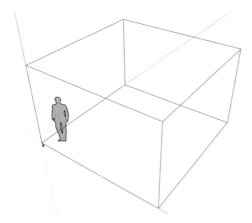

3. Now double-click it to go inside the space component (similar to SketchUp's usual group-editing mode).

4. Using SketchUp's standard modeling tools, draw a box inside this component. This will be the building. As you can see, the outlines of the Space group adjust to the size of the geometry that you add.

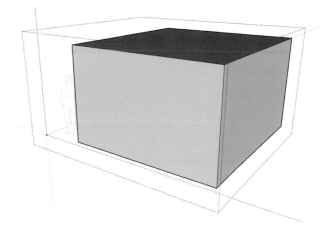

5. Without leaving the space component, draw some windows and a door onto the front surface of the box. You should notice at this point that when the door is attached to the sill level, it has a different color than the windows, which are in the middle of the wall.

6. Check to make sure you did everything right. Click on the Inspector tool on the OpenStudio toolbar. This brings up a dialog, which shows object properties when you highlight a face. Select the single face of the door and check that the dialog identifies it as a door.

7. Also highlight the windows and the walls to see how OpenStudio classifies them.

8. Let's add a shading device to the windows. To do this, you first need to create another group. Click the New Shading Surface Group icon on the toolbar and place it above the windows. It shows up in the same way the Space group that you placed earlier did.

9. Now double-click the Shading Surface group to be able to add shading geometry inside. If you can't double-click it, open the Outliner window and double-click it there.

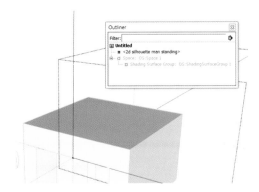

10. Finally, add any shading geometry you like. As before, keep it simple. This example simply adds a horizontal rectangle. Verify in the Inspector dialog that it is added as a ShadingSurface.

11. When you exit editing mode for both the Shading Surface and the Space groups, this is what you should see as your (very basic) finished model.

This exercise was a short introduction to setting up a building model in SketchUp for energy analysis using OpenStudio. As you can imagine, refining this model and analyzing it is more involved and, therefore, beyond the scope of this book. It is well documented on NREL's website, though, and I encourage you to explore this further.

Your Turn!

The following tasks allow you to practice the topics in this chapter:

1. **Make a physical 3D model of a building on a site.**
   Create a 3D model of your house or any other building you like. Use the Slicer extension and SketchUp's location tools to create an accurate model of the site.

Then make a textured 3D model of your house and use the Unfold tool to flatten, print, and fabricate it. (See **Figure 4.6** for a thermography example and **Figure 1.2** for the finished house model.)

2. **Make a glazed atrium roof shell.**

   Model the rough outlines of an inner courtyard (e.g., of a museum). Use any of the shell tools to create a glazed shell over it by modeling all mullions.

3. **Convert from a laser scanner to 3D printing.**

   If you have access to a laser scanner (or at least to its data), load a point cloud (e.g., of a small sculpture or the outlines of a building) into SketchUp and turn it into a watertight solid. Then, preprocess the object for 3D printing and send it to a printer (see Chapter 6 for details).

Figure 4.6: Unwrapped infrared house model, ready for fabrication

4. **Work with interactive SketchUp WebGL models.**

   Use one of your already modeled projects and upload it to either the 3D Warehouse or Sketchfab. Assume you are using this tool for a client presentation, so make it look good.

5. **Create walk-throughs for clients.**

   Get an architectural model and use any of the extensions discussed here to create a walk-through animation. Export this as a video.

6. **Create an assembly animation video.**

   Create an assembly animation in which components move. A good example is a steel connection where bolts move into place. Export this as a video.

7. **Estimate your home's energy usage.**

   Using the extensions and instructions given here, set up a very basic house for energy modeling and run an analysis. Keep it simple to begin with, so that you can thoroughly understand all the parameters. Also investigate insolation and daylighting if the extension supports it.

Chapter 5
Rendering in SketchUp

This chapter introduces methods for creating photorealistic renderings of SketchUp models and using them for highly polished presentation images. It covers how to create a rendering workflow, gives an overview of rendering methods, and presents techniques for setting up the rendering environment, lights, and materials.

Key Topics:

- Non-photorealistic rendering methods in SketchUp
- Principles of photorealistic rendering
- Overview of rendering software
- Employing free rendering software for a sample model
- Using commercial rendering software
- Rendering components: environments, lights, materials, objects
- Tips for successful renderings
- Making renderings presentable

Let's Get Visual!

An important—arguably the most important—aspect of a designer's workflow has always been the presentation of the work. In school, this consisted of desk crits and pinups; in work life, it encompasses presentations to clients and banks, for example, and even town hall meetings. In any of these situations, the designer's work has to be presented clearly, accurately, enticingly, and convincingly. This is the case for anything from hand-sketches through renderings to fabrication drawings.

Let's take a look at how SketchUp can help you with this.

What Is Already in SketchUp?

A major strength of SketchUp has always been its inclusion of presentation capabilities in the modeling environment. Many other CAD and 3D modeling software packages do not offer this combination—they typically separate modeling from presentation (think of *model space* and *paper space* in Autodesk's AutoCAD, for example). With SketchUp, however, it is possible to easily create a model, add annotation and dimensions, save the view of the modeling environment as an image, and then present it. It is even possible to present an annotated model interactively right inside SketchUp using its tabbed animation capabilities (you saw that in Chapter 3).

Several of SketchUp's built-in features support this workflow, in particular:

- **Font and dimension settings**—As mentioned in Chapter 2, these can be customized to the user's liking. Dimensions also display nicely and are easily readable in 3D space.

- **Shadow settings**—SketchUp has a built-in shadow feature that allows accurate display of date- and location-based shadows. Particularly architectural models benefit from the display of shadows—surface features are enhanced by giving them the perception of depth, and buildings look more realistic when "the sun gets turned on." (See **Figure 5.1**.)

Figure 5.1: Building without and with shadows enabled

- **Fog**—The Fog window in SketchUp lets you specify a distance from the view beyond which the view's background will fade away in what looks like fog. As you will see later, this feature is actually quite useful beyond simply making your scenes look "foggy."

- **Styles**—Most customization options for SketchUp's views are available as Styles. They can contain custom (and even "sketchy") lines, backgrounds, or watermarks. Many excellent styles have been premade and ship with SketchUp or are downloadable from the Internet. Styles can also be saved within animation tabs, allowing multiple styles to be used in the same file.

Styles are applied from the Styles window—where you can also make customizations and edits (see **Figure 5.2**).

Figure 5.2: The Styles window

PRO ONLY

SketchUp Pro Includes LayOut

If you own SketchUp Pro, you also have access to LayOut, a presentation and drawing-preparation software program that ships with it (see **Figure 5.3**). LayOut provides sheet-based presentation options that are not available in SketchUp itself. For example, you can add a sheet border as well as a text field, and you can arrange multiple SketchUp views—complete with Styles—on the same sheet. This allows for the inclusion of SketchUp in the document-creation process without the need for third-party software. Those model views then remain live-linked, so that whenever you update the model, all sheets also update.

Figure 5.3: LayOut main screen

Unfortunately, LayOut is beyond the scope of this book. To learn more about it, consult any of the books mentioned on the Further Reading page of the companion website: **http://sketchupfordesign.com/the-book/further-reading**.

The Magic of Styles

Because Styles are central to SketchUp's own presentation options in the sense that they allow customization of the view as well as linework, let's review working with Styles with a simple example.

Example 5.1: Creating Your Own Branded Sketchy Style

Follow the next steps to set up an easy-to use, personalized sketchy display style that doesn't even require exporting the SketchUp view into Photoshop for refinement. Once this style is set up, you just need to add it to a model and export the view using **File → Export → 2D Graphic…**. Of course, adjust any of the style components to your liking.

When you export the screen view to a higher resolution for an image, edge and profile line thickness will be scaled. Adjust those thicknesses until they look good at the desired resolution.

Beyond using sketchy lines, we will be working with layered watermarks here to create a faded-out style. **Figure 5.4** explains that layering visually. The transparent images and texture overlay build up the three layers that combine for the final view of the model. Please note that **Figure 5.4** just visualizes the layering; the images are not actually added to the 3D space.

Model

Texture

Washout frame

Logo

Figure 5.4: The watermark layers of the sketchy style (left: resulting style; right: the three watermarks shown in order)

1. You first need to get a logo or other wordmark as an insertable image. Because it should just sit on top of the model (rather than on a blocky colored background), it is important to place your logo on a transparent background, like this:

2. Do this in your photo-editing software (Adobe Photoshop shown here) and export it as a PNG file. Contrasting with the JPG format, PNG is able to save transparency.

3. For the watercolor-like, faded-out look, you also need to get a washout frame that is white around the edges and fades to transparent in the center. In the example, this frame also provides a bit of texture, which works nicely with the added texture in the next layer.

You can create such an image in your photo-editing software by starting with a white fill and then removing the center in several passes using a "natural brush" eraser.

4. Next, as shown in **Figure 5.4**, you need to get an image for the texture that makes this style a bit rougher and gives it paper-like qualities. For example, you could take a photo of a concrete wall or any other random-texture surface. Just make sure it is not too stark and gives you the look you are after. Modify it to your liking in photo-editing software. It is also a good idea to make it grayscale, so that it doesn't affect the model's colors. This image can be in any supported image format because you won't use transparency here.

5. Having assembled these three images, you can now open the Styles window in SketchUp. Start making your own style by first selecting the Default Style. Then click the small *plus* button (+) to create a new style based on this one. Give it a name and update it by clicking on the circular arrows style preview.

6. Now go to the Edit tab and click on the fourth icon that gives you access to the Watermark settings. Click the *plus* button (+) there to load the first watermark, the logo.

7. This logo needs to appear in front of the model; therefore, select Overlay in the Create Watermark Wizard dialog and then click Next.

8. Now increase transparency by moving the Blend slider a bit toward Model. Click Next again.

9. On the last page of the Wizard dialog, select Positioned On The Screen, and position the logo wherever you like. In the example, I placed it in the bottom-right corner. Adjust the scale as necessary.

10. Now repeat these steps with the washout frame and the texture image using the following settings:

Washout Frame: Pick Overlay, set Blend to Image, position Stretched To Fit The Screen, and uncheck Lock Aspect Ratio.

Texture: Pick Overlay, set Blend to halfway between Model and Image, position Stretched To Fit The Screen, and uncheck Lock Aspect Ratio.

11. To finish the watermarks, adjust their layering using the Up and Down arrows in the Styles window in the order shown here.

12. Update the style again by clicking on the circular arrows in the style preview.

13. Next, you need to apply the sketchy linework to your style. To do this, click on the Mix tab in the Styles window. Here, you can take components of other styles (such as edge or face settings) and apply them to your style. This is done by browsing to a style in the bottom part of the window and then dragging the style to the respective settings area above.

Browse to the Sketchy Edges styles in this tab and find one that you like (e.g., the Tech Pen style). Then click and drag the style right over the Edge Settings area above it to apply it to your style.

14. You are almost done now. There is just one more step: hide the axes and other unsightly elements. Go back to the Edit tab in the Styles window and select the Modeling Settings button (the rightmost one). In this sub-tab, you can uncheck what you don't want to see. At minimum, make sure the Model Axes are not shown.

15. At this point, you have a style that looks exactly the way you intended. Just update the style once more by clicking on its preview icon to finalize it. It is also a good idea to save this style somewhere so that you can always use it in other models.

TIP	Feel free to experiment with the style settings (there are quite a few more). For example, try placing the texture under the model instead of above it. You can also load a photo (e.g., of a building site) as an underlay; however, illustrating buildings in context is often better done with the Match Photo tool.

Starting with SketchUp 2015, look for the Fast Styles icon (a small stopwatch) in the Styles window. While graphically more complex styles can slow down SketchUp (especially in a large model), these styles will keep good performance. Things that affect performance are sketchy edges, profiles, depth cue, line extensions, endpoints, jitter, and some transparency face settings.

As you just saw, styles in SketchUp let you customize:

- **Edge (line) appearance**—Edge/profile size, depth-cue, and jitter, but also whether you want to use a sketchy style.
- **Face appearance**—Visual styles such as hidden lines or transparency.
- **Background colors**—Colors for the background, sky, or ground.
- **Watermarks**—As you saw, you can add an image as a watermark in front as well as in back of the modeling environment.
- **Visibility of nonmodeling items**—You can turn visibility on or off for items like axes and section cuts.

You can download new and interesting styles from several websites. One great resource is this page: www.sketchupartists.org/sketchup-styles.

See **Figure 5.5** for a comparison of the face display styles that are possible in SketchUp.

Figure 5.5: Comparison of different default SketchUp display styles (left to right: textured, x-ray, solid color, conceptual, hidden line, wireframe)

Style Builder

SketchUp Pro ships with a small program called Style Builder. This software allows you to use your own hand-drawn pencil strokes in a custom style—giving you the ultimate means to customize and personalize the visual appearance of the SketchUp-generated view.

What If I Want More?

A review of SketchUp's built-in visualization tools makes it clear that photorealistic rendering is a missing feature. While shadows add a level of reality to lighting, the only light source accurately used to display shadows is the sun. Artificial lights (such as streetlights or interior lighting) and indirect lighting effects cannot be displayed.

Materials are similarly limited. SketchUp's materials—while giving a surface more realism—look flat and are unable to display reflectivity or accurate light transmission, let alone refraction (as would be the case with glass, gems, or water).

These shortcomings can be remedied only by using photorealistic rendering software. Fortunately for today's SketchUp user, many options are available—from free programs to movie-quality (and expensive) software packages. The following sections present some of these options and introduce you to common techniques used to create high-quality photorealistic renderings.

Overview of Rendering Methods

Photorealistic rendering in SketchUp (or any 3D modeling software, for that matter) uses a different approach from what you saw when we looked at SketchUp's own styles. In the case of styles, SketchUp uses your computer's graphics card to *render*—or calculate—the view appearance. In that process, the view and all visual features (such as custom linetypes) are being created pixel by pixel by your graphics card at a rate that is faster than your eye can perceive it being refreshed. As a reference, your monitor has a refresh rate of at least 60 hertz (60 screen updates per second).

Because SketchUp's visual styles can be displayed at roughly the same frame rate your monitor uses, you can actually move around a model that has styles applied and view or edit it in real time (performance depends on the model complexity and style complexity, as well as the graphics card and CPU quality, of course—the higher the demand on the graphics card, the slower it can process the view and the more jagged any motion becomes).

Photorealistic rendering, on the other hand, has the capability to accurately estimate material properties such as reflection, as well as light properties such as colored lights or soft shadows. This, however, comes at a computational cost. In most rendering software, these computations are not performed by the graphics card but by the CPU (your computer's "computational heart"). Only the newest rendering software also processes some or all of these computations in the graphics card itself (commonly called the GPU). In any case, the necessary calculations typically are too slow to allow for real-time rendering at a high level of quality. Therefore, whenever you set up a view for rendering, you will send it from SketchUp to the rendering software and then wait for the rendering calculations to finish.

As you will see in the following sections, software is available that tightly integrates itself into SketchUp and that will execute all of these steps without requiring you to move files between different software. Some of the available programs are actually very fast (mainly because they now use both the CPU and the GPU), which will give you near-instant feedback on the rendered appearance once you apply a change (e.g., a material change or a camera move).

Before we look at rendering techniques, let's quickly review how rendering works.

What Is Photorealistic Rendering?

In real life, a light source like the sun or a desk lamp emits light particles (photons) in either a single direction, as is the case with a highly focused lamp or a laser, or radially in all directions, as with the sun or an unshielded light bulb. Briefly ignoring Einstein, let's assume that, for all intents and purposes, these particles travel in a straight line.

These light particles then land on an object (your work desk or this book, for instance), where they are either absorbed by the surface (and turned into heat in the case of a black surface), reflected (as is the case with most surfaces), or refracted while they travel through the material (their direction is bent, as is the case with water). Different materials exhibit different absorption, reflection, and refraction properties—water, a mirror, and a brick are three fundamentally different examples.

If a light particle is reflected, it has the chance to land on another object—or many more, as happens in a hall of mirrors, for example. Depending on the surface properties of the materials these particles land on, reflection is either very directional (e.g., with a mirror) or scattered (e.g., on a painted wall). See **Figure 5.6**.

Figure 5.6: Various reflections in real materials (brushed metal, coated wood, natural stone, shiny metal)

Finally, as you likely have observed multiple times before, light has the tendency to become dimmer the farther away you are from its source. Imagine looking along a street with street lamps at night. This effect, called *attenuation,* means that light particles can't travel forever—they lose energy the farther they travel. (See **Figure 5.47** for an example.)

As you can see in this brief description, materials and particularly surface qualities such as color, reflectivity, and refractivity have a large impact on how light travels and how our natural environment becomes visible to our eyes or a camera lens.

Photorealistic rendering software must be able to re-create these physical phenomena as accurately as possible. If you want your renderings to look like photos (or even better), the software you use must be able to represent all of the aforementioned light and material properties as realistically as possible. However, it must also be able to do that in a time frame that users can live with. As you can imagine, any computational simulation of complex natural behaviors can be extremely resource-intensive. Therefore, rendering software is often designed to take some shortcuts that approximate the "correct" solution just to keep computation time low. It is a measure of good software that it is able to create high-quality renderings in a short amount of time.

So how does rendering software work? Without getting too deeply into the technical details, it is fair to say that it basically works like nature, in that it uses light particles that travel through space. Depending on the computational approach, however, it may be more efficient to send out these particles "in reverse" from the viewer's eye (i.e., the camera view), instead of from the light sources. Sometimes a combination of both techniques is used.

When these particles meet a surface, the software queries the surface material's properties and modifies the particle's color, direction, and intensity to reflect the material's absorptive, reflective, or refractive properties before sending the light particle back on its way. (See **Figure 5.7.**)

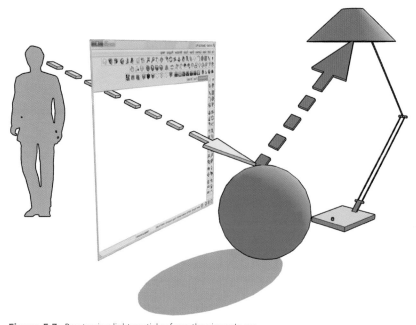

Figure 5.7: Ray-tracing light particles from the viewer's eye

It should be noted here that for computational efficiency, the number of *bounces* (or material interactions) is typically limited to a number that is low enough to reduce computation time, yet high enough to make the rendering look realistic. You can often experiment with this setting in your rendering software.

The following natural phenomena can be simulated by rendering software. Actual implementation and quality of the effects can vary among rendering software programs, though.

- **Material appearance**—This is commonly called *shading* and includes the interaction between light and a surface's material.

- **Texture**—This is the photographic appearance of the material. Often, seamlessly repeating images are used to represent a particular material (e.g., a brick pattern), but this could be accomplished by single images or a computational method as well (e.g., for solid colors or a patterned surface). SketchUp's materials are all seamlessly repeating *tiled* texture images. (See **Figure 5.8**.)

Figure 5.8: Various surface textures (rusty metal, wood, paper, canvas, rubber, solid colors)

- **Surface roughness simulation**—*Bump mapping* or *displacement mapping* can add the appearance of geometric detail and surface irregularities to an otherwise flat surface. Displacement mapping typically goes further than bump mapping in that the underlying geometry is modified. Bump mapping modifies only light reflection behavior. (See **Figure 5.9**.)

Figure 5.9: Material bumpiness: patterned rubber, natural stone, canvas

- **Reflection and shininess**—This adds fully or partially reflective properties to a surface. In rendering, this property is often adjusted using a *specular* texture or color.

- **Refraction/diffraction**—This describes how light direction changes when it moves from one material onto another.

- **Translucency**—This is the degree of opacity of a material.

- **Subsurface or particulate scattering**—When light travels through any material, particles (in the air, for example) reflect it, and we can see effects like the "beams of light" that we notice in the forest when sunlight breaks through fog. A similar behavior occurs with a material that lets light travel into it, where the light then scatters and makes the material appear as if it is partly illuminated from inside—good examples are milk, wax, and alabaster. (See **Figure 5.10**.)

Figure 5.10: Materials with subsurface light scattering: milk, soap, candle

- **Indirect illumination**—When a lighter-colored surface becomes illuminated by a light source, it invariably casts a light reflection on adjoining surfaces. This effect is called *indirect illumination* or *global illumination,* and it is a must-have in rendering software.

- **Caustics**—When light travels through glass or water, the internal refraction makes caustics appear. We know these from light ripples on the bottom of a pool or as light focusing behind a lens or a glass object. (See **Figure 5.11**.)

- **Shadows**—In reality, shadows are never as crisp and sharp-edged as in SketchUp. Depending on the light source, shadows either have blurred edges or are completely blurry.

- **Camera properties such as focal length and aperture shape**—When we take an image with a real camera, depending on the aperture settings, part of the image may be blurred because it was out of focus. If a light source is located in the blurry region, its outline will have the shape of the aperture of the camera, which is typically polygonal. (See **Figure 5.12**.)

Figure 5.11: Caustics behind a glass of water

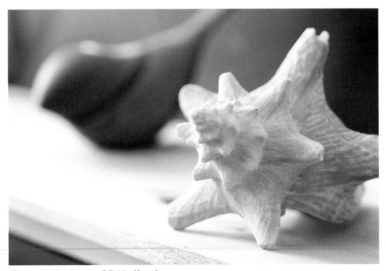

Figure 5.12: Depth-of-field effect from an open camera aperture

Both of these effects can usually be simulated by rendering software.

- **Motion blur**—Another camera effect is motion blur. When we take an image of a moving object, such as a car, at a slow shutter speed, the image becomes blurry in the direction of its motion.

- **Animation**—Instead of just creating a single rendered image, it is possible to render animations. Those are commonly created as successive renderings of single images, which then are stitched together into video using editing software. Because video frame rate can be anywhere between 25 and 30 frames per second (for fluid motion), quite a large number of single images need to be rendered to create a video of usable length. Advanced effects in rendered animations are animated objects (such as water ripples or driving cars) and light animations (e.g., a morning-to-night shadow animation).

Rendering Techniques

A variety of rendering methods exist, and every manufacturer of rendering software has its own proprietary modifications to common techniques. As previously mentioned, the typical trade-off is between quality and speed. Software implementations of even the same methods can vary widely in those categories between manufacturers. I recommend, therefore, that you test any rendering software that interests you and find out if quality and speed are satisfactory for your needs.

It is also common for rendering software manufacturers not to offer too many different methods in one software package. This may be a good idea because too many (and too technical) choices may actually be counterproductive by being confusing to the user.

Some common methods include:

- **Ray-tracing**—This is the basis of every rendering method. Light particles are traced as they travel through the model and are reflected or absorbed by surfaces. By itself, this method often does not include light bounces (indirect illumination) and only relies on direct illumination from the sun or artificial lights.

- **Global illumination**—Any good rendering software will include global illumination. This technique considers light bounces, which yield interesting effects such as illuminated shadows and colors *bleeding* (reflecting)—from a colored wall onto an adjoining white surface, for example.

- **Biased and unbiased methods**—Rendering always consists of computational simulation. As with any computational method, the more precise it is, the more resources and calculations it needs. Therefore, many rendering techniques are actually efficient approximations of the accurate solution, which by its very nature introduces a *bias* of one form or another. Only *unbiased* methods can accurately evaluate light behavior and, therefore, can be considered to produce "perfect" renderings. Unfortunately, those methods require considerably more computation than a biased method.

   Examples of unbiased methods are path tracing (PT) and metropolis light transport (MLT).

- **Ambient occlusion**—This rendering method approximates shadows based on how many light particles can potentially arrive at any point on the model. As a result, inside edges or occluded parts become darker and outside surfaces are lighter. This method often produces soft shadows reminiscent of what can be seen on overcast days.

Rendering Software

Adding rendering capabilities to SketchUp can be a surprisingly easy and/or cheap step (admittedly, it can be quite expensive, too). At this point, various software programs are available that accomplish this task. In general, they can be classified as follows:

- **SketchUp-integrated software**—This group of programs installs into SketchUp as an extension. The programs generally are accessed using either the menu system or a custom toolbar that becomes available after installation.

  When you start a rendering, your SketchUp model is processed in the background and a window with the rendering result typically shows up right within the SketchUp environment.

  Materials and lights are often handled within SketchUp as well and commonly use SketchUp's materials, components (for lighting components), and sun/shadow settings directly.

TIP

If you use only SketchUp for rendering and like the convenience of having an easy and integrated workflow, look for integrated rendering programs. The only downside can be that these programs are designed to be so user-friendly that they might not allow much customization.

- **External programs with exporter extension**—These are often stand-alone programs that can render scenes from a variety of 3D modeling packages (SketchUp, Rhino, Autodesk software, etc.).

  The user interface in SketchUp is similar to those of the first software group, because they integrate into SketchUp using their own exporter plugins. When you start the rendering, however, the 3D model data is exported and directly loaded into an external program, which renders the image.

  Depending on the rendering software, you may be able to modify any of the rendering settings (materials, lighting, etc.) even up to a very high degree in the external rendering software.

TIP

This approach is ideal if you use multiple 3D modeling software programs and would like to use the renderer with all of them. Because some of these programs offer extensive customization capabilities, they are often well suited for advanced users who look for more control.

- **External programs**—A large variety of rendering and 3D modeling/rendering software exists that is capable of loading 3D models using a generic file format (e.g., 3DS, OBJ, FBX, DAE, etc.). They can then be enhanced within the rendering software's environment by adding materials and lights.

  As long as the available import file formats are compatible with SketchUp's export formats, it is possible to use SketchUp's models with those programs. Some even use the SKP format as an input format.

  It is important to keep in mind that because they don't tie into SketchUp directly (and haven't been developed for it, either), rendering a model successfully often involves more work.

These programs are best for advanced users and those who seek custom features that only these programs offer. A benefit of external programs (which is, therefore, also true for the second software group) is that they usually can handle a large number of polygons and detailed textures quite well.

Depending on your preferences and your workflow requirements, you can choose between easy-to-use or highly customizable software. It is often a good idea to create a sample rendering using a trial version before you commit, especially to the more expensive programs. Other aspects to keep in mind when choosing are quality of help files and tutorials, availability of good materials, activeness of the user community (e.g., in forums), availability of plugins, and additional features such as animation support—if needed.

Multithreading and Network Rendering

In both of these techniques, a single rendered image is processed by multiple processor cores or even several computers at the same time (i.e., in parallel). Given that today's workstations (and even notebooks) have multiple processor cores built in (as in a quad-core CPU, for example), software can use each of these cores by sending a chunk (often a square portion) of the image to a different processor core in a *process* (or a computational *thread*). This can result in a significant increase in rendering speed. With enough computing power, near-real-time rendering is possible using this technique.

Almost all available rendering software can take advantage of *multithreading*. This means that if you have a computer with four processor cores, the image can be split up and rendered by all of those cores at the same time. As mentioned, modern rendering software can often use the graphics card's processors (the GPU) to process some of those calculations, increasing the number of computational cores even more.

Keep in mind: Because your operating system (and any other running software such as your e-mail program) uses processor cores, too, it may become necessary to limit the number of cores used for rendering so that the operating system doesn't freeze up during a rendering. If this is a problem for you, look into the rendering software's settings—often there is an option to limit the number of processes used for rendering.

If you are an advanced user or you are setting up a rendering solution for a larger company, it may be a good idea to look into the network rendering capabilities of any of the software in question. *Network rendering* is a technique whereby a single rendered image is processed by multiple computers (and their respective processor cores) at a time. These computers can be located in your office (e.g., using computers that sit idle overnight) or in what is commonly called a *render farm,* which is a similar setup of networked computers, this time with dedicated rendering computers that are provided (for a fee) by third-party companies.

The following list is a sampling of currently available rendering software for SketchUp. Because all of these software packages work with any version of SketchUp, you do not need to own the Pro version to experiment with rendering. For an updated listing, go to this book's companion website and look for this chapter's page.

SketchUp-integrated:

- ArielVision—Win only—**www.renderplus.com**
- Caravaggio—Win/Mac—**www.caravaggio3d.com**
- Indigo—Win/Mac/Linux—**www.indigorenderer.com**
- IRender nXt—Win only—**www.renderplus.com**
- LightUp—Win/Mac—**www.light-up.co.uk**
- Raylectron—Win only— **www.raylectron.com**
- Render[in]—Win/Mac—**www.renderin.com**
- Renditioner Pro—Win/Mac—**www. imsidesign.com**
- Shaderlight—Win/Mac—**www.artvps.com**
- SU Podium—Win/Mac—**www.suplugins.com**
- Twilight—Win only—**www.twilightrender.com**
- Visualizer—Win/Mac—**www.getvisualizer.com**
- VRay—Win/Mac— **www.vray.com/vray-for-sketchup**

External programs with exporter extension:

- 3D Paintbrush—Win only—**www.3dpaintbrush.com**
- Artlantis—Win/Mac—**www.artlantis.com**
- Bloom Unit—Win/Mac—**www.bloomunit.com**
- Kerkythea—Win/Mac/Linux—**www.kerkythea.net**
- KeyShot—Win only—**www.keyshot.com**
- LumenRT—Win/Mac—**www.lumenrt.com**
- Maxwell—Win/Mac/Linux—**www.maxwellrender.com**
- Thea—Win/Mac/Linux—**www.thearender.com**

Sample of external programs:

- Lightwave— **www.lightwave3d.com**
- Vue—**www.e-onsoftware.com**

These programs typically install easily from the Extension Warehouse (see Chapter 4 for details on this) or an installation file. In SketchUp, they usually create a new toolbar that can be docked anywhere on your screen and a menu entry. Many also add tools to the right-click menu (e.g., when you hover the mouse over a light object).

Renderings in this book were created using Twilight (see **Figure 5.13**), Kerkythea, and Shaderlight (see **Figure 5.14**) rendering software.

Figure 5.13: Twilight user interface

Figure 5.14: Shaderlight user interface

Please note: This book can be used with any rendering software. Except for the Kerkythea-tutorial, all principles and methods covered in this chapter apply with minor modifications to all rendering programs and the instructions are not presented in any software-specific format.

Setting Up Kerkythea and Creating a Rendering

At this point you have read enough about the theory behind rendering and available software. It is time to actually get to work. To keep things simple (and cheap, because all the software used in this short tutorial is free), this section will give you a brief introduction to setting up the freely available rendering engine Kerkythea and testing some renderings with it. This rendering software is available for both the Windows and Mac platforms. As you saw earlier, many other rendering software packages exist—all with their own strengths and weaknesses.

Let's get started by setting up Kerkythea:

1. Download the Kerkythea installer from the official website: www.kerkythea.net/cms/index.php/downloads/software.

2. Download the SketchUp exporter plugin (SU2KT) from the same page as well.

3. *Optional:* Download Kerkythea sample materials and models (trees, etc.) here: www.kerkythea.net/cms/index.php/downloads/resources.

4. Install Kerkythea. The provided installer will install it like any other software. As you can see now, Kerkythea installs as a completely separate program (and can, therefore, be used for rendering 3D models even without SketchUp running). The only part that is contained in SketchUp is the exporter plugin.

5. Install the SketchUp exporter extension according to the instructions given in Chapter 4 for extensions of the ZIP file format. You should see two new items in SketchUp: (1) An entry in the **Extensions** menu with the title "Kerkythea Exporter" and (2) a toolbar.

6. *Optional:* Start Kerkythea and under the **File** menu, select Install Library… to install the material libraries by selecting the downloaded ZIP files.

7. When you do the first rendering, the exporter will ask you for the location of the `Kerkythea.exe` file, so that it can open Kerkythea right after it exports a file for rendering, making the transition quite smooth. If for any reason, you are not able to set this up correctly, don't panic! You can always save a scene for rendering using the exporter plugin (as an XML file) and later open it from within Kerkythea.

Once you have the software environment set up correctly, you are ready to give rendering a try. Create any 3D model you like—this tutorial uses an indoor scene where you can test some materials and lights. **Figure 5.15** shows the basic scene used for this example.

Figure 5.15: Room setup in SketchUp (box for walls and floor, sofa, window, and plant from the sample components, custom-modeled mirror)

Next, you need to apply some materials. Use SketchUp's built-in materials for this—add a wood material to the floor and any color material to the walls. Make sure all surfaces have a material applied and are not just painted with the default white color.

TIP

An important quirk to know about Kerkythea is the fact that the exporter groups geometry by material. The implication of this is that once you are in Kerkythea's environment and you want to edit a material, clicking a particular face selects all faces that have the same material applied to them. Therefore, all faces that do not contain a material will be grouped because they actually contain SketchUp's default material.

As a good rule, make sure all the faces in your model have some nondefault material applied.

Let's also look at the scene with the sunlight on. Go to the Shadows window and make sure shadows are enabled. Adjust object placement and sun position (i.e., modify time and day) to your liking. (See **Figure 5.16**.)

Figure 5.16: Room in SketchUp with materials applied and shadows turned on

To explore one of the most important features of rendering software—artificial lighting—you'll next add a few lights to the scene. Let's first add two spotlights to the ceiling above the sofa. You'll use the exporter's built-in tool for this. Alternatively, you could place some of Kerkythea's light components into the scene, if you downloaded them when you were installing the exporter earlier.

Click on the Insert Spotlight icon on the SU2Kerkythea toolbar. The tool lets you pick a point where the spotlight will be located (click above the sofa on the ceiling). Then you need to pick a target point for the spotlight (just move down on the blue axis). Finally, a dialog will open with some light properties. You will also see a conical object appear in your scene, which represents the spotlight and its direction (it will not be shown in the final rendering). In the dialog, change Light Power to 5 but leave all other settings at the defaults.

Now you have set up the scene properly for export to Kerkythea. All geometry has been created, materials have been applied, and all lights have been placed. As a final step, you could create several scene tabs in SketchUp, each showing a different view of your model. These would be exported to Kerkythea as differently named camera views.

To start the first rendering, click on the Export Model to Kerkythea button on the SU2Kerkythea toolbar. This opens the Export dialog, from which you need to select the options shown in this image.

Now simply save the XML file that the exporter creates in a convenient location.

If you look at the file location, you will notice that the Kerkythea exporter saved not only an XML file but also a folder with a name that starts with TX_. This folder contains all texture images for the exported scene. If you used SketchUp's texture positioning tools, you will also notice that the exported textures have been "straightened" and exported exactly as they were visible on faces.

If you set up the link to Kerkythea in the SketchUp exporter correctly, then the 3D scene should open in Kerkythea right after exporting. If this doesn't happen, simply start Kerkythea and open the XML file from within Kerkythea instead. It should look like **Figure 5.17**.

Kerkythea's user interface is quite self-explanatory; nevertheless, take a minute to familiarize yourself with it. Here's what you see in the window:

Left of the model view is a tree outline of what is contained in the 3D space (models/objects, lights, and cameras). You can select something by double-clicking on the entry in this list, and you can modify parameters (e.g., light intensity or material properties) by right-clicking on it.

Figure 5.17: Room in Kerkythea after importing

Right of the model view is a material browser as well as a preview image of the rendered view. To view and apply materials, click on Library Selection and select one of the installed libraries. A double-click on a material applies it to the current selection.

Above the model view is a menu as well as a toolbar. On the toolbar you can find tools to change the view as well as start or stop a rendering. The menu offers many more tools, of which possibly the most important ones are under the **Settings** menu—you can control scene and light parameters as well as organize your material libraries there.

To be able to evaluate materials in Kerkythea's model view, press the V key to switch from wireframe to solid (or textured) view mode. This makes it easier to understand what is contained in your view.

Before you make any modifications to Kerkythea's settings, let's just start a test rendering. Select the **Render** → **Start** menu item or click on the round, green runner icon in the top toolbar to do this. The Camera and Settings dialog should open with various settings.

In this dialog, select the proper camera view that you want to render (choose ## *Current View* ## for the perspective shown in the viewer). Also, set all other options to the ones in the preceding image.

It is usually a good idea to test a new rendering setup with low-quality and small image size settings. The higher the quality and the number of pixels in an image, the longer a rendering takes. Increase those settings only after an initial draft rendering gives you adequate results.

To determine final pixel dimensions, multiply the size at which you want to print the rendering (e.g., 5 × 7 inches) by the desired resolution (e.g., 300 dots per inch). This gives a minimum resolution of 1500 × 2100 pixels.

Your first rendering should look like **Figure 5.18**.

Figure 5.18: Kerkythea rendering with default parameters

As you can see, the window material didn't transmit any light. This can happen sometimes. Let's go ahead and fix that by applying the Thin Glass material to the window glass. This step also shows you how to apply a material in Kerkythea.

Select the window glass to start this process. If you used a window like mine in your model, you can select all of the polygons that make up the window by simply clicking anywhere on it. Next, open the basic materials palette that came with Kerkythea in the Material Browser on the right side of the window. A double-click on the Thin Glass material will apply it to the selected window polygons.

The result after a repeated render should show the sunlight and its shadow on the sofa.

As you can see in **Figure 5.19**, the mirror has a plain material and doesn't reflect at all. Let's fix this by applying a mirror material to it. This time, we'll make a custom material.

Figure 5.19: Rendering with window glass and sunlight visible

To do this, select the mirror polygons in your model first. You will then see the material highlighted in the tree view on the left side of the screen. Right-click on it and select Edit Material… from the context menu. A Material Editor dialog will open, where you need to make the changes shown here.

You won't see much of a change in the viewer, but if you redo the rendering, as shown in **Figure 5.20**, you'll see that the material now reflects like a perfect mirror.

Figure 5.20: Rendering with reflective materials

It might be a good idea to apply the same material to the sofa's legs, because they are likely made of polished chrome.

Let's modify some other settings. In the next step, let's give the sun's shadows some fuzziness—the crisp outlines of the window's shadows are not realistic. To do this, find the Sun item under Lights in the tree view on the left side of the screen. Right-click on it, and in the Scene Settings dialog, modify the parameters as shown here.

Test these settings with another trial rendering. Your room should now look like **Figure 5.21**.

Figure 5.21: Rendering with fuzzy shadows

At this point, you have set up a quite usable rendering, and it is time to do a final render-ing. Select *08. PhotonMap—Fine + AA 0.3* as the setting and start a new rendering. When it finishes, notice that the blurry shadows look much better than they did using the trial settings. Furthermore, you most likely noticed that it took much longer to create the better-quality rendering.

To familiarize yourself with the various rendering methods that Kerkythea offers, try ren-dering the same scene with these settings:

- **02. Ray Tracing—High + AA 0.3**—This setting does not calculate indirect light and considers only the direct sun and spotlight for illuminating the scene.

- **08. PhotonMap—Fine + AA 0.3**—PhotonMap is the technique used for this tutorial so far. This method calculates indirect light and fuzzy shadows well.

- **02. Metropolis Light Transport (BPT)**—This method is unbiased, which means that it uses real light properties and does not just approximate them. You will see that indirect light and some materials look much better using this method—especially in complex scenes. Stop the rendering process when you are happy with the result.

- **22. Clay Render (PhotonMap—Medium)**—This rendering method ignores materials and applies a default white material to all surfaces.

- **Path Tracing**—This is an alternative method used mainly for exterior scenes. It doesn't work well in this case.

Once you have created the final rendering, keep the Rendered Image window open and adjust the Tone Map settings to your liking. Then click on Save and save the rendered image as a JPG, PNG, BMP, GIF, or HDR file.

This tutorial helped you understand how to use a rendering program—Kerkythea, in this case. For more information about Kerkythea than we can cover here, read the Getting Started tutorials that you can download from this website:

www.kerkythea.net/cms/index.php/downloads/documentation

A more thorough reference is Thomas Bleicher and Robin de Jongh's *SketchUp 2014 for Architectural Visualization* (Packt Publishing, 2014), which explains rendering with Kerkythea in more depth.

As this tutorial demonstrates, Kerkythea offers many modification options that are useful for advanced users. Nevertheless, they can be daunting for others who may prefer simplicity. Thus, I encourage you to peruse the list of software presented earlier to find the rendering software that is right for you.

Perfecting the Components of a Rendering

As mentioned earlier, the approaches and techniques presented in this section are applicable to any rendering software. Therefore, they are presented in a very general but usable form. Be aware, however, that you may have to adapt the concepts slightly to work with your software.

Use this section as a reference when you are working on photorealistic renderings.

Modeling

First, let's look at some modeling-related issues. You will need to consider much of what is discussed here in SketchUp while you are creating your model and before you send it to the rendering software.

Edges and Faces

A SketchUp model of any size is made up of many faces that are bounded by edges. When you look at a shape such as the sphere shown here and turn on the display of Hidden Geometry (in the **View** menu), you'll see that it is made up of several polygonal faces, which in turn are bounded by edge lines (four in this example).

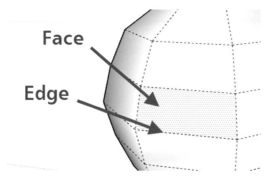

In addition, a model can have temporary guidelines (dashed lines) and guide points (little crosses) that you may have created when you were modeling using the Measure and Protractor tools.

When you send a model like this to rendering software, it typically uses only faces for rendering. Points and lines are assumed to have zero thickness and, therefore, cannot reflect any light, so they are generally ignored.

Two cases in which you might actually want to see lines in your renderings are (1) models that contain thin wires and (2) renderings that are intended to have outlines (either for more edge definition or for a more cartoonish look).

Let's evaluate this by working with a wire-supported tension-fabric structure model, as shown in **Figure 5.22**.

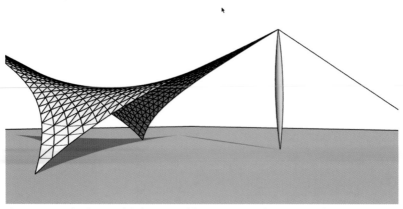

Figure 5.22: SketchUp model of a tension-fabric structure with guy wire and post

For the first case (making the wire visible), simply model it as a thin object to make it visible in the rendering. One consideration here is that it is likely very inefficient to do this with round objects (even though the wire may actually have a round cross-section). For example, the default circle in SketchUp has 24 side segments—extruding it along a straight line creates 26 faces (24 sides plus the top and bottom faces). Extruding it along a curved line creates many more faces because the geometry needs to fold around bends. (See **Figure 5.23**.)

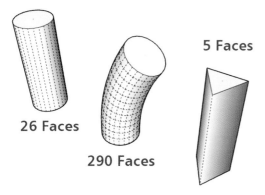

Figure 5.23: Number of faces after extrusion (left: default circle extruded along line; middle: default circle along arc; right: triangle along line)

Therefore, a good rule is to use the minimum number of faces when you model any object—especially when it is barely visible, such as in the case of a guy wire. To do this, you can preset the number of segments when you create a circle or a polygon by entering the number right after you start the tool.

The result of this approach can be seen in **Figure 5.24**, where the guy wire has been modeled using a triangle as a cross section.

Figure 5.24: Rendering with guy wire modeled as extruded triangle

Now let's look at the second case: If you want to show the lines in the tension structure in your rendering, you have two options—the first one depends on your rendering software, however.

When you use your rendering software to assign a material to the faces that make up the tension fabric, look for a material feature called something like "Show Edge Lines." If this feature is available, the rendering software can actually render edges as a line (or even, in some cases, using a different material). If this feature is not available, a good approach is to overlay a rendered view with an edge-only view exported from SketchUp.

To do this, switch to hidden-line view in SketchUp (go to **View** → **Face Style** → **Hidden Line**) and turn off all shadows. Then export the view from within SketchUp. Before exporting, adjust any line properties in the Styles window to your liking.

Also, do a rendering of the same view (make sure the image size in pixels is exactly the same) and export it as well. You can now take these two images into Photoshop (or any other graphics software) and combine them using a layer arrangement similar to the image shown here.

For this example, I also used a feathered white paintbrush to reduce the impact of the lines in some areas. The result of the combination looks like **Figure 5.25**.

A further effect related to faces can be seen in **Figure 5.26**. Whenever you render a tessellated surface (like the fabric in this model), the polygons that make up the shape will render as flat shapes. As a result, the surface may not appear smooth in the rendering. This can often be solved with yet another material-related setting.

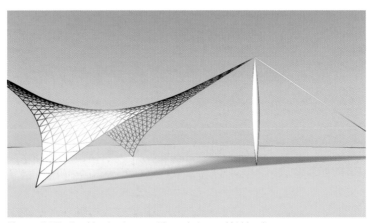

Figure 5.25: Combination image with rendering and hidden-line export

Figure 5.26: Smoothing of tessellated surfaces (left: SketchUp model; middle: no edge softening; right: full edge softening)

When you apply a material to the fabric in your rendering software, look for a feature called Hard Edge Angle. This may also be available in the general rendering settings. Similar to what you can set in SketchUp using the Soften Edges window, it is possible to pick an angle value below which adjoining faces will become smooth. For example, a value of 45 would mean that all neighboring surfaces that have an angle of 45 degrees between them will appear as one smooth surface. **Figure 5.27** shows an example of this method. Often, rendering software will simply use what is set in SketchUp's Soften Edges window.

Of course, you can also smooth surfaces by increasing the number of polygons that make up the surface. You will have to do this using an extension because SketchUp has no native function for this task. In addition, increasing the number of polygons may likewise increase render time, so having fewer polygons and visually smoothing them may be the most efficient approach.

Front Face and Back Face

SketchUp's faces have two sides to them: a front and a back. You can distinguish them easily by the default color with which each face is painted. The front is painted white, and the back is painted light blue. Extruding a polygon and then removing some faces reveals the two colors quite nicely.

This has various implications for rendering. First of all, many 3D modeling and rendering programs display only the front side of faces—the back side is often simply not displayed. In addition, SketchUp has the ability to assign two different materials to the same face—one to the front and one to the back. This is not always supported by other software.

Back face color

Front face color

While many exporter extensions and integrated rendering software deal with this internally (where you don't have to think about it), it is important to know about this in case you need to troubleshoot. In any case, the best rule is to *always have fronts of faces point outward* (or toward the camera).

Fortunately, SketchUp has a built-in function that flips a face's orientation. To use it, select the faces you need to flip and then right-click on one of them. Select Reverse Faces from the context menu, and you will see the face color change. If you already have materials applied to those faces, switch the Face Style to Monochrome (in the **View** menu) beforehand. This suppresses all textures and lets you find reversed faces by showing you default face colors.

If you need to export a SketchUp model to use in any other 3D modeling or rendering application, look at the exporter options. Some of the options, accessible through the **File →** **Export → 3D Model...** menu item, allow for transfer of two-sided faces. (See **Figure 5.27**.)

Figure 5.27: Option in the DAE Export dialog to use two-sided faces

Triangulation

Unlike many other 3D modeling software packages, SketchUp has the ability to use polygonal faces that have more than three edge points (or *vertices*). This allows us to use rectangular faces for walls—or even hexagonal faces (as shown in an earlier example).

While this is very useful for texturing—SketchUp's built-in texture positioning functions work on single faces only, for example—3D model export and processing by rendering applications typically leads to a triangulation of these polygonal faces.

This does not often cause problems, because the textured 3D model export into a rendering application is handled automatically by an exporter plugin. It is important to know this, however, for troubleshooting and for special cases.

One of these cases occurs when you use faces with a light-emitting material (e.g., to simulate a light box or a neon tube). While this can make a very nice-looking, diffuse light, it is important to keep in mind that the geometry of the faces that have the material applied should be as simple as possible—best is a triangle. If you use a circle with a light-emitting material, for example, the circle will be exported into the rendering application with many more faces than the one it has in SketchUp (see **Figure 5.28** for an illustration of this). The higher number of faces can increase rendering time significantly.

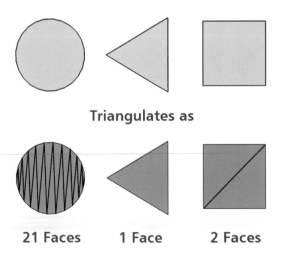

Triangulates as

21 Faces   1 Face   2 Faces

Figure 5.28: How similarly sized shapes triangulate upon exporting

Environment

All objects rendered in SketchUp exist (if only virtually) in some environment. A building, for example, is situated in a landscape or urban environment, which at the ground level may have objects like trees, but above that has a sky (possibly filled with clouds) and a sun (as the obvious exterior light source). Another example is a small object, such as a statue, that would be rendered in a studio setting, with virtual artificial light sources such as point lights and spotlights. In the first case, the environment might be quite visible through windows, but in the second case, the background can intentionally be quite abstract and blurry. Either way, the background provides some context, scale, and possibly color balance to the rendered scene.

Another feature that can be accomplished by the environment is lighting. Background objects can reflect or diffuse light and influence the mood in the scene. Likewise, if an image is used for the background in a rendering, it can actually be the main or even the only source of lighting in the scene. This technique is called *image-based lighting* (IBL), and it is useful for creating realistic lighting scenarios—especially when high-dynamic-range (HDR) images are used as a background.

Let's explore some of these effects.

Sky (Physical Sky, Sky Color, or Sky/Environment Image)

Any rendering software available for SketchUp usually is at least capable of rendering a physical sky. This is useful because SketchUp already has a physically correct daylight (and shadow) system built in, which can be enhanced by adding sky color, clouds, and haziness to the accurate sun shadows. The physical sky calculations ensure that atmospheric haze and sky darkening toward the zenith are reproduced properly.

Figure 5.29 shows the effect that a physical sky adds to a rendering. It still looks barren, but at least the lighting mood and the sky look more realistic and true to the time of day. Depending on your rendering software, the physical sky system may also add clouds and provide a parameter for cloudiness.

Typical settings for a physical sky system include:

- **Turbidity**—The amount of haziness is set by this value. This affects brightness as well as light color based on the underlying algorithm.

- **Sun intensity and color**—Modify these to fine-tune the settings beyond what is built into the physical sky calculation.

Figure 5.30 shows the effect of varying the turbidity/haziness parameter.

Another option that may be appropriate for some renderings (especially studio-type setups) is to not have a sky at all and instead select a color (gray, for example) to provide the rendering with a uniform background. **Figure 5.31** illustrates this approach.

A third option is to have a full-screen image aligned behind the scene. Typically, this is possible within the rendering software by simply selecting an image from your hard disk. A drawback of this approach is that you must take care to match sun angles and light mood between the background image and the rendered scene before you use the image. Depending on the rendering software, these images also may not appear in reflections. Furthermore, this approach is not useful for animations where the camera or the sun is animated. A benefit, however, is that you can easily take a photograph of the environment of, for example, a new building from exactly the position where a window will be and then use that image as a realistic-looking backdrop for an interior rendering. (See **Figure 5.32**.)

Figure 5.29: Physical sky (top: late morning light; bottom: sunset light)—the sky color is based on the time of day

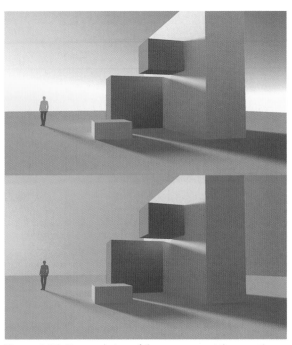

Figure 5.30: Two renderings of the same scene at the same time (top: low turbidity; bottom: high turbidity)

Figure 5.31: Rendering with uniform sky color

Figure 5.32: Rendering with background image of a sky stretched to fit the rendering size

A side benefit of using this approach is that later you can easily remove the sky (and replace it with a photograph) in Photoshop or any other graphics software by selecting and erasing the background color. This is especially true if you *green screen* the back with a bright green color (0,255,0 in RGB values).

TIP

It is a good idea to have a few neutral-color gradient images handy for use as backgrounds in these studio setups. For example, create an image with a gray gradient (from light gray to dark gray is usually best). Experiment with gradient directions, too. The accompanying images show some sample gradients that you could use. Always remember that a subtle gradient is usually better than a stark one—for example, a white-to-black gradient or a gradient between two primary colors.

If you intend to use this gradient as a wraparound spherical background (discussed later), make sure the gradient is oriented perfectly vertical.

IN DEPTH

Backdrop Images in Your Model

If you need the ability to realistically move the view (or the camera) through the scene and have the background adjust accordingly (in what is called a *parallax shift*), a good approach is to set up your model as a studio scene with a backdrop. This usually gives you more control in the appearance of the background than if you applied a background image as an environment or sky image. **Figure 5.33** illustrates this setup.

Figure 5.33: Studio setup with backdrop and lights

As you can see, I simply applied an exterior street scene photo to a vertically oriented rectangle (keep in mind that sometimes arched surfaces are better) that I placed a certain distance behind the window. Having this in place, I can then move the camera (the viewpoint) around within the room, and the background view shifts in a realistic manner. The result is shown in **Figure 5.34**.

Figure 5.34: Two rendered views from inside the room (note the background shift)

In order to make this rendering work, though, I had to place additional light sources in the inside and the outside of this scene. Because the sunlight shines into the window, the backdrop would have been in the shade. Placing a point light above the room (and giving it a high light intensity) illuminated the backdrop and even gave it a bit of overexposure—an effect that would be expected if you took a photograph from the inside of a room toward the outside.

Alternatively, you can make the backdrop image a light-emitting material and give it enough light power to make it look realistic. These materials are covered in a later section.

TIP

When creating renderings with difficult light situations (as in this case, where we show the inside of a room that is artificially lit as well as the sunlit exterior), it is a good idea to not create renderings that are "too perfect."

One approach is to look at photographs with similar light situations and evaluate the imperfections, and then try to apply a subtle effect that is at least similar to the rendering. Don't overdo it, though, or your rendering will look fake.

Examples include:

- Overexposed exterior backgrounds for interior renderings
- Light blooming in interiors (overexposure of light sources)

- Vignetting (a fuzzy darkening toward the edges of the image)
- Lens flare (a flare within a photographic lens caused by a point light source with high intensity—e.g., the sun)

Typically, you can apply many of these more effectively when postprocessing in your image-editing software, as opposed to in the rendering software itself. However, some rendering software lets you add these effects automatically.

Night Renderings

A common problem with sky renderings occurs when we want to render night scenes. In these scenes, we typically rely on artificial lights such as point or spotlights for illumination. However, when we use only those for our renderings, we generally find the result to be dull, badly illuminated, and uninteresting. You can see an example of this at the top of **Figure 5.35**.

The bottom of **Figure 5.35** illustrates a solution to this problem. Instead of using a solid background or sky color, this rendering uses a subtle gradient image. Furthermore, the scene is illuminated not just by the artificial lights but also by the sun—in this case, doubling as moonlight. After all, the night sky is seldom absolutely dark.

This approach gives the image more depth and general illumination. While this method isn't always appropriate, it is easy to execute. Just set the sun intensity very low in your rendering software and apply a bluish color to it. You may have to experiment a bit with the settings, but it is quite easy to create a moonlight effect using the sun.

Alternatively, you could go with an evening mood in your rendered image instead of a night shot. Try to create a sky that looks like the sun has just set, and start illuminating the scene from there.

Figure 5.35: Night rendering (top: only artificial lights and dark blue sky color; bottom: gradient background, light blue low-intensity sun to simulate moonlight)

TIP

For exterior night renderings, a good approach may be to create some color contrast between artificial lights and the night sky. To do this, apply a light yellow color to your artificial lights and a light blue color to your general illumination. This effect can be very subtle or quite dramatic. Adjust the settings to your liking, but keep in mind that subtle is usually better than overly dramatic.

360° Environments

Another approach to applying a sky and ground environment to a rendering is to use hemi-spherical skies, spherical skies, or a sky probe. The images in **Figure 5.36** illustrate what these look like. In essence, all of these are seamless images of the entire sky and ground as seen from a single vantage point. While a spherical sky image or a sky probe contains the entire 360-degree view, the hemispherical sky contains only the sky and omits the bottom half—the ground. The latter images are useful for oceanside renderings or any other setup where the visible ground is actually modeled in 3D.

Figure 5.36: Sky probe (top left); planar, spherical sky image (top right); hemispherical sky (bottom)

Using these environments has several benefits. First, the image provides a complete sky and ground environment, which can eliminate the need to add some background entourage (e.g., trees or a field) to the 3D scene. Another benefit is that if a spherical panorama has been created at exactly the location in which the virtual scene will be rendered (e.g., a location for a new house or a table in a studio where a statue is to be modeled), the rendering will have accurate reflections and a correct background image for that location. Because the image "wraps around" the entire scene, it can also be positioned by rotating it around a vertical axis. Moving the camera view also looks realistic because the view of the sky background will change.

The most important benefit of using these environments, however, might be that the image can be used as the sole light source for the scene. This is called image-based lighting (IBL) and is discussed in the next section. For now, you can simply imagine that the entire 3D scene can receive lighting and color information from the image that was applied to the background. As a result, a scene that is illuminated in this way is lit in exactly the same mood (light color and general lighting ambiance) as the location where the environment image was created. See **Figure 5.37** for an example.

Figure 5.37: Scene with spherical sky image and image-based illumination

There are many places on the Internet where you can find spherical skies and sky probes. The following list of URLs is not at all exhaustive but should help you in your search for the perfect background image.

- www.cgtextures.com—This site has several panoramic (hemispherical) skies
- www.kerkythea.net/cms/index.php/downloads/resources—Various skies and HDR sky probes, ready for use with the Kerkythea software
- http://hdrmaps.com/freebies—Has many free and for-purchase HDR maps
- http://ict.debevec.org/~debevec/Probes—A collection of various HDR light probes
- www.hdri-hub.com/hdrishop/freesamples/freehdri—Various HDR environments

You can also find more links on the companion website to this book under the Chapter 5 page.

TIP

You can very easily create sky probes yourself as long as you have a good-quality digital camera that has high image resolution. All you need is a perfectly reflecting chrome sphere. You can get one for less than $20 at some material suppliers—the one shown here is a precision-ground 2″ steel-alloy ball from McMaster-Carr (**www.mcmaster.com**).

To create a sky probe, clean the sphere meticulously and place it in the desired environment. Then position your camera on a tripod and align it horizontally. Take a picture (RAW image format is best) of the sphere with a telephoto zoom and at a high aperture setting. Finally, crop and scale the image in your editing software so that the sphere completely fills a perfectly square image (as shown in the top-left image in **Figure 5.36**). If you loaded the image as a RAW file, export it as an HDR image; otherwise, just save it in the format the image came in. You can now use that image as a sky probe in your rendering software.

If you don't need to have the 360-degree environment as an HDR file, look for smartphone apps like Google's Photo Sphere, which will create high-resolution JPG files instead.

Ground

Whenever your scene includes a "ground" (terrain, an ocean, etc.), you can create it using any or a combination of the following approaches:

- **Model the ground**—At least the ground next to the viewer should be modeled in SketchUp and textured, which gives it a good level of detail. If you have something akin to an *infinite ground* (e.g., a view out toward the ocean), you will need to create a large plane for your ground and texture it.

- **Infinite ground**—Some rendering packages allow you to add to your scene an infinite ground at some height level. This is most appropriate for seascapes, where the water plane can easily be modeled this way. SketchUp by itself does not support infinite planes.

- **Sky environment**—If the sky environment (as discussed previously) includes a ground (e.g., in a spherical sky image), it may be sufficient to use the ground from this image as long as the image quality is detailed enough. Just make sure you can render shadows on the (imaginary) ground plane or your model will appear to be floating.

Figure 5.38 shows a sample scene of an ocean scape in which the water plane was modeled with a simple (albeit large) rectangle. The water ripples were added as a bump map, a technique that is discussed in a later section of this chapter.

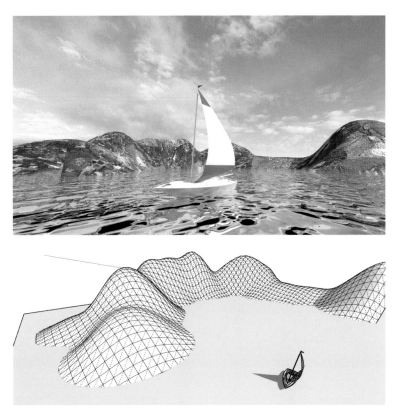

Figure 5.38: Ocean scene with water plane

Lighting

Lighting is arguably the most exciting part of creating photorealistic renderings. This is where you can create spaces and moods that can't be visualized with the same level of realism within SketchUp. You can be very creative with light and approach your rendered scene like a theater stage where *you* are in charge of placing interesting lights and illuminating the space in various ways. The following sections review some of the common issues encountered when executing lighting. Feel free to combine any of the following methods to get the best result.

Ambient Lighting and Image-Based Lighting

In the absence of any direct light source, such as the sun or point lights, the scene must be lighted by environmental illumination. Depending on your rendering package, this can be done in one of two ways, both of which are global illumination (GI) techniques that rely on the rendering software's capability to calculate light scattering.

The first method is general illumination caused by a uniformly colored light that is emitted from an imaginary sky dome (a sphere that fully encompasses your model). Typically, you can simply select a sky color and then use any rendering method provided with your software. Because the result will look very much like an ambient occlusion (AO) rendering, that rendering method can give sufficient results. See **Figure 5.39** for an example.

Figure 5.39: Ambient occlusion *clay* rendering of Notre Dame (model from 3D Warehouse)

This method is often used for *clay* renderings (like the one in **Figure 5.39**) where the material has been painted with either the default material or a neutral-color material (such as light gray). Often, this is not even necessary—the rendering software simply ignores all textures during rendering if Clay Render is selected. A benefit of this rendering method is that it allows you to evaluate shapes without being distracted by color and other surface textures.

A second method—which works well for clay renderings but especially well for textured models—is image-based lighting (IBL). In this method, an image is applied to the imaginary sky dome similar to what was described in the "Environments" section. If this image contains a spherical projection of the sky and ground, it can be used to represent a full 360-degree background. Even if the image will not be visible in the final rendering, its color information will be used to apply environmental lighting to the rendered scene. The three images in **Figure 5.40** are examples of IBL with a high-dynamic-range (HDR) image as a light source. Note the different shadows and overall light mood and color.

This method is especially powerful when HDR images are used for the environment map. Because an HDR image stores color information at a much higher level of precision (32 bits) than a standard *low-dynamic-range* (LDR) image (e.g., 8 bits for a standard JPG image), lighting in the HDR renderings is very natural-looking. This approach also permits reuse of a particular interesting light setting (e.g., the environment in a church), whereby you can apply it to a completely different scene.

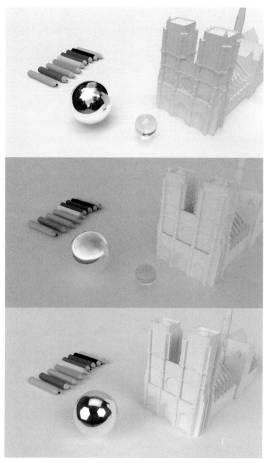

Figure 5.40: The same scene illuminated with different HDR environments (you can see them in the sphere's reflection)

It is often a good idea to combine image-based general lighting with in-scene lighting such as spotlights or even the sun. Experiment with your scene to find the best combination of lighting approaches.

You can find a large number of reasonably good-quality HDR skies on the Internet. Follow some of the links that were presented in the "Environments" section to download some, and try this method for yourself.

TIP

If you are rendering an interior scene where all the ambient light is entering the scene from the outside through a window, one feature you want to look for in your rendering application is *sky portals*. A sky portal is a material that you apply to a window, where it basically functions as a light collector for the ambient light that exists outside of your model.

Using a light portal can yield a more even interior light and lead to better rendering times.

Sun

A scene that is illuminated by the sun primarily allows you to evaluate the interplay of shadows and geometry at any given day and time and at any location on the earth. Set these visuals in SketchUp's Shadows window. You can use them to easily create shadow studies that evaluate a building's overhangs and the reflecting properties of materials to add to the general illumination of a room, for example. It can often be useful to have the ability to create a rendered animation of sunlight and shadows over the course of a day. (See **Figure 5.41**.)

Figure 5.41: Solar studies on shading devices and windows using sun illumination and physical sky

TIP	In SketchUp Pro you can adjust the north direction in your model by using the tools that install with the Solar North extension (get it from the Extension Warehouse). Use either the graphical (second button from the left) or the numerical (third button) method to adjust the north direction in your model.

While this is obviously useful for architectural visualization, turning on the sun can be practical for many other uses, too—for example, to simply bring out detail in a model when rendering it. The sun is also a convenient default light source over which you have full control simply by changing the Time and Day sliders in SketchUp's Shadows window. **Figure 5.42** illustrates a case where the flat sun angle was used to illuminate the model and bring out the shadows on the front of the Notre Dame building model.

Figure 5.42: Sun illumination to enhance facade detail

When creating renderings using the sun, it is important to remember that the real sun's shadows are not as crisply outlined as they are in SketchUp. It is, therefore, important to give them a realistic fuzziness around the edges (see **Figure 5.43**).

Rendering software is usually capable of doing this. The only drawback is a potentially longer render time. If soft shadows are not enabled by default, look in your rendering software for settings related to the sun's radius (or something similar)—a larger-diameter light source produces softer shadows.

Omnidirectional Lights

Among the artificial light sources, omnidirectional lights—often called *omni lights*—are usually the simplest ones to work with. As long as the light is placed correctly in 3D space, all the information that is needed for it to work is its light intensity and color.

An omnidirectional light can be imagined as a point light that emits light particles from its location with equal intensity in all directions. A

Figure 5.43: The sun's shadows: (1) close shadows are sharp; (2) distant shadows are soft; (3) shaded areas in shadows are also soft.

common use for these lights is, therefore, as lightbulbs in lamp fixtures. Another use case can be as a fill light in a dark area of a rendering; if you have an area that is quite dark given the light sources used, you can add a low-intensity omni light in that area (taking care to avoid unnatural shadows) to enhance detail.

Being a point light, the omni light by default creates hard and precise shadows. This may not be desirable in a particular rendering because natural light produces soft shadows. Therefore, rendering software usually includes the ability to create soft shadows by representing the point light as a sphere with a given diameter.

In some situations you may not want omni lights to produce shadows at all—for example, when using them as fill lights. In such cases, some rendering software adds the capability to turn off shadows on a light-by-light basis.

It is advantageous to use a studio-type setting to evaluate light properties. Therefore, in the following discussion I will use the studio setup shown in **Figure 5.44** for rigging lights. As you can see, it features one of SketchUp's default dummy 3D person as a model and has a continuous back and floor "canvas," as well as reflective sides. The lines visible in the setup have been divided into equal parts to provide points to which we can attach lights (simply by snapping them to endpoints of the line segments). As discussed, lines are not rendered and can, therefore, remain in the SketchUp model.

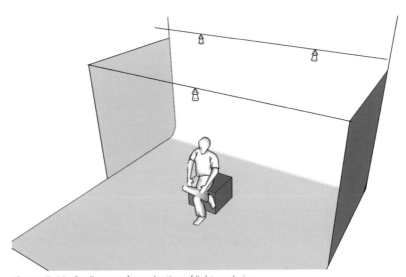

Figure 5.44: Studio setup for evaluation of light rendering

First, let's evaluate a default lighting setup consisting of three omni lights. **Figure 5.45** shows the result (on the left) and the setup for this (on the right). Two lights were placed above and slightly behind the model and one above and slightly in front of the model. This case used a white light color and the same light intensity for all three omni lights.

As you can see, the model is well lit with shadows that are not too dark. However, two problems are apparent.

First, the two rear lights are too bright. Their proximity to the background creates two overly bright areas. You might be tempted to think that what you see there are the actual lights. After all, if we take a photograph of a lightbulb, we get a similar result—a very overexposed area around the lightbulb. That is not the case here. None of the standard lights that we use in rendering (omni lights, spotlights, IES lights) typically show up on renderings because they have no physical representation; they are merely computational light sources.

Figure 5.45: Setup with three similar omni lights

The second problem is that the front of the person is too much in the shade. Although this gives the scene a dramatic look, such an effect might not be intended.

Let's start by fixing the first problem. **Figure 5.46** shows a modified version of the same setup, in which light intensity of the background lights has been reduced drastically (to about 1/10 the intensity of the front light). These lights also received a blue light color (via the renderers light settings) to give the background more depth and interest.

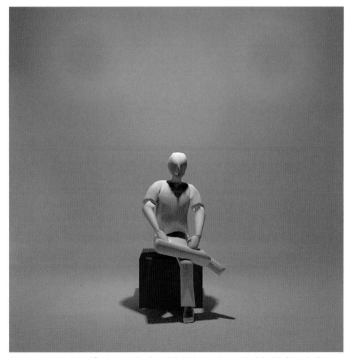

Figure 5.46: Modified setup (reduced light intensity and added light color)

We can now go a step further and add one more omni light—this time, directly in front of the person (see **Figure 5.47**). This light functions similar to a flash that would be mounted on the observer's camera and is needed solely to brighten the shadows on the model. Because such a light would create a shadow on the background, shadows were disabled for this light (again in the light settings).

Figure 5.47: Setup with added light source in front of model

Ideally a stage setup like this should have omni lights for the background and a spotlight for highlighting the person in the foreground. We'll discuss spotlights in a later section. First, however, let's look at an important light property: attenuation.

Attenuation

Any light (except IES lights) that you add to a 3D scene has a property called *attenuation,* which relates to the way light particles lose intensity the farther they travel from the light source. In reality, you likely have already observed this phenomenon. Just imagine looking down a street at night—the streetlights closest to you usually look brighter than the ones farther away.

Figure 5.48 illustrates this phenomenon and the various settings, using three spotlights. The top spotlight in the figure shows no light attenuation at all. As a result, the spotlight is as bright on the right as it is on the left—the only reduction in intensity comes from a flaring of the light.

The bottom two spotlights exhibit light attenuation—the middle one uses a linear model and the one on the bottom a squared one. These two look more realistic simply because of this property. It is, therefore, usually a good idea to use light attenuation for your light sources. If you want your rendering to closely resemble reality, opt for the inverse squared method.

Figure 5.48: Light attenuation in spotlights (top: none; middle: inverse linear; bottom: inverse squared)

Spotlights

The second light type that any rendering software is capable of handling is spotlights. As the name implies, these shine light from the source in one direction only, producing a cone of light that can be used to illuminate details or provide dramatic light scenarios. Real-world equivalents are recessed lights in a house and spotlights on a stage.

To evaluate spotlights, let's apply some to the same scene that we used in **Figure 5.47**. **Figure 5.49** shows the result on the left and the setup on the right. The only difference is the replacement of the three omni lights in **Figure 5.47** with spotlights, all pointing down, in **Figure 5.49**.

Figure 5.49: Setup with three similar spotlights

This scene already looks good and realistic even without any modifications. The two spotlights in the back are close to the background and therefore produce nice-looking light cones on the wall. All three have soft edges and produce soft shadows.

As we did with the omni lights, we can now modify some of the properties of the spotlights. For example, **Figure 5.50** shows what happens when we change the light color of the two in the back to blue. Together with the spotlight in the front, this immediately produces very nice stage lighting.

Figure 5.50: The same setup with some light colors changed

It is usually desirable that spotlights have soft edges. This is likewise rooted in reality because light cones, even from the most focused stage spots, don't have perfectly sharp edges. Nevertheless, let's explore what happens when we modify the related properties. **Figure 5.51** illustrates what happens when we switch from a soft-edged spot (on the left) to a hard-edged one (on the right).

Figure 5.51: Examples with different hotspot and falloff properties

The two spotlight properties of importance here are typically called *hotspot* and *falloff,* illustrated in **Figure 5.52**. Hotspot typically is an angular measure of the central light cone that will have 100 percent light intensity. Falloff describes the outer cone (again, as a value describing the "opening" angle) where light reduces in intensity from 100 percent strength to zero (at its outermost edge).

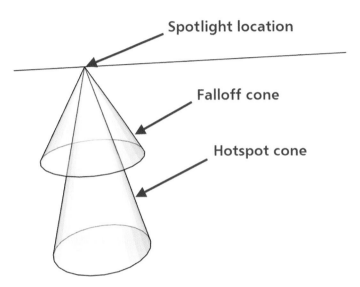

Figure 5.52: Spotlight properties

In **Figure 5.51**, the left image has a hotspot angle of 30 degrees, while the falloff angle is 60 degrees. This is what gives the spotlights the soft edges. The image on the right, in contrast, has both values set to the same amount (30 degrees). This is the other extreme and gives the spotlights perfectly hard edges.

For your renderings, evaluate how a light would look in real life and adjust the values accordingly. As mentioned, always use at least a slightly larger number for falloff rather than making both numbers equal.

IES Lights

One method for adding realism to a light source without using either an omni light or a spotlight is to use Illuminating Engineering Society (IES) light definitions. As long as your rendering software supports this, using IES lights will immediately provide a high level of realism because the file that describes an IES light source has been generated by measuring a specific light fixture's light distribution. Using a specific luminaire's IES data (from an ERCO spotlight, for example) in your renderings gives you an accurate preview of how the actual light will look in a scene. (See **Figure 5.53**.)

Figure 5.53: IES light data (left: data visualization; right: rendering—created with IES Generator 4)

Using IES lights is usually fairly simple. The first step is to get the appropriate IES file for a luminaire. Nowadays, manufacturers of high-end light fixtures usually allow you to download one file for each luminaire from their website. The following are a few websites where you can find IES tools and files:

- www.rip3d.net/web/en.html#/free/downloads—This site provides a free IES file viewer and file-creator software.

- www.lightolier.com/home/file-finder.jsp?ftype=ies—One manufacturer's download page for IES files. Also browse other manufacturers' websites for their data (e.g., ERCO, Philips).

> **TIP**
>
> If you are curious about what IES light data looks like, open an IES file with a text editor. You will see several lines of text describing the light fixture and the manufacturer. Below that are several numbers that simply describe (in 2D) the light distribution—in other words, the location of the yellow points in **Figure 5.53**. Your rendering software can use this to reproduce the light distribution accurately in 3D space when you use IES lights in your scene.

Once you have the IES file you want to use, go into your rendering software and start applying it to a spotlight. Because the IES light data is directional (it can have uplight as well as downlight properties), you must make sure the orientation (rotation and tilt) of the light is appropriate. **Figure 5.54** shows how IES data is applied and visualized using the Twilight rendering software in SketchUp.

Once you render your scene, you should see the light distribution that was provided by the IES file (it should look less uniform than a standard spotlight). If the light intensity is not as needed, you will need to modify that property. Also, you can usually add a color to the IES light, if desired. It may be necessary to adjust light attenuation to even out light distribution as well.

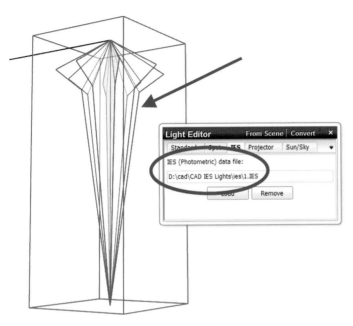

Figure 5.54: Applying IES light data to a spotlight

Figure 5.55 shows the standard scene that we have been using throughout this chapter—this time, illuminated with IES lights. It is interesting to note that the IES data for the lights on the right indicates a vertical cutoff (it does not contain any data above the light source), which leads to the horizontal line between light and dark. I should also mention that if you applied IES data that describes an uplight (e.g., a wall sconce) to a downward-pointing spotlight, the spotlight will only emit light upward.

Figure 5.55: Our standard scene illuminated with two different IES lights

Recessed Lights

A common feature of contemporary buildings is recessed lights (also sometimes called *potlights*). They are often a convenient choice in architecture because they do not project below the ceiling and they create an attractive-looking light cone. The question for us is how to render them.

Assuming that we might want to accomplish this with a simple spotlight, we could just model the rim of the recessed light and then add a spotlight in its center. When we do this, we get a rendered result like the one shown in **Figure 5.56**. Although the light cone looks appropriate, the light source itself is not visible and the center of the recessed light is not illuminated. As discussed, we would likely not see the lamp, even in a photograph, due to overexposure, but the center of the light *can* should at least be illuminated and appear white.

Figure 5.56: "Flat" recessed light without illuminated light source

There are a few ways to fix this problem. Depending on the situation you are dealing with, you might need to combine some of these. **Figure 5.57** illustrates three common approaches in SketchUp: spotlight, light-emitting face, and IES light.

Figure 5.57: Three methods to create recessed lights (left: spotlight; middle: light-emitting face; right: IES light)

The spotlight approach is similar to the one we used previously, with the main difference being that this time we modeled the recessed light as a true recessed *can*. This allows us to use the internal walls of the light fixture to capture light and, therefore, render the light source as an overexposed circle. The important property to change when using this approach is the falloff angle value, which must be large enough to include the side walls of the recessed fixture (e.g., 90 degrees).

The second approach, which uses a light-emitting face (a triangle, in this case), will be discussed in more detail in the next sections. Basically, it uses a SketchUp face and applies a light-emitting material to it. This approach has the benefit that we can control the size of the light source simply by modifying the size of the face. If you want to use this approach, make sure you use the simplest face possible. Remember that a triangle is exported to your rendering application as one face, while a circle has many more faces (which increases rendering time). It is also not as easy as with the other two approaches to tilt the spotlight (e.g., toward a picture on the wall).

The third method uses an IES light that contains a certain amount of horizontal light spread in addition to the downlight behavior (the same IES file used in the right image in **Figure 5.58**). The benefit of using this approach is that the IES light very likely reproduces the wall reflections of a true recessed light much better than either of the other two. **Figure 5.58** shows a comparison of all three approaches—note the double-arc light-beam projection with the IES light.

Figure 5.58: Rendered potlights from Figure 5.57

Use whichever approach is more applicable for your project. One thing to keep in mind, though, is rendering time. In the previous example, the spotlight produced the fastest rendering times by a factor of more than 2 (1 minute, 35 seconds) over the IES light (3 minutes, 15 seconds) and the light-emitting face (3 minute, 45 seconds).

Neon and Other Self-Emitting Light Sources

In addition to point lights and spotlights, there are many other light sources that you might need to render. One example that cannot be accomplished with the tools mentioned so far is a simple neon tube, which is basically a linear light source. Another example is a 2' × 4' neon ceiling fixture, as installed in suspended ceilings; this is an area light source. Neither of these consists of just a point that emits light—it is the entire surface that (with some intensity variations) emits light. As it turns out, these light sources are actually quite easy to set up—the only drawback is that rendering time can quickly increase if you are not careful with the settings. (See **Figure 5.59**.)

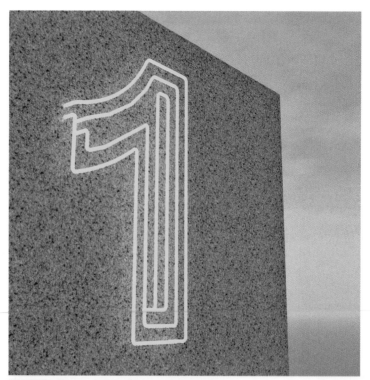

Figure 5.59: Neon light rendering

Rendering software usually enables this kind of setup by allowing you to apply a light-emitting material to a surface. Typically, you can just select one or more surfaces and apply the material to those surfaces as you would apply any other material. The software then assumes that every location on this surface emits light at a given intensity and without any single direction—light particles emit in all directions and produce a very soft, scattered light (similar to a light box).

Figure 5.60 shows an example of this approach. In this rendering, the model of a compact fluorescent lightbulb (CFL) was used as the sole light source in the scene. The faces that make up the light tubes were assigned a light-emitting material.

Figure 5.60: Model of a CF lightbulb with light-emitting material illumination

Although this approach is quite easy to implement and the resulting light is very even and scattered, keep in mind that rendering time is affected by using light-emitting materials. It is generally a good idea to keep to a minimum the triangle count of the faces to which this material is applied. Use this material preferably on triangular and rectangular faces, rather than circular or irregularly shaped faces.

When you use light-emitting surfaces, it is often possible to apply an image to the surface—some material properties, such as texture, also work for a light-emitting material. **Figure 5.61** uses an image of a plain 4′ drop-ceiling light fixture as a texture on a single rectangular face to not only illuminate the scene but also give the light the appearance of two neon light tubes behind a frosted glass cover. This eliminated the need for actually placing light-emitting surfaces (representing the neon tubes) behind a frosted-glass material, which would likely have significantly increased rendering time.

Figure 5.61: Using an image texture as a light-emitting surface (left: rendering; right: photo of neon light fixture)

TIP

If your rendering software provides different rendering methods, it may be more efficient to render scenes with light-emitting materials using an unbiased renderer (e.g., MLT) rather than a photon-map GI renderer. This can vary with the software package, however.

Combining Lighting Scenarios (in Photo-Editing Software)

Various rendering packages nowadays have the ability to apply lighting scenarios once the rendering is completed. The benefit of such an approach is that after just one rendering it is possible to view a scene at different lighting stages—for example, with daylight, at night, or with different artificial light sources enabled. You can easily use this technique to create many different images from just one rendering.

Even if your rendering software does not provide this functionality, it is possible to simulate changing light scenarios in Photoshop (or any other image-editing software). The steps are as follows:

1. Render the same scene with different light groups enabled for each rendering. The left-hand image in **Figure 5.62** shows the three base renderings with (1) only daylight, (2) only the floor lights, and (3) only the downlights. It should be easy to disable lights individually or in groups in your rendering software. If that doesn't work, place all similar lights on their own layer and then enable only the appropriate layer before you do the renderings.

2. Load the rendered images into your photo-editing software's layers (**Figure 5.62** shows this for Photoshop).

Figure 5.62: Three renderings with different lights are combined in Photoshop using "screen" layer blending

3. Apply the "screen" layer-blending mode to all layers. This adds light for each pixel when the individual layers become visible. You can also now adjust the Opacity sliders for all layers to adjust the intensity or visibility of each of the light groups.

Figure 5.63 shows two resulting images that use a combination of the three base images from **Figure 5.62**.

Figure 5.63: Two images created using various combinations of the base images

Light Analysis in SketchUp

Especially if you are creating interior spaces in SketchUp, one common task in lighting design is figuring out light intensities (e.g., over workspaces). As part of this task, light amounts must be quantifiable (typically, in a unit called a lux). Depending on the rendering software you are using, this may be a possible output that it can deliver. If the software is calculating light paths realistically anyway, why not use that data for analysis?

Figure 5.64 shows such an analysis. As you can see, light intensity has been colored in a false-color pattern, where the brightest areas are red and the darkest areas are blue.

To make such an analysis possible, you must use correct lighting data. Instead of using just light intensity factors for luminaires, make sure you enter correct wattages. Some rendering software also accepts watts per square area as a unit. This is especially useful for area lights such as light boxes and neon fixtures.

Figure 5.64: Light intensity analysis in the LightUp rendering software

For other approaches to light analysis, look up some of the analysis extensions discussed in Chapter 4.

Materials

Figure 5.65: The SketchUp Materials window

Much of the realism of a good rendering comes from using good-quality materials. In this section, we'll review various material types and how to set them up in your rendering software.

Fortunately for us, SketchUp already comes with a good array of materials—from simple colors to photorealistic repeating textures and even transparent materials. You can find them all in the Materials window (see **Figure 5.65**).

These materials work well in many situations. They are all seamlessly repeating textures, which allows their file size to be small and efficient. The main problems with them are related to close-up renderings, where it becomes obvious that the images have quite low resolution, and in some cases repeating patterns that make the textures look artificial. You can see both problems in **Figure 5.66**. In most other cases—especially when the view of the textured object is from a certain distance—the quality of the materials is sufficient for a good rendering.

Depending on the quality that your rendering is supposed to have, you will always need to choose among using SketchUp's materials, the materials your rendering software provides (if available), and making your own from scratch (e.g., from photographs). When you do this, you can vary these parameters:

- **Texture image quality**—A smaller texture image size often means more efficient rendering times (and a more responsive SketchUp display). For close-ups or large-size renderings, however, it is important that texture size is large enough to bring out detail.

- **Tiled versus single texture image**—Tiled, or repeating, textures (such as SketchUp's materials) are efficient because a small image can fill a large area simply by repeating itself. As **Figure 5.65** illustrates, tiled textures can create repeating patterns that can appear unrealistic. It is, nevertheless, possible to use good-quality tiled textures (e.g., SketchUp's roofing or brick materials) that do not have the patterning problem.

Figure 5.66: Problems with some default SketchUp materials (left: repeating pattern; right: low texture resolution)

In some cases, it may be more appropriate to use a single texture image (that does not seamlessly repeat). A textured concrete wall that has graffiti on it would be such a case. For this, a single good-quality and reasonably straight image would be enough to provide an adequate texture as long as it fills the entire required area (e.g., the face of the wall).

- **Nontextured material properties**—Materials such as glass, reflective metals, a mirror, or a light-emitting surface do not need a textured image as long as an appropriate color is chosen for them and the rendering software deals with physical parameters such as translucency, reflectivity, light-emitting properties, and surface light scattering.

As demonstrated, it may be necessary to use an image-based texture along with these material properties to get the desired effect.

In general, it can be stated that adding reflectivity, translucency, and any other physical properties to a texture invariably increases rendering time. Therefore, if a material is farther away from the viewpoint or a material is not reflective at all, it is typically sufficient to use the unmodified SketchUp materials in your rendering software.

The images in **Figure 5.67** show a few materials that can be created by rendering software. They are (top, left to right): a default SketchUp color rendered as a matte material, a shiny plastic, a colored glass; (bottom, left to right): fully reflective mirror, a light-emitting material, and surface-textured water (notice the ripples).

Figure 5.67: Various rendered materials

Components of a Material

Let's look at the components that make up a material and discuss the various options related to them.

Depending on your rendering software, you have either very detailed or very little control over all these parameters. The upside of having rendering software that lets you control many material parameters is that you have ultimate flexibility and you can affect appearance in many creative ways. This often comes at the cost of convenience, though, and getting it right might involve more practice. On the other hand, the main benefit of having rendering software that gives you only the most important parameters is that the results are automatically of good quality. You might not have the option to tweak them, however.

When you shop around for rendering software, take a close look at the material editor and the options and check that the process and the quality work for you.

For each material that you use in your scene, evaluate the need for any of the following properties and use them as needed.

Texture or Color (Diffuse Texture)

The texture of a material is provided either by a color or by an image that is applied (*mapped*) to the surface of an object. By itself, the texture has no glossiness or translucency. Note, however, that in a global illumination (GI) rendering environment, the color of a texture can affect colors of surrounding materials by reflecting indirect light onto them—a good example of this can be seen in **Figure 5.29**.

You can apply a color to an object by simply painting it with one of SketchUp's color materials. Most rendering software uses SketchUp's materials as a foundation for adding features such as glossiness.

To apply a material to all connected faces in SketchUp, hold down the Control key when you apply the material to a face.

If you want to use a photo-based texture, then you can choose one of SketchUp's materials and paint it to the surface, or you can apply your own image to a surface. To do the latter, you have two options:

- **Insert the image as a texture.** Import the texture image using the dialog under **File → Import...** Then select All Supported Image Types in the File Type selector in the dialog and make sure Use As Texture is selected on the right side of the dialog.

  You can then paste the image onto a face as a texture by clicking on its surface and dragging the image until its size looks correct (texture positioning will be covered later). Remember that the surface can't be in a group or a component. If that is the case, double-click it first to get into editing mode before you paste the image.

- **Make a new SketchUp material.** In the Materials window, click the Create a Material... **plus** button (+). You can then load a texture for this material and apply it like any other. Make sure you adjust the size reference in the material editor to reflect the accurate dimensions. The next image illustrates this process.

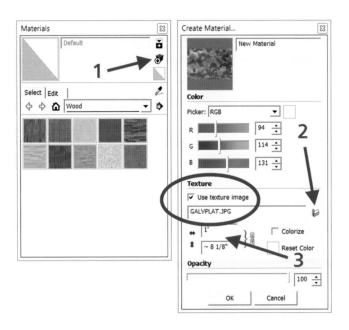

In **Figure 5.68**, you can see these methods in action. The tiles and the sand under the trees use materials that come with SketchUp. To give the concrete wall a rougher appearance than would be possible with SketchUp's tiled concrete material, a single image of a concrete wall was applied to its surface. This image does not tile well; therefore, it was necessary to position it so that it covers the entire wall surface.

Figure 5.68: Two texture types (single image and tiled)

TIP	You can modify any texture in SketchUp after it has been applied to a face using the **Texture → Edit Texture Image…** right-click context menu. This opens the image in the editor that you have preselected in SketchUp's preferences.

After editing and saving the texture image, the texture in SketchUp is automatically updated with the modified image.

Besides the textures that are contained in SketchUp's materials, there are many online resources where you can get good-quality imagery. Here are some examples:

- www.cgtextures.com—An extensive resource with lots of good-quality (and even some tile-able) textures.

- http://texturify.com—A similar site.

If you search for "textures" or "cg textures" online, you will find a lot more. In addition to the texture images, software is available that can generate tileable textures based on a source image or a standard pattern (often complete with bump and other maps). A good example can be found at www.bricksntiles.com. Finally, many tutorials are available online that show you how you can take an image and create a tileable texture simply using your image-editing software.

Reflection

When you render a SketchUp scene in your rendering software using default settings, you may notice that all the materials look quite flat. They look very much like matte paint. In reality, however, most materials have some degree of shininess and maybe even reflectivity. Good examples are semigloss wall paint, the plastic or aluminum enclosure of your computer, magazine covers, and tabletops. Although their degree of shininess varies, most of them do have some. Only very rough materials (e.g., uncoated paper or soil) do not. (See **Figure 5.69**.)

Figure 5.69: Reflectivity of a walkway's stones

As you likely know, this is related to surface smoothness—the smoother the surface, the shinier a material is (up to perfect reflection). Polished metal and glass are materials that are very reflective—a mirror is a good example. Brushed aluminum (with its roughened surface) is quite reflective, but its surface scatters all light, thereby lacking a shiny and polished-looking reflection.

Figure 5.70 shows two materials that illustrate this. The ground material on the left has default properties and, therefore, looks quite flat. The material on the right has reflectivity similar to polished stone. As you can see, the reflection of the omni light (in the center of the image) is quite different from that of the material on the left. The light's reflection is visible on the ground, and there is not as much scattered light reflection close to the light source. Also, the checkered pattern on the back wall is reflected in a realistic fashion: Close to the wall, where the view angle is quite small, the pattern has a blurry reflection. Farther away from the wall and closer to the viewer (where the viewing angle is larger), the reflection fades out. This material appearance is typical of vinyl flooring or a semigloss tabletop, for example.

So what should you do to materials in your renderings? It is usually a good idea to give flooring, furniture, leather, and other partially or fully reflective materials at least a subtle reflectivity. This goes a long way toward realism in your renderings. Having said that, it is important to keep in mind that reflectivity invariably increases rendering time. Only perfect reflection renders fast, but that is obviously limited to mirrors and water or glass. Therefore, whenever a material is too far away from the viewpoint or nothing exists in the scene that could actually reflect in the material, it is usually okay to ignore reflectivity for that material. But this very much depends on your scene, and you should evaluate this need on a case-by-case basis.

Figure 5.70: Comparison of flat and reflective floor materials

TIP	
	You can sometimes cut down on rendering time if you don't assign reflective properties to a material but rather use a subtle gradient for that material (which simulates a soft reflection). You must make sure it works with lighting and the general environment, however.

If your rendering software allows you to do this, consider adding a *specular map* to the material. This is similar to the bump map (discussed later) and is a grayscale image. When added to a shiny material, the grayscale values in the image determine the shininess distribution of your material (the darker it is, the shinier it will be).

Refraction

When you have transparent materials in your scene (such as glass, water, or gems), it can be important that these materials have realistic refraction properties. As mentioned, *refraction* refers to how light direction changes when it travels through a material. In reality, you likely have observed this—imagine holding a straight stick into a swimming pool, and notice how the lower part of the stick looks as though it is bent (see rendering in **Figure 5.71**). You can also see this behavior when you look at a thick glass or a prism from an angle.

Figure 5.71: Refraction in water

Especially when your glass object has an observable thickness, it is important to include realistic refraction properties. This is the case when you model a glass vase or water in a swimming pool. Having said this, it is often not important to add refraction to architectural uses of glass. Windows can usually be modeled only with a transparent texture—as long as their reflection properties are accurate. Refractive glass would actually increase rendering time too much without adding much visual benefit.

Table 5.1 shows some refractive indices for various media. Use these as a guide if your rendering software gives you the option to enter them for a material.

Table 5.1: Refractive Indices

Material	Index of Refraction
Air	1.0
Water	1.33
Crown glass	1.52
Sapphire	1.77
Diamond	2.42

Figure 5.72 illustrates refraction in three prismatic transparent objects.

Figure 5.72: Refraction in three transparent materials (from left: glass, diamond, and frosted glass)

Bump

A *bump texture* or *bump map* is a very useful tool in a rendering software's material editor; it can add significant realism at minimal (computational) cost to any material that has a surface roughness.

The best example to illustrate where you could use this might be a brick wall. In such a wall, the mortar is slightly recessed from the surface of the bricks. Depending on where the lighting comes from, you should see shadows in the mortar lines and highlights at the edges of the bricks. If such a wall were textured with a simple photograph of bricks, then changing light direction would not change the shadow appearance of the mortar lines, which would lead to a flat-looking wall. A bump map remedies this by giving the rendering software information where it needs to modify surface appearance so that the texture looks as though it is flat or recessed. (See **Figure 5.73**.)

Figure 5.73: The same texture rendered without bump (left) and with bump (right)

Other examples where bump maps are appropriate are bevel siding, flooring, paving, rough soil, and other textures where surface roughness creates gaps, creases, and depressions of less than approximately 1″ in depth. **Figure 5.74** shows a classic case where material bump should be used.

You can easily apply a bump map to any texture by providing a black-and-white image of the map and applying it in your rendering software's material editor (if the software supports this). It is important to remember that the map image has to have the same pixel dimensions as the texture image for both to align properly. During rendering, parts of the map that are dark will appear to recede while white parts will stay at the material's surface.

Figure 5.74: Brick walls—a classic case where bump is warranted

A common method that is often built in to rendering software is to use the desaturated (*grayscale*) inverse of the texture image as the bump map. This is a bit of a rough approximation that can work well, but it is usually a good idea to create higher-quality bump maps in image-editing software and then use two separate images for the texture and the bump map.

TIP

Some rendering software also offers a more advanced technique, called *normal mapping*. While bump mapping applies various levels of brightness to any location on a material depending on the depth information in the bump map, normal mapping modifies light properties based on a surface's "normal," or perpendicular, vector at any given point.

One method for creating a bump map in image-editing software is to start with a black-and-white version of the texture image and then invert it. Then use Brightness/Contrast adjustment to increase the black-and-white contrast in the image. Finally, use a white brush to remove any unwanted gray or black areas from the image. Don't forget to save the image at the same pixel size as the original texture. (See **Figure 5.75**.)

Figure 5.75: Two different bump maps (left: texture; middle: inverted black-and-white map; right: high-contrast black-and-white map created in image editor

Displacement

Depending on your rendering software, you may be able to add a displacement map to a texture as well. This technique goes one step further than bump mapping in that it doesn't simply modify light properties but modifies the surface of the object itself. Small or even larger details can be added to a surface through a displacement map—requiring less initial modeling and providing a higher level of realism because surface depressions or extrusions exist as actual geometry.

A good use for a displacement map would again be a brick wall—especially if larger bricks or round boulders were used for the surface texture. While bump maps fail to model wall edges properly (they don't show a mortar recess at the edge, for example), a displacement map can do this by creating geometry at this location. Other uses are terrain generation, whereby an entire three-dimensional terrain can be created from a black-and-white image (typically called a *heightfield*) in which pixel grayscale corresponds to altitude values.

Emittance

This material feature was already partly covered in the lighting section. What emittance can add to a material is its behavior as a light source. This is most useful for aerial light sources such as neon lights and light boxes. It is also a good way to add lighting to display (or advertisement) boxes and television screens in your model. In those cases, it is also important that an appropriate texture is applied to the material, in addition to it being a light emitter.

You can see this in **Figure 5.76**. The "Stand Up!" text at the back wall is a neon-backlit sign that features the image of an evening sky as its texture. It was modeled using SketchUp's 3D Text tool and by applying the light-emitting texture only to the front faces. Side faces and back faces of the text were left as is, which gives it the appearance (and shadows) of a display box.

In contrast, the light globes in the back corners are plain 3D spheres that have a white light-emitting texture painted on their entire surface.

Figure 5.76: Emitting materials used for light globes and text-logo display

Some rendering software allows you to add a physical light property to a material, such as 100 W/m² illumination. Even if this is offered, it is often necessary to try out various settings until scene illumination looks just right.

Remember that the number of faces that have light-emitting materials applied to them directly influences rendering time. Try to keep those faces as simple and as few as possible.

Subsurface Scattering

Beyond materials that are opaque and fully reflect light and materials that are transparent and, therefore, let light pass through, there are some materials that let light filter through the surface of the material but then scatter it internally. The thicker the material, the less light travels through it. Good examples of these kinds of materials are wax, milk, alabaster stone, and translucent rubber.

To render these materials accurately, your rendering software must be able to handle a material feature called *subsurface scattering* (SSS). This material feature can then be assigned to any closed object (an object that has a volume and no openings in its surface). You can see the effect in **Figure 5.77**, where the candle wax material has subsurface scattering properties. As you can see, it is a white reflective material that internally also scatters some of the flame light, which was modeled as a combination of an omni light and a light-emitting flame object.

Figure 5.77: Three candles with subsurface-scattering wax materials

Using SSS for materials in your scene can put a strain on rendering time, and you should carefully evaluate whether you actually need it. For example, if you render a kitchen that has a few candles standing in a corner, you will likely get away with applying a simple white material (maybe with some glossiness) to the candles. However, if you render a close-up of a milk glass lit only by candles, you should use it for those two materials.

When you model translucent materials (as in the lampshade shown next), you have several options:

■ **Use an SSS material**—This requires your lampshade to have an actual thickness and will likely result in a relatively long rendering time. Use the Joint Push/Pull plugin (see Chapter 4) to thicken the surface.

■ **Use a partially transparent material**—This may work, especially if light can bounce inside the lampshade.

■ **Use fake transparency**—Add an emitting material to the outside of the lampshade to give it a luminous glow.

Putting These Features Together

Once you start working on materials for a rendered scene, it is usually a good idea to ignore the material features from the last few sections for the first test renders. Simply use the materials that you applied in SketchUp and work on lighting the scene. Then run a few low-quality and low-resolution test renders. Once you are happy with the view and the lighting, start refining materials and their properties.

When rendering, it often makes more sense to focus first on geometry, then on lighting, and on materials last. Often, however, it is a back-and-forth process among all of these until you get the result you want.

When refining materials, keep your focus on the big picture. In other words, don't get lost refining materials that will barely be visible in the final rendering. That contributes only to the rendering time and not much to the result.

Follow these tips when you work on materials:

- First, evaluate which objects in the scene need reflective (e.g., a mirror) or transparent (e.g., a window) properties. Since the scene will not look real without them, add those first. For reflective objects, start with a fully reflective material, and for transparent windows, use a simple transparent-reflective glass material that does not feature refraction or even dispersion—both of which render quite fast.

- If you need any material-based lighting (e.g., from a neon tube), add light-emitting materials next. As mentioned, keep this as simple as possible to reduce rendering time.

- Next, look at large-area (in relation to the image size) objects, such as a wall or floor, and add appropriate properties such as reflection and bump. If you notice when doing a low-quality test render that adding these properties has no effect on the final result, undo especially the reflection properties, because your scene will render faster without them.

■ Then focus on your key objects. Do you have a "showcase" object such as a kitchen counter-top or a piece of furniture located close to the observer? Adjust its properties accordingly. If this object is made of glass, try a physically accurate glass material and see if its appearance improves. This will likely increase rendering time, but for the added realism it may be worth it.

■ Finally, see if you need to manually adjust any of the material textures. In SketchUp, you can export a material's texture for editing in an image editor. This is useful if you need to add "edge dirt" (e.g., at the base of a wall) or fix tiling problems by making textures appear more random.

Tweaking Texture Positioning

One of SketchUp's best features is its ability to easily place textures from various sources and position them. As you have seen in this chapter, you can add textures using the Materials window or by importing images and placing them on faces as textures. Beyond these meth-ods, you can also model using the photo-matching technique (which will not be covered in this book—if you are interested, you can find information in SketchUp's help system).

Once you have a texture for a particular object, it is important to get its positioning right. Fortunately, SketchUp offers tools to help with most common situations. Beyond those, you can use extensions. The following examples showcase techniques for this.

Example 5.2: A Wooden Tabletop

This example is relevant for any situation where a texture should extend from one face to other faces—be they in the same plane or not. You will use a positioned texture as reference and "paint" it onto other faces.

1. Let's assume that you need to place a texture of a slatted wooden board correctly on this 4' × 4' panel with a 2" thickness. To be able to place the texture, this object must not be grouped. If it were, you would have to double-click it and enter group- (or component-) editing mode. All surfaces have to be selectable.

You can use SketchUp's texture positioning tools on textures that have been directly applied to faces. If you apply (or *paint*) a texture to a group of faces (or a component), all faces with the default texture will receive the new texture.

Remember: You cannot position texture applied to groups/components—even after double-clicking the group and getting into editing mode.

2. An easy way to get the initial positioning right is to import the image as a texture using the **File → Import...** dialog. Alternatively, you could create a new texture with the image and then adjust the positioning.

3. When placing the image on the surface, stretch it so that it fills the entire surface. After placement, SketchUp will simply "cut off" any excess (or tile the image). Because the texture image in the example doesn't tile, I opted for filling the entire surface with the image.

4. Since the texture has now been imported and a new material has been created, it is possible to use it from the Materials window by simply selecting it and painting any surface. The drawback here, as you can see in the accompanying image, is that its orientation is not correct—the wood grain on the edge runs perpendicular to the top surface's texture.

5. A better method here is to use the Sample Paint tool in the Materials window (the eyedropper) and sample the top surface's material before placing it on the side of the board. This method retains the orientation of the sampled material and then extends it to the painted faces, which gives our tabletop the appearance of properly aligned boards.

6. Although the texture already looks good, its positioning could be improved so that the board alignment looks more accurate. To do this, right-click on the texture you just placed and select **Texture** → **Position** from the context menu. This gives you SketchUp's alignment pins. As you can see in the image shown here, you now have pins to move, rotate, skew, and stretch the texture. For the purpose here, just use the move pin (click and drag) to position the texture to your liking.

TIP

If you work a lot with textures in SketchUp (be it for rendering or geo-modeling), it is imperative that you become familiar with the pin positioning system. You can find more information about it in SketchUp's help system.

For now, keep in mind that you can click-drag to move, skew, or rotate the texture. If you want to position a texture relative to reference points, another method is to click and position (don't drag) the pins and then click-drag them to where you want the reference points to end up. This latter method takes some practice, however.

To reduce the visual impact of patterns that may appear when you use some of SketchUp's tileable textures, rotate them slightly. This is especially helpful when the texture tiling occurs along a straight edge in your model.

7. In this example (see accompanying image), I placed the side texture close to where the top texture ends so that color and seams line up better. Although this does not give us a perfect end grain for the boards, it provides us with something that looks similar to vertical-grain boards—especially if viewed from a distance.

These steps allow you to position most materials in SketchUp. In general, homogenic materials such as concrete, brick, and metals are easy to apply and straighten using the process outlined here. If you use nonhomogenic materials (where one side looks much different than another side), it may be necessary to use other methods. **Figure 5.78** shows some of these approaches for the case of a rough-looking old wooden beam.

Figure 5.78: Three different texture-positioning methods in SketchUp (1st image: no end texture, 2nd: sample and paint; 3rd: paint projected texture; 4th: adding an additional end-grain texture)

The second image shows the same technique that we used previously: The top-surface texture was sampled and then painted on the end of the beam. As you can see, this method fails in this case because the end grain of the beam should be visible.

The third image shows an approach whereby the top-surface texture was first converted to a projected texture (right-click on the surface and select **Texture → Projected**). Then it was sampled and applied to the end. As you can see, this simply extrudes the texture at the end, giving it unnatural-looking stripes. Although this method may work well in other cases, it fails in this case.

The right image finally shows the only feasible method: adding a separate end-grain texture to the beam. This gives the wooden beam the most realistic look. Especially with wood (but also some other materials) it is important to keep a few "end" textures handy. Close-up renderings benefit greatly from those.

Example 5.3: Texturing Curved Surfaces

Curved surfaces have traditionally posed problems for texturing in SketchUp (tiled textures, on the other hand, tile well on curves, too). Although it is possible to apply a continuous texture over a curved surface, positioning using the pin method previously described does not work on those surfaces (because they are made up of surface facets).

If you need to align a tiled texture on a curved surface, turn on Hidden Geometry in SketchUp and align the texture on one of the faces. Then, sample and paint the aligned texture onto all other faces.

One method to deal with this is to add a planar object close to a curved object, place the texture on the planar object, position it there, and sample and paint the *projected* texture onto the curved object. **Figure 5.79** shows how a texture would look after this operation.

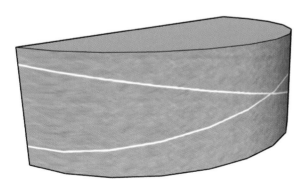

Figure 5.79: Placing a projected texture onto a curved object

As you can see, the texture looks good on the right side of the curve but stretches significantly on the left side. Therefore, this method works best for curved objects that feature only gentle slopes.

The steps outlined next describe how a texture can be precisely mapped onto a curved object using an unwrapping plugin. For this example, I will use the Unfold extension (see Chapter 4) on a surface with a simple curve.

1. To begin, make sure hidden geometry is visible. You will need to see the dashed edges of all faces.

2. Select the curved part of the object and make a copy.

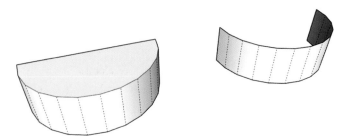

3. Now use any of the Unfold or Flatten extensions (as shown in Chapter 4) to unwrap the curved surface into a planar surface. Of course, this is possible only with a surface that lends itself to unwrapping (commonly called a *developable* surface) such as a curved wall, a cylinder, or a cone.

4. Use the eraser to remove all the dashed lines and create one continuous surface.

5. Now you can apply any texture image to this surface. Use the Positioning tool to stretch and place the texture to your liking. For this example, I placed a cross-texture on the surface that illustrates its placement on the curve.

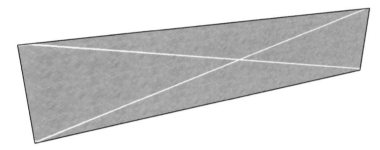

6. Right-click on the plane and select Make Unique Texture. This creates a new texture that retains the current positioning and gets cropped to the face's edges of the surface. You can find it in the Materials window (under the In Model textures). Simply pick this one and apply it to the curved surface. To do this successfully, you must turn off viewing of hidden lines—the texture will then correctly be applied to the entire curved surface, as shown here.

Example 5.4: Texturing a Sphere

One object that cannot be textured correctly using any of the methods presented here is a sphere. A sphere in SketchUp is commonly produced by revolving an arc around an axis. As you can see in **Figure 5.79**, it, therefore, consists of rectangular faces of varying sizes and aspect ratios. If you use SketchUp's materials to texture it, you will likely get a result similar to the one shown in the middle image of **Figure 5.80**—a jumbled mess of texture orientations. You could manually position the texture of every single face, but this is not practical.

Figure 5.80: Texturing a sphere (left: sphere showing hidden faces; middle: default mapping in SketchUp; right: spherical mapping using UV Tools plugin

Fortunately for us, there is another extension that can help out here. UV Tools by Whaat (Dale Martens) provides spherical and cylindrical mapping. All you need to do is select all faces on the sphere and right-click on one of them. The context menu will offer you both mapping options. If desired, you could also adjust texture size in SketchUp's Materials window.

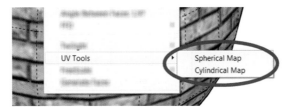

Alternatively, look for the Eneroth Texture Positioning Tools extension (EW).

Objects

As you can imagine, a rendering of a kitchen looks quite sterile and uninhabited if there are no objects (e.g., a vase, a plate with fruit, a wine bottle) on the countertops. Likewise, an external rendering of a building looks artificial unless there are a certain number of realistic-looking plants and exterior objects in the scene. Including people in a rendering often lends the scene realism and scale and gives viewers an intuitive way of imagining themselves in the environment.

As you can see in these examples, objects and entourage (defined in the widest sense) are important for our renderings. So how do you include them?

In general, there are two methods, each with its respective advantages:

- **Include in the rendering process**—This involves getting 3D or 2D models into SketchUp (or your rendering software) and placing them in the scene. While this seems to be the most intuitive method, it might be labor intensive to find or create a particular custom component you are after. Also, depending on the complexity (and number) of the objects, they might lead to an increase in rendering time. On the positive side, this method results in consistent renderings if several perspectives of the same scene are created.

■ **Add to rendered images using image-editing software (in postproduction)**—You can often easily and quickly create renderings without plants, people, and so forth, and then add them using your favorite image-editing software (e.g., Photoshop). As long as you master selection tools, brushes, and masks, you can very effectively add a large number of entourage elements to a rendering without making the actual rendering process too complex and time intensive.

A downside of this method is that the same elements might have to be inserted into various renderings, multiplying the workload in postprocessing.

The upcoming sections mention some of the techniques you can employ to include objects in the 3D environment and use them for rendering.

Entourage

When it comes to adding objects to your renderings, your best source may be SketchUp's own 3D Warehouse (see **Figure 5.81**). This virtual warehouse of SketchUp models has grown significantly over the past years and now boasts an impressive collection of user-submitted objects, brand-name appliances, 3D buildings, trees, and much more. A few years ago, the makers of SketchUp decided to move the object collection that beforehand installed with SketchUp into the Warehouse (leaving only a few sample objects behind in SketchUp's installation folder).

You can find the 3D Warehouse at http://3dwarehouse.sketchup.com.

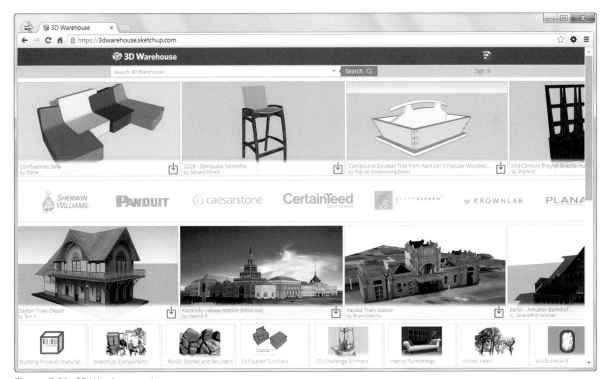

Figure 5.81: 3D Warehouse main screen

Get Models...

You can incorporate 3D Warehouse objects into your SketchUp project in a variety of ways:

- **Browse the 3D Warehouse using the Get Models... button.** This gives you a web browser that opens right within SketchUp and allows you to load any object as a component into the current model. This method is usually best if a search doesn't immediately return the desired object or if more detail about a model is desired.

  - **Search the 3D Warehouse from the Components window.** When you search for any term in the Components window, SketchUp displays the most relevant models it found in the 3D Warehouse. You can then load any component with one click into the current model.

  - **Browse the 3D Warehouse using your web browser of choice.** You can alternatively search the 3D Warehouse, download any models you like to your computer (as SketchUp's SKP files), and then import (or drag-and-drop) the components into the current model. This works well if you need to import multiple components.

  While the 3D Warehouse may be the largest resource for SketchUp models at this point, it isn't the only one. Various manufacturers offer 3D models of their products directly for download, and there are commercial websites that sell well-crafted generic models (e.g., www.formfonts.com or www.bimobject.com). Sample company sources include:

- www.maglin.com/sketchup.html—For landscape furniture such as benches.
- https://3dwarehouse.sketchup.com/collection.html?id=ua2569d7e-8851-4990-bf21-9e87834cd673 (Short link: http://goo.gl/5EBk7w)—Herman Miller has modeled many of their furniture items and uploaded them into the 3D Warehouse. Get your Eames chair for your renderings here!

When you work on lots of renderings, it is a good idea to create your own library of these entourage items. That way, you can dress up a standard scene very quickly. Select your favorite SketchUp components for their quality, good rendering appearance, and, possibly, low polygon count, and archive them. Although you could create a library on your hard disk, you can also create a Collection under your account in the 3D Warehouse and add your favorite components to it. Those components will then be available in SketchUp via the Get Models... button on the Getting Started toolbar.

Urban Context

If your entourage consists of neighboring buildings—as in the case of a model that is to be shown in its urban context—you can use the same technique as previously described to load those buildings into SketchUp. All you need to do is select the Nearby Models menu option in the Components window, and 3D Warehouse models that are located within a certain radius of your model's location will be offered for download.

TIP

Keep in mind that you can download only user-submitted (or SketchUp-submitted) content from the 3D Warehouse. Some buildings that you see as 3D buildings in Google Earth (especially in larger cities) were created by commercial companies for Google and are not available for download. You can identify those buildings in Google Earth when you hover over them and they don't get highlighted.

It is important to note that you must make sure your model is properly geo-located before you can do this (otherwise SketchUp doesn't know where it should search for buildings). To locate your model, select the Add Location... button from the Getting Started toolbar or the **File** menu.

Figure 5.82 shows a scene after several models have been loaded into the file.

Figure 5.82: Building models loaded into SketchUp

People

People are an important component in a rendering. Not only do they add scale to a scene, they also personalize the scene. For example, in a street-view rendering you can create very different neighborhood ambiances by either adding businesspeople in suits or families with strollers. Of course, you want to add people as appropriate and as necessary for the message you intend to convey.

To add people (or animals, for that matter) to your scenes, you can take any or all of these approaches:

- **Add 3D people to the scene.** These are complete 3D models of people—sometimes even with realistic-looking textures. The 3D Warehouse is a great resource for these kinds of models, but there are also other (sometimes commercial) distributors.

  The main benefit of using 3D models is that once you have staged a scene with people, you can create as many realistic-looking renderings from various perspectives as you need. A potential downside of this approach is that some of the models are composed of many polygons and may slow down rendering—especially if you use lots of people in your scene.

- **Use 2D people shapes or cutouts.** SketchUp allows components to be set up so that they always face the camera. This is very convenient (e.g., you need only a 2D photo to represent a tree from various perspectives), but it results in the people in your scene always facing the viewer—no matter the vantage point from which the viewer looks at them.

  You can find many 2D people in the 3D Warehouse. Some are created from photographs and, therefore, look very realistic. Others are "sketchy" people who look better in sketchy non-photorealistic renderings.

  In terms of rendering speed, these will render faster than true 3D objects. This is true especially if the rendering software allows for transparent image maps (e.g., using a PNG image with transparency) and the object has only a few polygons.

- **Add people as 2D cutouts in your image-editing software.** If you are comfortable using image-editing software such as Photoshop, then you can learn to place people cutouts realistically into any image. While this may require picking appropriate photos and some postprocessing work on shadows and layering (e.g., when a person stands behind a plant), this approach is very efficient. Because people aren't being added to the rendered scene, they don't add any additional time to the rendering itself.

  A downside of this approach is that it is not very usable when various perspectives of the same scene must be rendered and the people need to appear consistent in the different perspectives.

Figure 5.83 illustrates some of the people models that you can download from the 3D Warehouse (from left to right): sketchy 2D, silhouette 2D, photo-cutout 2D (model by TaffGoch), sketchy (untextured) 3D, and photorealistic 3D (model by Reallusion iClone).

Figure 5.84 shows how the three main types—2D follow-me, textured 3D, Photoshop-added image cutout—behave when two views of the same scene are being rendered. As you can see, the only one that looks appropriate in both views is the 3D model of the person in the middle. The left figure renders facing the camera independent of the viewer's location, which is convenient but may not be desired. The figure on the right works only in the top image because for the bottom image a different photograph (one taken from behind) would have to be available.

Figure 5.83: People models available from the 3D Warehouse

Figure 5.84: Different perspective renderings of people

Example 5.5: Adding a Person to an Image in Photoshop

To add a person using your photo-editing software, follow the procedure illustrated in **Figure 5.85**. These instructions are for Adobe Photoshop—modify them slightly if you are using another type of software.

1. Load the rendered scene image into Photoshop.

2. Load a photograph of a person into Photoshop. Make sure the view and the lighting roughly work with the scene and viewpoint of your rendering. It is best if the photograph has a uniformly colored background because you need to remove this background in the next step.

3. Cut out the shape using appropriate selection tools (the Lasso and the Magic Wand tools are very helpful here).

4. Paste the shape twice into your rendered image. You create two different layers this way.

Figure 5.85: Adding a person and her shadow using Photoshop

5. Turn off the topmost layer, which is the image of the person that will be visible in the end.

6. On the second layer, color the shape completely black.

7. Select the shape and stretch it until its perspective makes it appear as the person's shadow.

8. Apply a Gaussian blur filter to this layer. Go with a light blur for this one.

9. Copy this layer and apply Gaussian blur again—this time with a higher degree of blurring.

10. If you want a shadow that appears less fuzzy next to the person yet blurs farther away, apply a layer mask as shown in **Figure 5.85** to the two shadow layers.

11. Make the person's image visible again and place it on top. It should now look correct in the rendering.

Plants, Trees, Grass, Rocks, and Carpet

It is easily possible for computer-generated geometry (be it the model of a house, a landscape, or simply an object) to look artificial. In our SketchUp models, edges are always straight and most lines are parallel to one of the three main axes. As you know, nature doesn't look like that. When you stand in front of your house, you will see not just the straight lines of the facade but also a tree, a bush, some grass, some dirt, and other natural fuzziness. It is, therefore, important—even if landscape elements are not your main focus—to include them in order to add realism. This is, of course, even more important when you focus solely on the landscape and need to show not only vegetation but also consider species, growing season, and so on.

While this is very important for exterior scenes, interior scenes often benefit from adding plants as well. From a rendering perspective, adding a shag carpet and some fabrics (drapes or bedsheets) serves a similar purpose. Chapter 4 showed you how to use the Make Fur extension to create a carpet. We'll focus on vegetation in this section.

2D versus 3D versus Photoshop

When you want to add landscape objects such as plants to a scene, you face the same questions you did with people: Should you include complete 3D models in your scene? Can you get away with 2D (face-me) images? Or should you add them in postproduction (using Photoshop or any other image-editing software)?

As before, this often depends on various parameters—in this case, the most important is how close an object is to the viewer. The closer the object is to the camera, the more visible detail is and the more modeling might be necessary to include that detail.

Another aspect to consider in your model is polygon count. Natural objects are always crooked, random, edgy, or at least bent (imagine a blade of grass). Modeling this in detail often requires many polygons to make these objects look realistic. You might be able to use fewer polygons and add detail using a texture, but that is not always possible.

In general, follow these recommendations:

■ **Object is close to the camera**—Model as much as necessary. You might be able to model only one side of the object (e.g., the front side of a wall). Use as few polygons as possible and try to add randomness by using a texture. Prefer a single-image texture rather than a tiling image (tiled images often create patterns that can easily be spotted up close).

■ **Object is far away**—Use a 2D image of the object if you have one and its alignment works. This is a great method for adding trees as long as you can create some random variation in them (by scaling, etc.). Of course, the image must have transparency so that it doesn't include a background of its own (PNG and GIF file formats work well for this). Alternatively, use a coarse 3D model. You might be able to use simpler textures or just colored materials. If you use texture images, try using tileable textures, such as the ones included with SketchUp.

Figure 5.86 illustrates this approach. While the tree in the front is modeled in 3D at a reasonable level of detail, the tree in the back is a face-me photo-based 2D image. The sky and landscape beyond the hill come from a sky probe—you could even use it to add more trees, or other landscape objects, in the background.

Figure 5.86: 2D and 3D trees in the same scene

Adding 3D Plants

Let's take a look at how to add 3D plants and make them look good in a rendering. We'll add a tree here, but this works analogously for shrubbery, flowers, and the like.

For this scene, we will use one of the trees that come from SketchUp's 3D Warehouse. You can find it as "Aspen deciduous tree high polygon." The top-left image in **Figure 5.87** shows how it looks when you insert it into your model. As you can see in your model, the trunk is textured but the leaves are simply colored. For my purpose, I replaced the trunk texture with a browner one. This is not correct for the species but works better for now.

Figure 5.87: Adjusting a tree for rendering

When you render the tree as is, you should get a result similar to the top-right image in **Figure 5.87**. Although this already looks quite good, it could use some refinement. The leaves are green, but they look very flat. Also, their color is a bit too stark to look natural. Furthermore, although the trunk has a good texture, it also looks flat. To improve the rendering, I made these changes:

- **Leaf texture**—To add a bit more texture to the leaves, I added a tile-able leaf image to their material. You can see it in a bit more detail in the bottom-right image.

- **Leaf transparency**—When you hold a leaf up to the sun, it lets light through. Therefore, in SketchUp, it also helps to add a slight transparency to the leaves. In the Materials window, adjust the opacity slider to 80 percent.

- **Leaf reflectivity**—In my rendering software, I gave the leaf a slightly reflective preset. Don't go overboard with this setting—unless you are modeling a rubber tree (or wet leaves), of course.

- **Leaf and trunk bump**—As always, some material bumpiness helps a lot. This is true especially when we have something as coarse as bark. I gave both the leaves and the trunk texture a bump, reserving the higher magnitude for the trunk. You can see the result of this in the bottom-right image.

You can evaluate the result of these setting changes in the bottom two images in **Figure 5.87**. You can also see that, although the tree model works well at the distance shown in the bottom-left image, the bottom-right image is too close and would require some additional modeling of secondary branches. It is also not realistic that leaves intersect the stem—this would need to be fixed, too.

Adding Grass

Grass is a rendering component for which quality and preparation effort are very much dependent on the distance between the viewer and its blades. Imagine looking at a lawn from several houses away. The lawn (at least, if it is well maintained) looks like a uniformly colored and textured green plane. As you get closer, you see the individual blades of grass—especially at the edges of the lawn, where blades overlap walkways. If you bent down to get even closer, you would then see that not only is each blade curved; it also has a V shape in cross section. As you can see from this example, your approach to modeling and rendering must vary, depending on the distance of the viewer from the object.

Figure 5.88 illustrates the four approaches you can take.

Figure 5.88: Grass rendering methods (left to right: SketchUp's grass texture, same with bump, individual blades, 2D image patch)

When your distance to the grass is quite far, it might be enough to simply use SketchUp's grass texture (or any other uniformly patterned tiling grass texture). This is shown in the leftmost image of **Figure 5.88**.

This method improves when you add a strong bump to the grass material in your rendering software. The deep shadows that appear give the grass more realism, as you can see in the second image from the left. You can evaluate the appropriateness of this approach when you are at arm's length from the image—this rendering should appear reasonably realistic.

The third image shows the other end of the effort spectrum. This is what you get when you model each blade separately. I used the Make Fur extension (from Chapter 4) to do this and went with its default arch shape. As you can see in the third image from the left, this approach leads to an excellent degree of realism—even when the viewer is as close as we are to this image. A major downside of this approach, however, is the very large number of polygons that this method creates, which not only increases rendering time but can also slow SketchUp significantly if you are not careful. Use it mostly for close-ups.

A good compromise between those two approaches is to use a 2D image of a grass patch (see **Figure 5.89**), which contains a transparent background (a transparent PNG, in my case). Especially when you use a low-resolution image, this approach can significantly reduce the polygon count in your model. I also used the Make Fur extension, as before, but this time let it place copies of the image component instead of individual blades. You can evaluate the result in the far-right image in **Figure 5.88**.

As you can see, this leads to quite a good rendering. Each grass-patch image (representing many blades) triangulates as two polygons, while each individual blade in the last method turned into five—making this method much more polygon-efficient. The only problems with this approach are occasional patches (you can see some in the foreground) and a bit of a scruffy appearance. Because these images are all vertically placed, it is not possible to get a good result when you look down onto the grass. Nevertheless, this approach is very efficient, and any problems can easily be fixed later in your image-editing software.

Figure 5.89: Using transparent images for grass

Figure 5.90 combines both approaches. The blades close to the camera were modeled as single blades (with a striped green texture), while the grass in the background consisted of randomly placed images.

Figure 5.90: A grassy hill

Example 5.6: Making a 2D PNG Cutout Face-Me Component

Follow this procedure to make your own 2D cutout SketchUp components for trees, people, and so forth. This example uses a tree image from www.cgtextures.com and turns it into a face-me component.

To be able to remove the background in an image, it is best to start with a uniformly colored background. If you are taking the pictures yourself, look for a white wall, a gray sky, or any other uniform texture as a backdrop. To make sure the image can be used as a component, take it straight on, not looking down on or up at the main subject. It is also a good idea to take the image when the sky is overcast—this eliminates any unsightly shadows in the component.

1. Let's start with the raw image. Note that it has a relatively uniform background.

2. Load it into your favorite photo-editing software. This example demonstrates the process in Photoshop, but you can do this with other software, too (e.g., Gimp).

3. Remove the sky background and the portion that includes the hills. Use the Magic Eraser tool, set Tolerance to 50, check Anti-alias (to smooth the edges), uncheck Contiguous (so that areas inside the tree will also be removed), and keep Opacity at 100 percent. Next, click anywhere in the sky area. This removes the sky but not the hills in the background. To remove the hills, click anywhere on them. The result should look like the image shown here.

As you can see, the background has largely been removed and replaced by Photoshop's default checkered pattern.

4. Let's check how well you did. Add another layer in Photoshop, fill it with a dark solid color, and place it underneath the tree layer.

5. As you can see in the image, the background was removed quite well in the darker area (at the bottom left), while the right side of the tree still has a slight white halo.

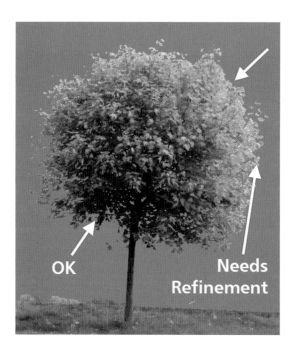

6. On the tree layer, use the Magic Eraser tool again. Experiment with the Tolerance setting and click at the right edge of the tree until just the white halo is removed.

7. Now let's focus on the base of the tree. To remove the grass and other ground, use any combination of the Eraser, Magnetic Lasso, and Magic Wand tools that works well for you. Because the tree trunk is reasonably straight in this image, I was able to just erase everything around it.

8. Use the Eraser tool to cut the base of the trunk parallel with the ground and clean up the image as necessary. This is what you should have now.

9. Crop the image to the edges of the tree, scale it to your liking, and save it as a transparent PNG file.

10. In SketchUp, change your view to a parallel-perspective front view, which reduces errors in the next steps.

11. Import the image into SketchUp using the **File** → **Import...** menu item. Make sure you check Use As Image in the import options.

12. Double-click on the origin to place the tree in your model. Scale the tree to your liking.

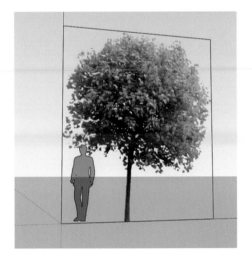

13. Right-click on the tree image and select Explode from the context menu. This turns the image into a rectangle with the tree image as its texture.

TIP

If you want the tree to have appropriate shadows in SketchUp, trace its outline with the Pen tool and cut away the remaining parts of the rectangle using the Eraser tool.

14. Before you turn the tree into a component, you need to hide all the bordering edges. Do this by holding Shift while clicking the edges with the Erase tool. This hides them instead of erasing them.

15. Select the tree again and click the Make Component button in the toolbar (or use the right-click menu). In the dialog that comes up, make sure you check the Always Face Camera box. Don't click on the Create button yet!

16. In the same dialog, click the Set Component Axes button to place the axis at the base of the tree. This will be the insertion point for the tree component.

17. When you click on Create, your new face-me tree component will be created (see **Figure 5.91**). Orbit around your model and see that the tree component behaves properly. Also, add a few more component instances from the Components window (or copy them).

Figure 5.91: Finished face-me tree component in SketchUp

Rendering Tips

- **Keep your scene simple, well modeled, and organized!** These are three important principles to reduce the chance that rendering your SketchUp scene will give you a headache. Here's what I mean:

  - **Keep your scene simple.** Model only what you absolutely need for your rendering. Often, there is no need to model geometry that is out of view or inside an object. If your model is complex, it might be a good idea to make a copy of the file and then prepare the copy for rendering (by deleting and cleaning items) rather than using the original.

    Delete any face that does not contribute to the rendering. Make sure there is no left-over geometry (e.g., from a previous intersection operations).

  - **Craft your model well.** You will run into trouble if you have small holes between surfaces, overlapping surfaces, or crooked planes.

    Any gaps in your model will increase the chance of light leaks—bright spots where there should be none, as, for example, in a corner. If your scene has overlapping surfaces, intersect them and trim excess geometry. If you have planes that should be flat but aren't because one vertex is out of plane, this surface will be triangulated during rendering, and you might see edges appear in your images.

- **Keep your model organized.** If you use many copies of the same object, make sure they are components rather than groups. Many rendering software packages nowadays are able to handle object instancing just as SketchUp does. This means that instead of exporting lots of faces per copy, these tools use the more efficient method of component definitions and instance locations.

- **Name your materials, objects, and layers.** Especially when models increase in complexity, it is a good idea to apply a consistent naming scheme to those (instead of just letting SketchUp name everything as it likes). This makes life easier when you are editing or searching for those later.

- **Reduce the number of polygons.** Every additional polygon increases rendering time and makes your model more complex. This is true especially if you assign translucent, reflective, or light-emitting materials to the polygon. Therefore, keep your model's polygons to the necessary minimum.

  This is the case particularly with natural objects such as trees or grass. When they are at a certain distance from the viewer, it is often a good idea to either reduce their complexity or replace them with a photograph of the object.

  Also keep in mind that while SketchUp is able to handle multivertex polygons, rendering software usually uses only triangular polygons and triangulates any nontriangular face coming from SketchUp.

- **Use fully reflective materials or fake reflections.** Reflective surfaces in your scene increase rendering time, especially if they are just partially reflective (such as brushed aluminum). Unless you absolutely need this effect, try going with full reflectivity (a mirror or highly polished chrome material) or a gray gradient texture (faking blurry reflectivity) instead. This works especially well when the object is not too close to the viewer.

- **Consider using fake caustics.** If you need caustics (the light ripples that reflect off a pool, for example) but don't want to expend the additional rendering time that caustics require, consider faking them by projecting a caustics texture image onto a wall, ceiling, or other surface.

- **Handling depth of field, light rays, and motion blur.** All of these effects increase rendering complexity. Consider adding them in postproduction using your photo-editing software's filters.

  Depth of field can usually be added using Gaussian blur, and motion blur is a filter that is typically available in your editing software. Experiment with the settings and master masking techniques to perfect these effects.

  Light rays (as you would see coming through trees on a slightly foggy day) require your rendering software to simulate particles in the air (this is often called *volume lighting*). They can often be added in postproduction, especially if they are produced by simple geometry (a window, for example).

- **Use postproduction to your advantage.** Depending on your image-editing skills, it might be more efficient to add people, vegetation, sky effects, and some shadows in your favorite photo-editing software after the rendering is done.

  A great resource for learning and discussing rendering and illustration techniques is this website: www.sketchupartists.org.

Making Renderings Presentable

Although photorealistically rendered images can be produced with a quality similar to that of actual photographs, sometimes this is not desirable. For example, you might want to create sketches that have a watercolor appearance but contain effects such as lighting or reflections that you can produce only using rendering software.

To this end, it is often useful to expend as much effort on your renderings in postproduction as you do in setting them up. The following examples give you some ideas for paths to follow.

Combining SketchUp Output and Rendered Output in Photoshop

Because SketchUp has very good built-in support for hand-drawn linework through its styles, adding a handmade touch to your renderings can easily be accomplished by exporting a sketchy image of your current model in addition to creating a rendered image.

Let's start this process by using the rendering shown in **Figure 5.92** as it came from the rendering software.

Figure 5.92: Raw rendered image

Although the grass and the soft shadows look good already, you might still want to add some sketchy linework to the image. To do this, try out various styles in SketchUp until you find one you like. Let's use the one in **Figure 5.93**. Export it using the **File → Export → 2D Graphic** menu item.

Figure 5.93: Sketchy view exported from SketchUp

Alternatively, you could also print the SketchUp view, overlay it with tracing paper, and sketch onto it yourself. Then just scan the sketch, scale it, and overlay it onto the rendered image in Photoshop if you go this route.

TIP	Create both images—the rendering and the SketchUp exported sketch—from the same view and at the same pixel resolution. This makes it easier to combine them in your image-editing software.

Figure 5.94: Layer arrangement in Photoshop

To combine the two images, I imported both of them into Photoshop and used the layer arrangement shown in **Figure 5.94**. As always, if you use different image-editing software, adjust this appropriately.

Let's go through the layers, from bottom to top:

- The Background is simply the rendered image.
- The Basic Fixes layer is a copy of the background in which I cleaned up some things (moved some knots around for diversity) and applied the Diffuse Glow filter.
- The High Pass Filter layer is a copy of that layer. I desaturated it (to make it grayscale) and applied the high-pass filter. I then applied the Soft Light blending mode to this layer, which basically uses this layer to make contrast a bit more interesting.
- The White Vignette is a transparent layer onto which I painted white edges and which has an opacity of 70 percent. This fades the image out nicely toward the edges (this is similar to what was discussed in Example 5.1).
- The next layer is a Hue/Saturation adjustment. I reduced saturation a bit because the colors were a little too bright.
- Next are two copies of the sketch. The lower layer of the two has a Soft Light blending mode (to soften colors even further), and the top one has a Multiply blending mode (to add crisp linework). Putting these layers on top of the White Vignette layer fades colors but continues lines.

The image created using this process looks like **Figure 5.95**.

Figure 5.95: Combination of sketchy and rendered image

Another example for this process is the cover image of this book, where a layer-blending technique was used to transition between a "sketchy" SketchUp image to a photorealistically rendered one.

Other Methods

The approach just described is a good staple to have in your tool kit. In addition, you can go after the looks shown in **Figures 5.96, 5.97**, and **5.98** (and combine as necessary). All of them used the free FotoSketcher software that you can download from www.fotosketcher .com to modify the source images. This software lets you convert an image into a sketch, a watercolor or an oil painting (complete with brushstrokes and canvas texture) that you can then layer onto a rendering using the aforementioned technique.

Figure 5.96: The same scene with an added "expressive brushstroke" underpainting

Figure 5.97: Layering of two pencil sketch types

Figure 5.98: Combination of a watercolor underpainting with sketchy linework

Your Turn!

The following tasks allow you to practice the topics in this chapter:

1. **Model a photo.**
   Take a picture of a small setup (one that is easy to model in SketchUp). For example, lay a metal knife on a wood block on a granite counter and take a close-up picture that shows all three materials. Evaluate the materials in the photo with respect to reflectiveness, bumpiness, irregularities, and other qualities. Then model the scene in SketchUp and re-create it in your rendering software. Your main challenge will be to re-create material properties and the lighting environment as closely as possible to the real world. Render the scene and compare it side by side with the photo.

2. **Create a loft sales brochure.**
   Model one or two typical loft scenes (a living room with a sofa and artwork on the wall or an open-floor-plan kitchen). Then apply good-quality materials, set up the scene with interesting lighting, and render it. Finally, put the images together on a single page, add some text, and turn it into a sales flyer for a new downtown loft.

3. **Render day and night scenarios.**

   Using the scene from the previous task, create good-looking night renders (complete with artificial lighting). Make sure the night renders don't just have a black sky. Then present the day and night renders side by side. Experiment with different lighting scenarios.

4. **Create visual styles.**

   Using any method described in this chapter, create three visual styles that cannot be done only by using renderings, SketchUp's Styles, or FotoSketcher. Use any model you like as the basis for this.

5. **Bring yourself into SketchUp.**

   Get someone to take a photo of yourself (or a friend). Then turn it into a cutout face-me component for SketchUp.

Chapter 6
Making Things with SketchUp

In this chapter, you will learn how you can turn your digital SketchUp models into physical objects. Making something has become such a popular application for SketchUp that Trimble even renamed their free version to SketchUp Make. This chapter will first cover the possibilities for making with SketchUp and then lay out specific workflows for cutting prep (manual fabrication planning), laser cutting, CNC machining, and 3D printing.

Key Topics:

- Using SketchUp for digital fabrication
- Services and tools for makers
- Manufacturing techniques
- Cutting prep with SketchUp
- Using LayOut for 2D cut sheets
- Laser cutting prep and techniques
- CNC milling prep and techniques
- Preparing models for 3D printing
- 3D printing from SketchUp

What Can I Make with SketchUp?

Almost anything, really! As a matter of fact, SketchUp has been used to create objects from small jewelry and robot parts to furniture, buildings, and entire landscapes. Trimble showed off a large-scale example a little while back when they used their construction technology to control excavators via GPS with SketchUp terrain data to shape a landscape. See **Figure 6.1** for some examples.

SketchUp's traditional application case has, of course, been architectural design and construction. This has produced anything from scaled models to physical 1:1 mockups to the actual buildings. Over the last few years and with the emergence of a worldwide "maker" movement and easily attainable and rather cost-efficient technologies such as 3D printing, laser cutting, and CNC milling, SketchUp's traditional application field has expanded significantly.

As it turns out, it is actually quite easy to make something with SketchUp. Naturally, the amount of work you have to put into this process increases with the complexity of the project, but especially smaller things—take a key tag with a name on it, for example—can be designed and 3D printed in less than a half-hour. This, of course, makes fabrication and rapid prototyping easy to incorporate into your workflow.

Figure 6.1: Examples of what can be made with SketchUp *(Models by International Masonry Institute, UMass Biology, John Bacus. Excavator image used by permission of Trimble Navigation)*

SketchUp has enough built-in tools and file exchange formats to make most of this possible without installing extensions. Often, though, extensions will at least make your life easier and will let you create more complex objects. Therefore, keep Trimble's Extension Warehouse or SketchUcation's Plugin Store bookmarked if you venture into the realm of making things (see Chapter 4 for details on extensions).

Often, making physical objects using a particular technology (e.g., laser cutting) requires you to rethink what you want to build in terms of what the technology can deliver and how it does so. You might have to clean up or simplify your 3D model, and you often will have to break it up somehow into parts to be "buildable."

While all of these technologies require tools and machines that can range in price from a few hundred to several thousand dollars, often it is not necessary to purchase them. Online services and networks of makers can help you out for quite reasonable fees. The following section introduces some of them.

Services for Makers

Depending on how handy you are with tools, what your budget is, and how many items you intend to produce, it might not make sense to equip a woodshop or cash in your retirement savings to purchase a top-of-the-line 3D printer or CNC router. Don't get me wrong! Many of these technologies have very affordable entry-level machines that produce high-quality objects. But if you only need to make two digitally designed wedding bands or if the 3D printer you actually own is already tied up with other projects, it's time to look online to see who can make that stuff for you. That's where fabrication services come in.

At the time of writing, the following services were the main ones offering one or two of the techniques (3D printing and laser cutting, for example) using an often quite extensive selection of materials. In addition to these large and internationally operating services, you are likely able to track down local or national services where you live as well.

- **i.materialise** (Belgium)—http://i.materialise.com—3D printing.
- **Ponoko** (USA, New Zealand)—www.ponoko.com—Laser cutting, 3D printing.
- **sculpteo** (USA, France)—www.sculpteo.com—3D printing.
- **Shapeways** (USA, Netherlands)—www.shapeways.com—3D printing.
- Select **Staples** and **UPS** stores (USA)—3D printing.

Many of the 3D printing services mentioned here let you create with colored plastics, full-color materials, and often also metals and ceramics (see **Figure 6.2** for some examples). Plastics, cardboard, wood, and metals are typically available for laser cutting.

Figure 6.2: Some materials available from Shapeways (small samples at left) and common PLA (polylactic acid) plastic (right)

Most of these services will also allow you to put your models into an online store that gives any visitor to the site the chance to fabricate them on-demand and gives you the chance to make some money back. Recently, copy-service type stores (with the larger chains being Staples and UPS) are getting into the 3D printing service business as well.

Another quite exciting approach to fabrication services is to use a shared machine where the owner rents out time on it. The following online services provide marketplaces for local fabricators (often worldwide) that either allow you to use their machines for a fee or provide the full range of design and fabrication services. A side benefit of this approach is that you will also get into direct contact with the fabricators and might meet other makers in your area.

- **100kGarages**—www.100kgarages.com—CNC milling, laser cutting, 3D printing.
- **3D Hubs**—www.3dhubs.com—3D printing.
- **makexyz**—www.makexyz.com—3D printing, CNC milling.

The main downside with any of the commercial or private custom making services mentioned in this section is likely the time it takes for the item to be produced and shipped to you. This can often take anywhere from a few days to several weeks. Local services, however, likely will provide a faster turnaround time. So if you want to go this route, make sure you plan ahead!

Selecting the Manufacturing Technique

What you intend to produce often determines the technique you will want to choose to make it. For example, laser cutting works only with rather thin sheet material. You will, therefore, likely have to assemble any cut objects in a secondary process once cutting is done. Material selection also has a large influence because not all materials are suitable for all techniques. Wood, for example, cannot be 3D printed (except for plastic/wood-fiber filament), but it can be used for laser cutting as well as CNC milling.

In some cases, combining techniques might make sense. You could, for example, make a beautiful geodesic dome model using cut rods, 3D-printed connectors, and laser-cut exterior panels. In other cases, you can fabricate the identical shape (e.g., a sculpture) using any of the available methods. You will, however, likely observe that this often leads to varying amounts of effort, time, and cost. Material quality and usability of the final object may also vary depending on chosen technique.

Manufacturing techniques can broadly be classified as *subtractive*, where you remove material (as in cutting, milling, and lathing), and *additive*, where you accumulate material (as in assembling and 3D printing). Two further categories are *casting*, where liquid material (e.g., resin, metal, or concrete) is cast into a mold, and *forming*, where material (e.g., sheet metal) is reshaped under pressure. For the purpose of this text, I am including casting only with cutting prep because you can use this technique well to prepare the molds. However, you can very much use a CNC-routed mold or a 3D-printed object for casting as well. For example, 3D printing wax filament that can dissolve in the casting process is now available, making it very easy to create accurate molds.

- **Cutting prep**—This technique is not a direct digital-manufacturing technique but rather an indirect one. You would use SketchUp and the 3D modeling process to figure out the geometry, intersections, and other details. Then you would use a printout-based transfer process to have templates guide your manual cutting.

This is likely the cheapest of all the presented methods because it uses only paper output. It is generally suitable for sheet products like plywood but also for larger objects such as structural beams and entire assemblies.

Due to the nature of the transfer process, this technique is not as precise as the following ones because it relies heavily on the skill of the user. It can be used for any material orientation, however, which allows you to work on back sides and undersides of a project piece.

See **Figure 6.3** for some examples.

Figure 6.3: A scale paper model of a shell from Chapter 7 and concrete formwork, made using cutting prep techniques

- **Laser cutting**—Laser cutting uses the light of a highly focused laser beam to etch or cut through sheet material like cardboard, plywood, or plastic. Depending on the strength of the laser, this can be done up to approximately 3/4" thickness. The work area and, therefore, maximum sheet size depends on the machine, but maxes out at roughly 2' × 4' for large machines.

As a result, this technique can best be used to process planar scale model objects such as walls and structural ribs. Laser cutting is a very accurate technique that produces crisp edges. Due to the high temperature of the process, wood and paper products are often burned black at the edges, though (see **Figure 6.4** for some examples).

Figure 6.4: Examples of laser-cut and laser-engraved pieces

While high-powered lasers are able to cut many different materials, even the strongest lasers will not cut ceramic materials like brick or granite. These can be engraved using the laser, however. Alternatively, water-jet cutting machines can be used to cut through thick steel and stone, and plasma cutters can be used for metals.

Most laser cutters have a fixed head that only cuts vertically (downward) while moving in the x-, y-, and z-directions. Only some industrial laser cutters are equipped with rotating heads that allow them to operate in any direction.

■ **CNC milling**—This technique most commonly uses router-type bits on a movable spindle that remove material from sheet goods or larger objects. Similar to laser cutters, they move on the x-, y-, and z-axes; however, the work area is typically larger (4' × 8' is a common size) and the z-range is significant, often allowing for at least 6" of vertical motion. Some CNC mills have rotating heads, allowing for 5 degrees of freedom—x, y, z plus two rotations—and making it possible to cut material from the side or even from underneath.

Five-axis CNC machines are used nowadays to process entire structural beams at full scale, and even tool-changers are not uncommon (where the drill head can be automatically changed by the machine). In the shop, however, they are often used for everything from engraving-like operations (e.g., for sign making) to part-building at a larger scale than is possible with a laser cutter. The vertical travel also allows interesting patterns and surfaces to be applied to a material (by not cutting all the way through).

Due to the inherent diameter and geometry of the router bit, some operations (particularly cutting of sharp, reentrant corners, and tight spaces) must be considered while detailing objects. **Figure 6.5** shows a building-scale and a furniture-scale example of CNC milled objects.

Figure 6.5: CNC-milled examples from Trimble's Maker Faire booth *(Images used by permission of Eric Schimelpfenig / sketchthis.net)*

■ **3D printing**—While all of the above-mentioned techniques are *subtractive* methods, 3D printing is an *additive* method because it relies on the layered deposition of material. A variety of technologies are available in this category, ranging from heating and depositing molten plastic (called Fused Deposition Modeling, or FDM) to the melting of granular material using lasers or other energy sources (as in Selective Laser Sintering, or SLS, for example) and the hardening of resin with laser beams (called Stereolithography, or SLA).

This process typically employs an extrusion (or laser) head that travels in an x, y, z pattern over the work area, and the object is then created layer-by-layer. Depending on the material used, those layers can be quite fine and the surface of the object can be reasonably smooth. The maximum build volume depends on the printer and can range from approximately 70 cubic inches for small machines to 20 cubic feet for the largest.

Thermoplastics are often used to print objects because the material has to melt and fuse during the process of being made (see **Figure 6.6** for some examples). Other 3D printers are able to work with metal powders or ceramics, which after some postprocessing leads to quite sturdy objects that can even have a smooth-surface preparation. All 3D printing methods typically require some postprocessing to finish or clean the printed objects. Although wood has been used with FDM printers, this typically requires a filament that is a combination of plastic and small wood fibers.

Figure 6.6: Some 3D-printed examples (left to right): vase, rotation shape (can you see the face?), house model

As anyone with marginal do-it-yourself experience knows, this list is not exhaustive. Other techniques are available as well; however, those mentioned in this chapter are probably the ones most relevant to practitioners and students. Other techniques of interest include CNC lathing, stamping, water-jet or plasma cutting, and foam cutting. Many of the methods introduced in the following sections can be modified to apply to these, too.

For the techniques covered next, it is very important to understand the machines and the materials that are being used. This typically requires a thorough reading of any manuals (including the safety section!) and a good number of tryouts. For example, in my foray into 3D printing, I have produced much waste just because some small setting was off. Another common misconception is that these highly precise methods lead to interlocking parts that automatically fit into each other. After all, they do so in SketchUp! Often, however, minor material deformation and fabrication leftovers require some cleanup after production.

Unfortunately, covering the various manufacturing techniques and machine or material intricacies in detail would extend too far beyond the scope of this book. I will therefore focus more on preparing and processing your SketchUp models for the various methods and showing you which intermediary steps are necessary.

A Word About Materials

Although digital fabrication offers amazing possibilities for precision manufacture, it is important to remember that all "real" materials have tolerances in their dimensions and mechanical properties. If you pull a face in SketchUp upward by 1/2", every point on the new face will be away from the original by that exact dimension. In the real world, material-thickness tolerances can amount to +/–10 percent and can vary across a piece. It is also important to understand a material's peculiarities, especially if it is natural (as with wood and other fiber-based products) and/or prone to dimensional changes under climatic influences (as with wood or metals, for example).

On top of this, even CNC- and laser-based machines have tolerances, albeit very small ones. Any assembly process that comes afterward introduces further inaccuracies.

Keep all of this in mind with the following techniques. For example, introduce gaps where needed to allow for tolerances and manufacturing peculiarities. Make it a habit to always have a set of calipers handy and check material sizes at several stages during digital fabrication work.

Cutting Prep

SketchUp is a great tool if you need to figure out detailed geometry for manual fabrication. This is mainly because the process of 3D modeling often replicates the steps that make up the fabrication process itself, thereby letting you practice the process virtually. Even if the model geometry is not overly complex, SketchUp can be useful for work preparation. Examples for this approach include: woodworking details, concrete formwork setups, rafter intersections, and many other applications, often produced manually using the tools shown in **Figure 6.7**.

Figure 6.7: The common (manual) tools of the trade

These processes commonly require full-scale or scaled-down templates or cut sheets. Therefore, a core skill here is the ability to print or otherwise export to scale from SketchUp. Many of the general modeling principles (beam trimming, geometry unwrapping, creation of shell geometry, etc.) have already been covered in earlier chapters of this book and won't be repeated here. Let's rather focus on the steps needed to get your model out of the software.

As an example, let's assume you want to export the tread geometry for a curved-edge stair.

Example 6.1: Fabricating an L-Shaped Stair

Let's start by modeling the stair treads and risers as precisely as needed in SketchUp. As you can see in **Figure 6.8**, the L-shaped stair follows a 90-degree wall corner on the outside but has a curve with a 1' 6" radius on the inside. The corner treads fan out and, therefore, widen toward the outside. All treads have 1.5" nosings. For the purpose of this exercise, I will not cover determining the stringer geometry (although that would certainly be an interesting exercise!). As you can see in the figure, everything has been trimmed accurately already. Also, the model is well organized with individually grouped geometry so that each actual piece can be moved separately (following the principles laid out in Chapter 3).

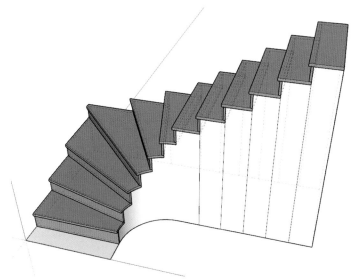

Figure 6.8: The modeled treads and risers for the stair

Independent of whether you intend to create full-scale paper templates (for cutting layout), a scaled model, or simply dimensioned cut sheets, the following steps are quite similar.

First, you will need to lay all of the pieces flat on the ground (the x-y plane). Starting with the treads, copy all of them to the side of the assembled model and then move each piece individually to the ground plane at z=0 (e.g., use the origin as a reference).

TIP

If you have lots of pieces, use the DropGC extension by R. Wilson (get it from EW, SM) and drop everything automatically onto a temporary rectangle on the ground plane. You can also manually move them one by one down along the vertical (blue) axis while constraining the move direction (hold down the Shift key) and inferencing the origin (or any other object on the ground plane).

For my layout, I also rotated all treads so that the front (nosing) part of each tread ended up parallel to the red x-axis. This assumes that the treads will be cut out of wood with its grain running parallel to that direction. The following graphic shows the result.

Now that the shapes are nicely arranged, switch your camera position to top view and use parallel projection. Using parallel projection here will ensure that there won't be any distortion because the perspective and sizes are accurately shown.

TIP

For easier visibility of all edges, switch the default display style to a hidden-line display style. You might also want to use a style that doesn't show textures. You don't need those right now anyway.

It is also a good idea to set up tabbed scenes via the **View → Animation** menu for each view that you intend to print/export separately. Make sure you name them logically, especially if you plan to export the model to LayOut for further documentation.

Next, we will print this to-scale right from SketchUp. Zoom in, so that only what you want to print is shown (make sure you have only minimal white space around it). It is also a good idea to arrange everything so that the aspect ratio of the combined items roughly conforms to the printer's paper (i.e., lay everything out horizontally if you intend to use landscape paper orientation).

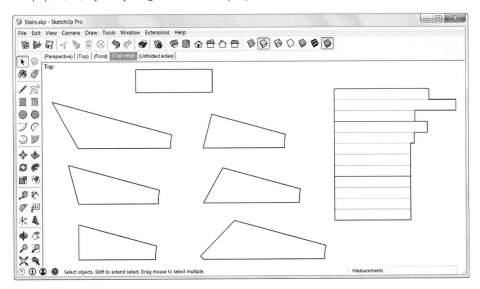

Now you are ready to select **Print...** from the **File** menu. The dialog shown in the following image comes up where you will need to make some adjustments.

First, set the print range to Current View, so that you have control over what is being printed. Also, in the Print Size settings, uncheck both Fit To Page and Use Model Extents. This will let you specify a scale at which to print the model view.

In the Scale settings, you need to provide a usable scale. In my case, the model components print well at a 1/2" = 1' scale, so I entered **0.5 Inches** in the first field and **1 Feet** in the second. Adjust to suit your needs.

TIP

If the scale ends up too large and your model won't print on one sheet, the "To" number of the Tiled Sheet Print Range will increase. To keep control over the model printout, keep this number at 1 and adjust the scale or pick a larger sheet size on your printer/plotter.

Don't forget: You can always try a print preview first using the appropriate **File** menu item.

Finally, you can adjust quality settings for the printout in the dialog. As you can see in the previous figure, I chose the highest quality setting here (Use High Accuracy HLR).

PRO ONLY

Using LayOut for Printouts

Instead of printing from SketchUp, with SketchUp Pro you can open your model in LayOut (using **File → Send to LayOut**) and print from there. This gives you more control over how the model components are arranged on a sheet and lets you add additional annotations such as angular dimensions.

Once your model has been loaded into LayOut, you can go to the SketchUp Model section of the right Default Tray area. As you can see in the following figure, this lets you select a specific scene in SketchUp to be displayed in the view and makes applying standard scales quite easy. You could also adjust display styles here, but we will again keep things simple.

With the model view available in LayOut, add linear and angular dimensions as needed. **Figure 6.9** shows how this can look:

Figure 6.9: Dimensioned treads in LayOut

After printing the flat model views shown previously, you can use the result either as a guide for measuring or as a 1:1 template (depending on the size and scale of your object, of course). **Figure 6.10** shows how the previously shown views were used to make a (rough) paper model of the stairs.

Figure 6.10: A paper model of the stair

TIP	If you have an arbitrarily oriented object that you need to print to scale, you can use the **Align View** context menu tool instead of moving it and laying it flat. This works only on faces, though. Go into editing mode for groups and components to be able to use it.

Entity Info
Erase
Hide

Select ▸
Area ▸
Intersect Faces ▸
Align View
Align Axes
Reverse Faces
Orient Faces

Figure 6.11 shows an application of this approach where 3D beam cuts were transferred to a sheet of paper at 1:1 scale and were later applied to the beam by wrapping the printout around it and scoring all the cut outlines.

Figure 6.11: Transferred cut outlines at 1:1 scale

Quite a few tutorials that apply processes like this to woodworking and carpentry are available on the Internet. As an example, *Design. Click. Build.* is a great blog that covers SketchUp modeling for woodworking:

www.finewoodworking.com/blog/design-click-build

Cutting Prep Tips and Tricks

- When making printed transfer sheets as templates, keep the actual material thickness in mind. Even if you are using a very thin material (sheet metal or thin plywood), a SketchUp printout from a 3D model that contains zero-thickness faces can make things not fit in the end. It is good practice to always model with actual material thickness.

- Likewise, consider bends when you are templating bent edges. Actual material tends to compress when it is bent. An exact 90-degree crease will almost always be impossible, contrary to what you see in SketchUp. Even thin material typically bends with a certain minimum radius.

- Pieces that are arranged flush on cut sheets might not cut at the correct size if you do not consider kerf sizes (the width of the material that is removed by the cut). For manual cutting it is often a good idea to place items apart on such sheets.

Laser Cutting

Depending on the cutting machine's power, material type, and cutting speed, laser cutters are able to either cut all the way through a sheet of material or just engrave a pattern onto its surface. While the majority of the following text assumes you intend to cut sheet material to size, engraving can be useful, too. One example would be adding a pattern to a material's surface to represent brick or siding in a house model. The process of engraving usually simply requires you to specify a lower power for certain lines (edges) or patterns (usually from raster images).

Figure 6.12 shows a typical laser-cutting machine.

Figure 6.12: Laser-cutter *(Image used by permission of Epilog Laser)*

Let's illustrate the process of preparing your SketchUp file and exporting it with a simple example: a mobile made of laser-cut plywood.

Example 6.2: Creating a Laser-Cut Mobile from SketchUp

This example will create the mobile illustrated in **Figure 6.13**. In this version it has only two levels, but you can easily increase its complexity by adding more, if you like.

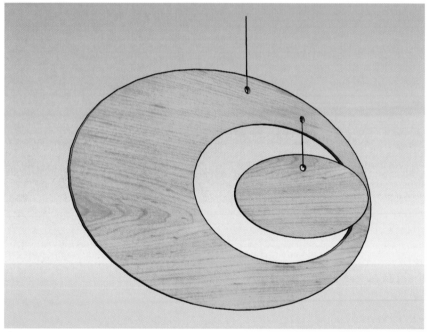

Figure 6.13: A simple, two-level mobile

Your first step will be to model the shape outlines in SketchUp using stretched circles (which turns them into ellipses). Turn the view to top (**Camera → Standard Views → Top**) and to parallel projection (**Camera → Parallel Projection**) before you start doing this because you will just be working on the ground plane. Once you are done, you should have these outlines:

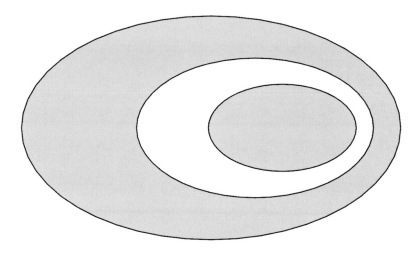

Because this mobile needs to hang in balance, you need to find the centroid of the area that is to be suspended. While this is easy to find for a symmetrical part like the inner ellipse, other shapes, especially curved ones with internal holes (as with the outer shape) require you to use an extension. So before you proceed, make sure you get the Face Centroid and Area Properties extension from the Extension Warehouse. To demonstrate how it works, let's start using it on the ellipse in the middle.

Select the ellipse and right-click on it, and then select the **Get Face Properties** context menu item. For now, ignore the dialog that follows (those properties will change soon anyway) and okay the placement of cross-hairs.

You could place a hole (with the Circle tool) at the center of the cross-hairs (at the centroid), but the mobile piece would not hang very stable vertically. Instead, place it a little higher along the center line, like this:

The hole will be the suspension point for this piece (using a thin thread with negligible weight). As you can see, I also placed a corresponding hole in the outer piece.

Next, you need to find the centroid of the outer piece. To make the extension work in this case, you need to add temporary, single connecting lines to all of the inner openings before you run it again. They are indicated by arrows in the following graphic.

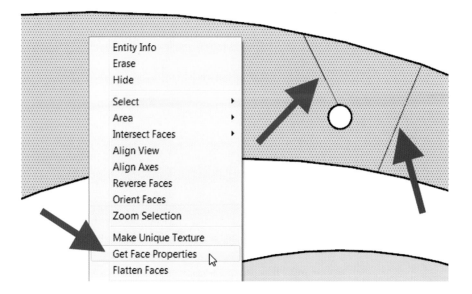

Once you have both centroids, it gets interesting. As shown in **Figure 6.14**, you now have all of the dimensions to get going on the calculations that will equilibrate all forces and give you the location of the suspension line.

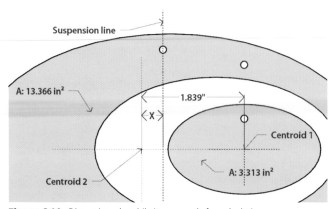

Figure 6.14: Dimensioned mobile items, ready for calculations

In this case, the x-value solves to 0.365 inches (I'll leave it up to you to find out why). You can, therefore, reposition the temporary suspension line and place the overall suspension point there. **Figure 6.15** shows the finalized mobile, ready for processing. As you can see, all of the faces have been removed because we only intend to cut the outlines instead of engraving a pattern on the areas.

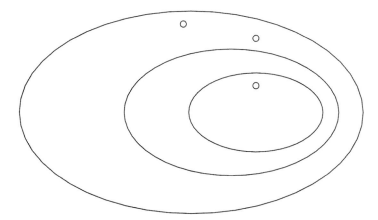

Figure 6.15: Finished mobile with all outlines and holes

At this point, you need a way to export the outlines as vector data from SketchUp. Depending on which version of SketchUp you have (Make or Pro), there are different paths to take.

For the free Make version, try this:

- **Export as a DXF or SVG using an extension.** SketchUp Make natively exports only to SKP and DAE (COLLADA) as save/export formats. You are in luck if you find a way to process DAE files in the laser-cutting driver software. But a working fallback is to find a DXF or SVG export extension (see Chapter 4 for examples) and use those instead.

- **Export as PNG or TIF image (not JPG for its lack of precision) and vectorize.** This method uses raster images as intermediaries and after vectorization requires size calibration of the output (only vector files export sizes, raster files don't). You can vectorize any raster image using the tracing tools in most vector graphics programs (e.g., in Adobe Illustrator).

PRO ONLY

The following export options are available only in the Pro version of SketchUp, which also includes the LayOut illustration software:

- **Export directly from SketchUp to EPS, DWG, or DXF.** This is easily done using File → **Export** → **2D Graphic…**. The default export options should work fine, but you might want to experiment with them. My only words of caution for DWG/DXF export: In the export options, select compatibility with an older version of AutoCAD (e.g., the 2000 version). This frequently makes importing into other software much smoother.

■ **Insert the SketchUp model into LayOut and then export as DWG or DXF.** This works best if you explode the SketchUp model view in LayOut after inserting (right-click on it and select Explode from the context menu). You can then assign line weights and colors as needed:

Depending on the driver setup for your laser cutter, you might even be able to print directly from LayOut.

In many of these file export procedures, you will have to edit the output linework in a vector graphics program (such as Adobe Illustrator, Corel Draw, or the free Inkscape). For the purpose of this exercise, let's assume you want to process the file for uploading to the Ponoko web service. Their specifications require all cutting lines to be 0.01 mm (0.0004 in) wide and blue in color (RGB values: 0/0/255).

Figure 6.16 shows how the linework looks in Adobe Illustrator. You can also see in that image that I ungrouped everything and removed all compound paths (right-click on the selected objects to do so from the context menu). The Stroke and Color tabs also show how you can then assign both line width and color to all of the lines.

Figure 6.16: Linework in Adobe Illustrator

TIP

If you can assign line weights only in the point unit (instead of inches), assign these:

0.72 pt = 0.01 in = 0.254 mm (Ponoko recommendation)

0.072 pt = 0.001 in = 0.0254 mm (Epilog recommendation)

If you upload your designs to Ponoko, you would want to place them onto the templates that they provide on this page (together with many tips and tricks): www.ponoko .com/make-and-sell/design-it-yourself.

If you instead have access to a laser cutter, you probably will have its printer driver installed. Adjust its settings in the Print dialog to your liking.

Laser Cutting Tips and Tricks

IN-DEPTH

- Make sure you set the paper/artboard size in the software from which you print to the laser cutter to the exact sheet size that is available in the machine.

- Always check for double lines in your exported linework. Overlapping lines could cause more cutting than necessary, which might damage the machine or simply cost you more money (if you use a cutting service).

- Cutting curves takes longer than cutting lines. This is a clear case where SketchUp's inability to create real curves can save you real money. Use the minimum number of curve segments necessary when you are working with curves.

CNC Milling

In some ways, CNC milling is similar to laser cutting: it uses a toolhead, which travels over an x-y–type work area and removes material from sheet goods to create shapes. The two main differences are a) the tool (a router bit) typically has a non-negligible width and shape, which leads to a larger milling kerf and affects the smoothness and appearance of the final surface, and b) the tool can travel a certain distance in the z-axis and can thereby provide cuts of varying depths. As mentioned before, industrial CNC machines also have the ability to rotate their tool head, which allows for milling operations from almost any conceivable nonobstructed angle.

Figure 6.17 illustrates the CNC milling process, where a router bit follows a toolpath (shown as a single-line curve), guided by motors that move it along the x-, y-, and z-axes. The workpiece (a wood panel here) is held down by vacuum or through mechanical means, and waste (e.g., wood dust) is pulled away with a dust collector system.

This illustration also shows the resulting kerf that needs to be considered when working with CNC milling. This is particularly crucial for small details and minimum clearances with dimensions that in turn are determined by the bit diameter. While not overly problematic in the previous example, **Figure 6.18** shows a case where you need to make design adjustments to accommodate this process.

Figure 6.17: A CNC toolpath and resulting kerf

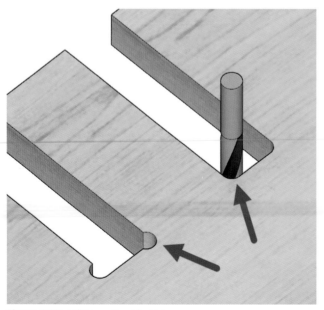

Figure 6.18: Milling reentrant (inside) corners

As you can see in the right example in **Figure 6.18**, inside corners can only be milled with a resulting filleted radius that is based on the router bit's geometry. This can lead to mating pieces (e.g., a tenon and mortise connection) that do not fit into each other after milling. While these corners could certainly be cleaned manually, it is better to *overcut* them as shown in the left portion of the figure. There, two different types of overcuts have been applied that both clear the rectangular area.

Fortunately for us, we typically don't have to worry about these (and other) machine details when we are working in SketchUp. The CNC processing (also called CAM—Computer-Aided Manufacturing) software usually will either automatically take care of these details for us or alert us to manually fix them. It is just important to know about them at this point.

CNC machines of many different sizes are currently available, but the most common ones have a work area of approximately 4′ × 8′ and a vertical travel distance of about 6″. **Figure 6.19** shows some of those.

Figure 6.19: A typical CNC router table and its smaller benchtop cousin *(Images used by permission of Shopbot Tools, Inc.)*

These machines are typically able to handle a variety of materials, from wood and foam to metals. The choice of material typically affects bit types and milling parameters such as cutting speed; however, they are machine-dependent and will, therefore, not be covered here. Follow your machine manufacturer's instructions for those details.

The following describes two cases and shows how you would process your SketchUp files for CNC machining. Both examples employ Vectric's VCarve Pro and Cut3D as the processing and toolpath software; however, the principles are applicable to other CAM software as well (e.g., Mastercam or CamBam).

Example 6.3: Cutting the Patterned Panel

This example uses the patterned panel from Chapter 7 and prepares it for CNC routing to cut out all of the circles. To start, run the Ruby code from Chapter 7 to get the following panel pattern (for a 3′ x 3′ panel).

As you can see, I removed the outline and all faces so that only the circles (i.e., edges) that make up the pattern were left. Because you are milling a work piece cut to exact size, you do not need to include the square perimeter to cut the outline. In this example, you will cut the circle outlines through the entire material thickness and not work with different depth cutting.

At this point, you need to export this geometry to the CNC toolpath-generating CAM software. If that software doesn't natively read SketchUp files, try exporting using the DXF format (via **File → Export → 3D Model...** in SketchUp Pro and a DXF extension in the Make version). In my case, I am in luck because VCarve Pro imports SketchUp SKP files directly.

Next, you need to apply appropriate material and machine parameters that as mentioned can vary between machines and setups. In my case, I went with a 1/4" bit and asked for the shapes to be cut on the inside of the geometry. As you can see in **Figure 6.20**, you can select for the bit to either follow the geometry paths or cut on either side of them. I also went with a full 1/2" drilling depth to cut all the way through the material (in three passes).

Figure 6.20: The cutting toolpath in VCarve Pro

In 2D view, all of the toolpaths become a bit clearer where you can even see in which direction the machine will travel while cutting.

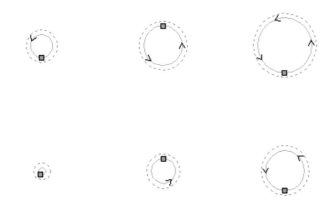

If you intend to apply different parameters to individual toolpaths (e.g., cutting depths, tools, etc.), separate them on different layers in SketchUp before you export the file. CAM software can typically read and process those layers separately.

In this example, all geometry was already arranged in the correct positions for CNC milling. What if you instead had a compound 3D object that was made up of parts, such as a piece of furniture? Let's take the stair from earlier in the chapter as an example here. As you saw in **Figure 6.8**, all of the risers and treads are separately grouped objects in the SketchUp model that need to be laid flat and arranged for CNC processing (e.g., for a scaled model).

You could do this manually in SketchUp akin to what you did in Example 6.1, but often CAM software is able to do that for you. **Figure 6.21** shows how this can look after the CAM software (VCarve Pro in this case) imports an SKP file, lays all the shapes flat on the ground, and then applies a nesting algorithm. This worked here because in the original SketchUp file, each part was grouped individually.

Nesting in CAM software is a process where elements are arranged to minimize material waste and reduce machining time. As shown in **Figure 6.21**, you can typically modify some parameters such as minimum spacing between objects.

All of these examples use CNC milling only for cutting out shapes. The next example goes one step further and investigates how you can mill something that has a bit more depth to it.

Figure 6.21: Nesting imported SketchUp parts in VCarve Pro

Example 6.4: Depth Cutting Profiled Models

For this example, let's assume you intend to process a model that has varying depths in the z-axis, such as a topographic model of a landscape or a sculptural object. To make things easy, let's use a model of the Grand Canyon here.

Follow the instructions from Example 4.5 in Chapter 4 to create the terrain model; only this time around, find some deep valleys from the Grand Canyon (just search for it in the Add Location dialog) to make things interesting. Once you have the "boxy" landscape model, scale it down to a size that your CNC machine can handle.

Next, you need to export this model. Which file format you use for that process depends on your CAM software, so check its manual to find out. In my case, I was able to export the model using the SketchUp STL extension (see Chapter 4) in the STL file format.

To process the machine toolpaths, I used Cut3D by Vectric, but—as mentioned earlier—other software should be able to do this, too. **Figure 6.22** illustrates the resulting steps.

Figure 6.22: Steps in the toolpath processing (top left to bottom right): Original SketchUp model, roughing toolpath visualization, finishing toolpath visualization, all toolpaths as lines

As you can see, a first, "roughing" pass with a coarser bit removes unneeded material efficiently and makes fine finishing passes easier on the machine. This process progresses by removing layers until the rough shape has been revealed.

The next pass uses a round-head bit and finer movements in a logical pattern to finish cutting and smoothing of all surfaces, resulting in the finished piece.

IN-DEPTH

CNC Milling Tips and Tricks

- Because the SketchUp model needs to generate a machine toolpath, it is a good idea to make sure the model outline or other geometry that ultimately defines the toolpath is clean, well-modeled (e.g., straight where it needs to be) and does not have any gaps.

- Of all the techniques in this chapter, CNC milling is likely the one that requires the most intimate knowledge of all aspects of the machine that is being used (and the materials, for that matter). Familiarize yourself with all of your manuals and experiment thoroughly with the various settings.

3D Printing

3D printers come in all sizes and cost ranges—varying from the $400 do-it-yourself kit (e.g., the RepRap printers, see http://reprap.org) to the industrial-size printer that costs as much as a good-size car. Some 3D printer models are shown in **Figure 6.23**.

Figure 6.23: Two 3D printer sizes: Desktop-size (left) and full-size (right) *(Images used by permission of MakerBot Industries LLC and Stratasys Ltd.)*

Let's start by making your SketchUp models printable.

Preparing Your SketchUp Model for 3D Printing

As you know, SketchUp is not a solid modeler, yet you are going to print a solid object. Therefore, there are a few rules to be followed regarding what you can print and how you need to prepare your model to be 3D printable. The main rule is, the more careful you are while modeling, the less hassle cleanup and processing will be. Make sure your object has only necessary geometry and no leftover edges or faces. Also make good use of groups and components to organize and build your model, and finally, use inferences, snaps, and dimension entry whenever feasible.

To be 3D printable, an object coming from SketchUp to a 3D printing processing software usually has to be a *solid* group or component. As discussed previously, this is also called a *watertight* object (that has no holes) or a *manifold* (that has no overlapping or errant geometry). In SketchUp, the Volume property in the Entity Info window is the main tool to find out if a group or component object is a solid. This property is shown only when a group or a component is selected *and* this object is a watertight solid. **Figure 6.24** shows the Entity Info window for two groups, where the left one is a solid and the right one is not (because its top is open).

In some cases, what you want to 3D print may in SketchUp have zero thickness. One example of this would be a very thin-walled vase, created by lofting a surface over three guiding curves. **Figure 6.25** shows the curves on the left and the vase on the right. As you can see, the top is open and the walls are made up of just faces (that have no thickness).

Figure 6.24: A solid group (left) and a non-solid one (right)

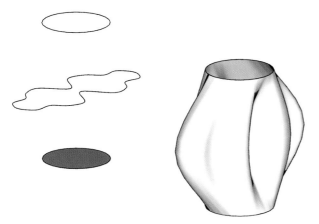

Figure 6.25: A lofted vase

To be able to properly 3D print this, you need to thicken the walls before you export this object. With a complex shape like this, none of the native SketchUp tools will be able to do this—at least not efficiently. You will, therefore, need to load an extension (see Chapter 4 for more information about extensions in SketchUp).

The best extension for this case is Fredo6's JointPushPull Interactive tool; however, another useful extension is ThomThom's Shell. I used the first here, which lets you easily thicken the walls by a given amount (1/8″ in my case) as the following graphic shows:

The result of this operation is shown in **Figure 6.26**, where you can nicely see the complexity of the original geometry and the thickness of all of the walls and the base.

Figure 6.26: After thickening the vase

As **Figure 6.27** shows, although important, wall thickness is not the only thing you want to consider at this point. You also need to look at tight corners in your model (e.g., at the bottom of the "e" in this case) and thicken thin bridges that could otherwise break off when you remove the print from the printer. This is especially necessary if any mechanical stress will later be put on the object.

You also want to avoid areas in your model that will not stay in place after printing (like the inner part of the "e") and provide attachments or other means of fixing those in place.

Figure 6.27: Problematic areas in a model

If you use a 3D printing service, check its material-specific tutorials, which will explain these parameters in sufficient detail. The various 3D printing materials usually have specific minimum dimensions, published in those tutorials.

The following example shows various techniques you can use to create a clean, solid compound model in SketchUp that is ready for exporting and processing.

Example 6.5: Cleaning Up a Model for 3D Printing

Let's assume for the purpose of this exercise that you would like to merge a letter (made with SketchUp's 3D Text tool) with a slanted block so that you can 3D print the combined object as shown in **Figure 6.28**. Let's also assume you want to do all model cleanup in SketchUp and not in an external program.

For my example, I grouped each object separately before placing the objects in their over-lapping position. This has the benefit that they don't stick to each other while moving, and I am starting off with two watertight solids (as you can see, the Entity Info dialog shows a volume). Of course, this is just one example and the following techniques work equally well with geometry that is completely created from scratch.

Figure 6.28: Two separate objects: a 3D "a" and a slanted block

---

For these images, I turned on Back Edge Display, which shows any hidden edges as dashed lines. This is a very helpful feature when you are "chasing edges" inside objects. You can show back edges via the **View → Edge Style → Back Edges** menu item. Alternatively, you can use the X-ray face style via **View → Face Style → X-ray** to see inside objects.

In addition, turning on hidden line display might be necessary, too. Do so via **View → Hidden Geometry**.

Method 1: Using the Outer Shell Tool

The Outer Shell tool that can be found on the **Tools** menu lets you select any number of individual, intersecting watertight solids (such as my letter and block groups) and will merge them automatically into one. In that process, all overlapping, internal geometry will be removed, leaving only the combined shell. This approach is often called *shrink wrapping* because it creates a single shell, similar to having objects wrapped with one layer of shrink wrap. As you can see in the following graphic, the result is a perfect combination.

This approach, however, requires that all of the selected objects are watertight solid groups or components. Otherwise, the tool will not work at all.

PRO ONLY   Alternatively to Outer Shell, SketchUp Pro users can work with other Solid Tools like Union, which combines objects one by one.

Method 2: Using Intersect and Manual Cleanup

This is the more tedious method because you manually have to remove any rogue geometry. It is a good idea to master this technique, though, because it might be necessary even in combination with other cleanup methods.

For a model like the example here, you would start by exploding everything, selecting all of the edges and faces, and then running the Intersect with Selection tool. The following image uses the context-menu item to do this, but you can also access the tool from the **Edit** menu.

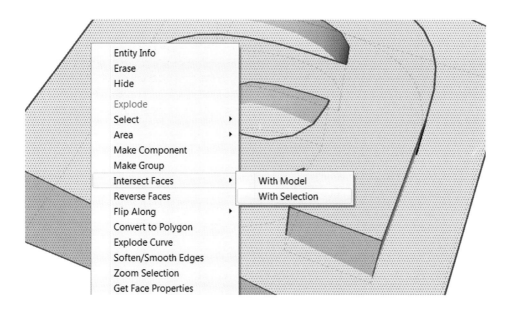

Once everything has been intersected (with itself), you will need to hide an outside surface (for example, the top of the "a" here) and then using the eraser manually, remove all of the internal geometry that is not part of the outer shell.

After cleaning up the geometry and unhiding the top of the "a" (**Edit → Unhide → All**), you can regroup everything and see if SketchUp now thinks of this as a watertight solid. If it doesn't (and the Entity Info dialog doesn't display a volume), it is time to go back into the model and search for whatever you missed. Fortunately, there are a few tools that can help you along the way:

■ ThomThom's Solid Inspector extension, which you can find on the Extension Warehouse, will identify holes and rogue geometry in your model. It doesn't fix those errors, but at least you can look for the colored circles and find what you have missed.

■ TIG's SolidSolver extension, which you can find in the SketchUcation Plugin Store, will try to fix any problems that it finds automatically. His approach works very well in some cases and completely ruins the model in others, requiring an Undo. The success of the automatic approach is very much dependent on how severely messed up your model was to begin with. The following graphic shows how it automatically filled in a hole, albeit with many faces.

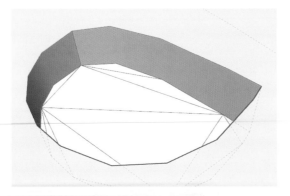

Finally, even if you correctly created a watertight solid and SketchUp happily shows you its volume, it is sometimes important for the slicing software that there are no reversed faces. Therefore, switch to monochrome view mode briefly using the **View** → **Face Style** → **Monochrome** menu item to see if there are any reversed (light blue) faces and flip them (e.g., using the context menu). **Figure 6.29** shows the completed object that still has one reversed face.

Figure 6.29: A watertight solid with a reversed face

At this point you are ready to export the model for further processing.

IN-DEPTH

How to Make Anything Printable

Admittedly, that is a tall order. Often you will find that a model you would like to 3D print (e.g., from the 3D Warehouse) has not been modeled with sufficient care or with 3D printing in mind. Short of remodeling the object, the nuclear option might be your best bet. Here's my workflow for those cases:

1. Load the object into SketchUp.
2. Explode the object all the way to its base geometry. Select everything and intersect it with itself (Intersect With Selection).
3. Clean up the most obvious errant geometry manually using the Eraser tool.
4. Group everything and try the Outer Shell or Union tools or the Solid Solver extension. Sometimes applying several passes can get you results.

It is usually helpful to go into the Materials window and delete all the materials in your model. This reduces the file size and makes it easier to see things. And unless you are 3D printing in full color, textures won't be needed anyway.

An alternative to this approach has been implemented by the SketchUp folks into 3D Warehouse (in collaboration with i.materialise). You can actually upload any model to it (using the methods described in Chapter 4) and select I Want This To Be 3D Printable in the upload dialog. This will automatically fix mistakes and create a 3D printable model that you can download as an STL file.

For some models and especially if you are just starting out with 3D printing, it might be best to work only with solids. To do that, load the Place Shapes toolbar or Shapes extension from the Extension Warehouse and use its standard shapes (box, sphere, etc.) to build your model. You can add text using SketchUp's 3D Text tool as well. Scale the shapes using the Scale tool and intersect and subtract them using SketchUp's Solid Tools (don't explode anything!). This will yield a 3D printable object where you don't have to worry about stray geometry.

In addition to cleaning up a model for printing, sometimes it is necessary to rearrange a model so that it can be printed easily. The following example illustrates such a case:

Example 6.6: 3D Printing a Cutaway View

Let's assume you want to print a scaled-down cutaway model of a two-story interior, complete with structure, columns, doors, and some furniture. As you can see in **Figure 6.30**, this model features several overhangs and cantilevers. The second floor overhangs the first, and the roof structure is only shown as half, which removes its support on the right side and forces it to cantilever from the left supporting wall.

Because a 3D print is built from the bottom up, the furniture, railing, and the doors on the first floor pose no problem at all, independent of which 3D printing method is used. Also, the overhangs over the door openings are small enough that even an FDM print can create them without requiring supports. In that case, the soft filament simply stretches over the opening and hardens in place (shortening slightly when it cools, thereby straightening itself out).

Figure 6.30: Interior cutaway model for 3D printing

The problematic parts are the second floor slab and the roof structure. If they were printed in place (as shown in **Figure 6.30**), they would require temporary supports during printing. As described previously, powder-based printing techniques use unhardened powder for temporary support and are better able to handle larger overhangs and openings than filament-based printers. Nevertheless, the roof structure might still fail since its connection to the rest of the model is very small.

If this were an FDM print, all of the overhanging parts would need to be temporarily supported with cutaway material. Printer processing (*slicing*) software can typically add those automatically. However, removing those supports after printing might be problematic and might break the model.

To facilitate printing of this model, we will employ a technique that breaks everything up into easily printable, bottom-heavy parts. This process is facilitated by the fact that every item in this model (each column, beam, door, etc.) was modeled as a separate group (components would have worked, too). Each of those was also carefully modeled so that they all constitute watertight solid objects (as described earlier). When this is the case, the next step in the process is to simply select all of the objects on each of the levels and fuse them into one object by the level. This is shown in **Figure 6.31** with numbers 1, 2, and 3 showing the final parts.

Figure 6.31 The model after the Outer Shell operations

To begin, the first floor slab, wall, doors, columns, and furniture were selected and combined with SketchUp's Outer Shell tool (**Tools** → **Outer Shell**). As mentioned earlier in the chapter, this tool only works on solid objects and will *shrinkwrap* everything.

Once the three main parts have been created, all that is left to do is to separate them and place them with their flat side down on the ground (see **Figure 6.32**). Use proper object snapping here so that you don't run into any alignment issues when you preprocess the model in your slicing software. You are now ready to export this model as an STL file.

Figure 6.32: Arranged parts, ready for 3D printing

TIP

Because of their relatively small diameter, the columns might still not print well in this arrangement. FDM printers move quite fast and therefore thin, vertical objects can deform while printing. In that case, try slowing down print speed or producing the columns with another material (e.g. cut-off wooden dowels).

If after printing and assembling this model the half-structure of the roof is still too unstable, then it might be a good idea to add a clear acrylic sheet to the right side of the model and attach it to the floor and roof structure (or simply model the other half).

Exporting and Processing Your Model Outside of SketchUp

For 3D printing, you will likely want to export your model either as an STL file or a DAE file. While COLLADA DAE export is natively available in SketchUp (both Make and Pro versions), STL export requires an extension. Fortunately, the SketchUp folks and a few users have developed an STL exporter extension called SketchUp STL, which you can find in the Extension Warehouse. The following graphic shows its export options.

After the export, you have an STL file that is readable by any 3D printing processing software. If you prefer to use the DAE file format instead, go to **File → Export → 3D Model...** and use the default options for the export.

For the purpose of this text, I will be showing how an STL-exported model now gets processed for the MakerBot Replicator 3D printer using the MakerWare software (see **Figure 6.33**). Depending on which 3D printer (or online service) you use, the following steps are likely quite similar. Many of the online printing services even do this step for you and will only let you know if they run into trouble with your model.

Figure 6.33: A house model loaded as an STL file into MakerBot's MakerWare software

In principle, this next step consists of slicing the entire model into horizontal layers, with thickness that is determined by the raw material used (e.g., plastic filament or granules), typically around 0.2 mm. Often, slicing software is also capable of automatically adding a raft (a base support for the print) and supports for overhanging features (especially if an FDM or SLA printer is used). Thick, solid volumes in an object are also often only partially filled (e.g., with only 10 percent of material) for economy. **Figure 6.34** shows MakerWare's Export dialog and illustrates these and more options (like the print speed and temperature).

Previewing this particular example's toolpaths (see **Figure 6.35**), we get a visualization of the printing process as well as an estimate of the material use and the time it takes to make this print. For example, we now know that based on a kg-price of a spool of filament, this print will set us back $5.56 in material cost. As you can see, larger prints are also best done overnight and shouldn't be started too close to a deadline.

Figure 6.34: Export options in MakerWare

Figure 6.35: Toolpath visualization

Finally, the 3D print can be started at this point. The slicing software generates all of the necessary G-code that drives the printing machine and the printer can now get to work.

One word of caution about the entire process: Sometimes neither SketchUp nor the slicing software can fix all of the problems in your model. This is especially the case if you are trying to print a 3D-scanned mesh that is completely free-form and often contains holes. In that case, you will need to use other software as an intermediary that is able to fix those models. Some of the options include:

- **Meshlab**—http://meshlab.sourceforge.net
- **Meshmixer**—www.meshmixer.com
- **Microsoft's mesh repair service**—https://modelrepair.azurewebsites.net
- **Netfabb** (Basic or full version)—www.netfabb.com

3D Printing Tips and Tricks   `IN-DEPTH`

- 3D printing can produce highly accurate objects, but there is a lower size limit. When objects get too small, plastic can't cool fast enough and might get distorted during printing. You might want to increase some sizes (e.g. for very slender columns) in your models manually to prevent this. If your processing software (the slicer) allows this, add cooling pauses after each layer. Alternatively, try rotating the object on its side; it may print better in that orientation.

- Simpler models are faster to print. Often you have no choice about including detail; but if you can, simplify your model as much as possible. It does not make sense to include detail below the size of the printed filament layer. Adjust the model resolution based on the available material.

- For very small parts or moving parts such as hinge pins in a 3D model, a change of material might be in order. Replace them with metal pieces, for example (e.g., small nails), so that the mechanical stress does not wear them out. As you can see in **Figure 6.6**, the muntin windows of the house model were printed flat to preserve their detail.

- The object you are intending to print must have its base on the 3D printer's bed (at z=0) before slicing. If you print a single object, then the slicing software can usually drop it to that level. If you, however, are printing many objects at the same time (e.g., a chess set), then you must make sure all of the objects are at the same base level. To check this in SketchUp, draw a rectangle on the ground (at z=0) and watch from underneath for flickering faces (called "z-fighting") at the base of all the objects. If one does not flicker, then it needs to be dropped to the ground.

For More Information About Making

The field of making and digitally fabricating is a large one, and lots of great information is available these days. For more detailed descriptions of some of the presented techniques and case-study examples, refer to the following books:

- Daniel Schodek, Martin Bechthold, James Kimo Griggs, Kenneth Kao, Marco Steinberg, *Digital Design and Manufacturing* (Hoboken: John Wiley & Sons, 2004).
- Nick Dunn, *Digital Fabrication in Architecture* (London: Laurence King, 2012).

You can find these and more relevant book recommendations in the "Further Reading" section of this book's companion website at http://sketchupfordesign.com.

Your Turn!

The following tasks allow you to practice the topics in this chapter:

1. **Make your own laser- or CNC-cut mobile.**
   Given the instructions in this chapter, design and fabricate a mobile. Apply all cuts and holes in the SketchUp model, so that you just need to tie the connecting threads to assemble.

2. **Create a useful object.**
   Design and fabricate an object using 3D printing that will make your life easier. For example, make a flashlight holder for your bike, a cup holder for your desk, or anything else you can dream up. For mechanical parts, combine 3D printing with hardware such as metal bolts as necessary.

3. **Cast an object.**
   Create a cast object where the formwork is made using any of the techniques in this chapter. Use low-shrinkage mortar or cheap concrete from the hardware store as casting material. Make sure you design your formwork fully in SketchUp.

4. **Make something four ways.**
   Produce the same object or shape with all four manufacturing techniques in this chapter. For example, design a chair and evaluate how you would have to break it down to fabricate it (at varying scales) using laser cutting, 3D printing, etc.

5. **3D print yourself.**
   If you have access to a laser scanner (or one of the various 3D scanning smartphone apps (like Trnio or Autodesk's 123D Catch), scan someone's head and fabricate it using any of the techniques presented here. This gives you the opportunity to 3D print yourself or make a great gift for a loved one!

Chapter 7
Creating Geometry
Using Ruby Scripting

In this chapter, you will create scripted geometry in SketchUp. Often called *computational geometry,* this is an exciting current topic that allows you to produce 3D shapes and arrangements that are impossible (or at least hard) to create by hand. Scripting in SketchUp also allows you to automatize repetitive tasks or facilitate data exchange with text files.

If you are new to scripting (or *coding*), then this chapter can serve as a great general introduction. You will learn principles that are common to many scripting languages, and you will apply those to creating items in SketchUp's 3D environment—items that you can even fabricate (using instructions from Chapter 6).

Key Topics:

- What is computational geometry?
- Using Ruby Scripts in SketchUp
- Working with multiline editors
- Introduction to Ruby
- Overview of SketchUp's API
- Creating scripted geometry
- Transforming geometry
- Modifying geometry based on attractors

Why Computational Geometry?

Even to the most seasoned SketchUp user, some tasks are challenging to complete by hand, using only the tools SketchUp provides. A good example is the creation of copies of a component where all the copies need to be placed at locations that vary not only linearly (e.g., "place a copy every 16 inches") but also in intervals that are determined by a formula (e.g., where the y-coordinate is determined by the square of x—which, of course, results in the shape of a parabola; see **Figure 7.1**).

Another example is a curved building with window-shading devices that need to be designed such that the degree to which they shade or open is determined by how far they deviate from the southern direction. (See **Figure 7.2**.)

Figure 7.1: A parabola-shaped park

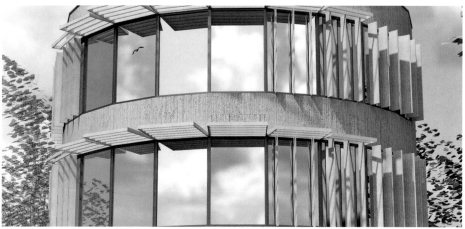

Figure 7.2: Parametric solar shading

Such tasks can sometimes be accomplished using one of the available extensions. However, those extensions are usually limited to the supplied feature set and are hard or impossible to modify to your needs. As it turns out, some complex tasks may actually be easier to script in a few lines of code than to model by hand.

Fortunately, for the user, both versions of SketchUp (Make and Pro) come with a scripting language preinstalled and readily available. Also, when it comes to scripting, there is almost no difference between the feature sets of the Make and Pro versions, providing the user of either version with a significant tool set. Only Pro-specific features (such as the Solid Tools' Boolean methods) are inaccessible from the Make scripting interface.

The scripting language SketchUp uses is called Ruby. This language, created in the mid-1990s by Yukihiro "Matz" Matsumoto in Japan, might be unknown to many software users (Microsoft Office products usually ship with another language called VisualBasic and websites typically use a language called JavaScript). However, it has been a very popular language among web application developers, and many large and popular websites (Twitter, Groupon, and Hulu are among them) run on code written in Ruby. Besides, it is a modern, object-oriented language that is actually quite easy to learn, as you will see. (See **Figure 7.3**.)

SketchUp itself provides a large variety of tools and procedures that are available to the Ruby scripting language using what is called an application programming interface (API). This gives you access to tools such as Move or Copy, as well as the entire collection of objects and materials in your SketchUp model, through many well-documented functions.

Having said all of this, it is important to note that any tool or method has its limitations. Consequently, scripting in SketchUp also has limitations. For example, curved shapes are not implemented as perfect curves, in SketchUp's tool set nor in the API. Because SketchUp is a polygon-based modeling software, it naturally does not have a way to define perfect curves. As you know, circles are always made up of several polylines in a SketchUp model. While this certainly is a limitation, it is also impor-

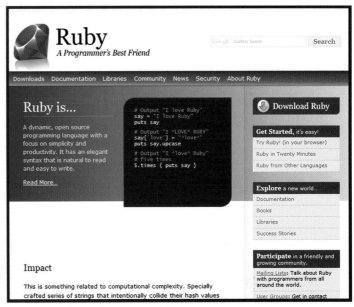

Figure 7.3: The Ruby language's website

tant to keep in mind that in real construction, curved shapes may be approximated by planar elements (e.g., plane glass panes on a curved-looking facade)—often for constructability and cost reasons. As a result, SketchUp's API does not natively support NURBS (nonuniform rational B-splines)—at least not without a plugin. This is better implemented in other software programs (McNeel's Rhinoceros and Autodesk's AutoCAD, Revit, and Maya, for example).

Nevertheless, creating scripted geometry is quite possible in any version of SketchUp, which lowers barriers of entry and offers the potential for everyone to dabble in this exciting field and create advanced geometry (e.g., for 3D printing).

This chapter approaches SketchUp scripting in a pragmatic way. This means that every step in the process of geometry creation and manipulation does not necessarily have to be scripted—after all, we are not writing an extension, and SketchUp already has a great set of built-in modeling tools. As shown in Chapter 4, there are also quite a few excellent extensions that tremendously help with our modeling. We'll script only what can't efficiently be modeled by hand, thereby using standard SketchUp modeling tools to start or finish a project.

First, let's set up your computer so that you can easily script using Ruby.

Setting Up Your Computer

Before you do any modifications to SketchUp, let's use Ruby as SketchUp provides it to get you started quickly. In SketchUp, look for a menu item in the *Window* menu called Ruby Console. When you click on it, you should see the dialog shown here.

This is the built-in interface for the Ruby scripting language. It works simply by accepting a line of code in the text box at the bottom. Once you press Enter, the line is executed, and the result appears in the field at the top of the box.

Let's try this out: Enter `puts "Hello World!"` into the text field and press the Return (or Enter) key. The result shown here should appear in the dialog.

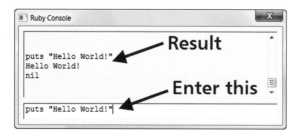

Because the `puts` command simply prints something to the result part of the dialog, all you get as a result is the `Hello World!` string.

You can even get a little more "programmy" by assigning variables. First, enter `a = "Hello World!"`, press the Return key, and then enter `puts a`. You will find that you get the same result. In this case, however, you assigned a text string to a variable first.

Let's try something a bit more useful—let's do some calculations. As it turns out, you can essentially use this dialog as a built-in calculator. Enter `2*16`, and you should get a result of `32`. You can use any of the common mathematical symbols here such as `+`, `−`, `/`, `*`, and `**` for power (as in `2**4` equals 16) as well as parentheses to structure calculations.

To make things more interesting, let's try a square root. Enter `Math::sqrt(10)` and you should see `3.16227766016838` as the result. Nice, isn't it?

As you might have guessed, you can use any of the usual mathematical operators and functions here. This is the complete list of all built-in math functions: `acos`, `erfc`, `asin`, `atan`, `cosh`, `sinh`, `tanh`, `acosh`, `asinh`, `atanh`, `exp`, `log`, `log10`, `sqrt`, `atan2`, `frexp`, `cos`, `ldexp`, `sin`, `hypot`, `tan`, `erf`. Just make sure you precede them with `Math::` (include the double-colon).

TIP	When using any trigonometric functions such as `sin` for the sine of an angle, keep in mind that the argument must be in radians. You must add `.degrees` (including the dot) to the angle to get the correct answer. Example: `Math::sin(45.degrees)` results in 0.707.

While this is all great, the preceding examples use only the scripting language Ruby itself. Let's try an example where you actually get SketchUp to do something. Enter the following line of code into the Ruby Console:

```
Sketchup.active_model.entities.add_face [0,0,0],[0,10,0],[0,10,10]
```

Once you press Return, you should see a triangle appear in SketchUp's modeling area (at the origin, to be exact). It should look like **Figure 7.4**.

You can even access some of SketchUp's user interface components. Just for fun, let's open a File Selection dialog. Enter this code:

```
UI.openpanel 'Select any file please'
```

As you can see, this one-liner opens a dialog, lets you select any file, and returns its location on your computer (the complete path) in the results part of the Ruby Console. Don't worry—nothing will happen to the file. All you did was ask yourself for a filename.

As you can see in these examples, the Ruby Console is already very powerful. Although it can execute multiline scripts (press Ctrl+Return to advance a line), it is not very comfortable to work with. For an easier approach, you need to enhance SketchUp with an extension.

Installing the Ruby Code Editor Extension

Throughout the rest of this chapter, you'll use the free Ruby Code Editor extension to edit and run Ruby code within SketchUp. While this extension is a convenient way to accomplish the task, there are other methods and extensions that work well—they will be described later.

Here's what you need to do:

Go to the Extension Warehouse in SketchUp and install the Ruby Code Editor extension from there (see instructions in Chapter 4 on how to browse the Extension Warehouse and install extensions). Alternatively, you can install the extension from the SketchUcation Plugin Store or download it from my website: www.alexschreyer.net/projects/sketchup-ruby-code-editor.

You should then see the following menu item in the **Window** menu (next to the **Ruby Console** menu item you used earlier). The extension also installs a one-button toolbar that you can use instead. Click on it to start up the code editor.

The Ruby Code Editor starts up as a dialog in SketchUp. **Figure 7.5** shows what it should look like on your screen.

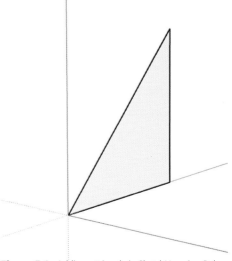

Figure 7.4: Adding a triangle in SketchUp using Ruby code

Figure 7.5: Ruby Code Editor

You can try it out by entering into the editor area any of the code examples that you worked with before. In the example shown in **Figure 7.6**, you perform these steps:

1. Insert the line of code that adds a triangle to the model.

2. Click the Run button, and the triangle will appear on the screen.

3. If you don't like what you just did, simply click the Undo button next to the Run button to undo the drawing of the triangle.

Figure 7.6: First example in the Ruby Code Editor

As you can see, the Ruby Code Editor has a few advantages over SketchUp's Ruby Console. For example, you can enter multiline text, the source code is highlighted appropriately, and you have Run and Undo buttons. Furthermore, you can save and open code snippet files and even work on files in HTML and other languages. There is also a handy drop-down that lets you insert common code snippets at the current cursor position. For now, we'll ignore some of the more advanced features. Just peruse the editor and discover some of its tools on your own terms.

Now you are ready to tackle all of the examples in this chapter.

More Extensions and External Editors

There are some alternatives (all free) to my Ruby Code Editor extension that have similar functionality. All of them work fine with the examples in this book.

■ **Ruby Console+**—An excellent code editor by Aerilius that also features many common scripting tools: autocomplete, code folding, etc. Get it from the Extension Warehouse.

■ **SketchUp Developer Tools**—A set of developer tools by the SketchUp folks that contains an improved Ruby Console. Get it from the Extension Warehouse.

■ **WebConsole** by Jim Folz and **Ruby Console Pro** by Martin Rinehart—Look for those on the SketchUcation forums.

■ **On-Demand Plugin Loader**—You can use the first menu item (Load Single Plugin/ Extension) to execute any Ruby code from an external RB file.

If you prefer not to use extensions at all, or if you like using an external code editor, you can use this method:

1. Using any text (or Ruby code) editor you like, create a text file `source.rb` (or similar) in any convenient location, such as in the root of the C: drive.

2. Add some Ruby code to it and save the file.

3. Open the Ruby Console in SketchUp and type the following line when you are ready to run the code: `load 'C:\source.rb'`.

4. This loads all code from the file and executes (runs) it line by line.

TIP

If you prefer the external-editor method and you become more familiar with writing Ruby code, then it might be a good idea to add the load script to SketchUp as a menu item (using a small plugin that you will have to write). This will give you one-click access to the function.

Another more-advanced method that even allows you to access SketchUp debugging from an external editor is the SketchUp Ruby API Debugger, which you can find here:

https://github.com/SketchUp/sketchup-ruby-debugger

Intro to Ruby and the SketchUp API

This section gives you a primer for the Ruby language as well as an overview of the most important aspects of SketchUp's API. If you need more in-depth information, follow any of the links at the end of the section.

For the impatient: If you prefer to just get things going without learning the basics of the language first, then skip this section and go to some of the code samples in the next section (starting on page 333). You can copy and paste them to get immediate results. Any of them work as they are when you run them in SketchUp. You can always come back later and read up on the basics here.

How Does Ruby Work?

Objects, Objects, Objects

Ruby is essentially an object-oriented language. Everything in the language is an object, and every object has properties and methods. You can always apply any appropriate method to an object. You can even add more methods, if you like. Here's what I mean.

Assume you have an object `an_object`, and the object has a method `a_method` that does something with it. You can apply the method to the object simply by adding it with a dot, as in `an_object.a_method`. If you want to apply more than one method, you can simply chain them, as in `an_object.a_method.another_method` (as long as they are compatible). Here are some examples that make this a bit clearer.

"Hello World!" is a string, as you saw earlier. It is also a string object that has some built-in methods. One of those is length. You can, therefore, enter "Hello World!".length, which yields 12, the length of the string in characters.

An example for chaining methods is 125.to_s.length, which gives the result 3. Now, what happened here? You started with 125, which Ruby automatically interprets as a number (an integer, actually). You then applied a conversion method to it (to_s), which converts the number object to a string. Finally, you added the length method that tells you the length of the string in characters, which, of course, is 3.

A similar operation in SketchUp is converting from one unit system to another. As you know by now, internally SketchUp uses inches as its base unit, no matter which localized version you are using. If you want to convert a number in inches to, say, centimeters, you can simply use the built-in numeric function to_cm to get the correct value. Therefore, entering 1.to_cm results in 2.54.

As you learn more about methods, you will likely come across these two strange-looking types of methods (shown here as examples):

- my_string.upcase!—A method with an exclamation mark at the end modifies the original object in place (in this example, it turns a string into uppercase). Therefore, you don't need to assign it to another variable.

- my_string.include?—A method with a question mark checks something on the object and results in a true or false (Boolean) answer. The example method shown here checks whether a string includes a substring.

One important principle to understand about object-oriented programming languages like Ruby is that objects (and the classes that define them) have one or more ancestors (*parents*). Analogous to the way we receive our parents' genes, objects in Ruby receive (*inherit*) their parent's methods and properties. For example, the Edge object in SketchUp, whose parent is the Drawingelement object, has a bounds property (its bounding box) that it inherits from that object, although by itself it doesn't have this property (as you can see in Appendix C). This may sound confusing at first, but you will soon find that it is a very useful principle.

Storing Stuff: Variables and Constants

As demonstrated, you can simply assign anything to a variable name of your choosing (e.g., a = 1.2). This works with a string, a float number, an integer, an array, or an object. You don't have to even declare the variable's type as you often need to do in other programming languages.

TIP

When using variables, start the name with a lowercase letter or an underscore (_). Uppercase first letters are reserved for methods and constants (e.g., for Math::PI). You can assign constants then like MYNAME = "Alex".

You can even mix types in your calculations, for example:

```
a = 1.2   # a float number
b = 2   # an integer number
a * b
```

This correctly gives you `2.4` as the result. Just keep in mind that numbers stored as strings don't automatically convert in your calculations; use `to_f` (for float numbers) and `to_i` (for integers) first. If you had started the three lines of code with `a = "1.2"` (with the quotation marks, thereby defining this as a string), the calculation would not have worked. The last line would have to be changed to `a.to_f * b` instead.

> **TIP**
> A useful constant is `__FILE__` (with two underscores on either side of the word `FILE`). It always gives you the current Ruby file's name and location.

It is important to remember that these variables are local variables. This means that they work only where they were declared (within a program or a function). If you need a variable to work everywhere (globally), add a dollar sign to the front: `$a`. Use those sparingly, though.

If you want to use a collection of items, it is often best to store them in an array. An array can, for example, contain a set of coordinates, names, or values. There are two ways to add elements to an array. Either do it when you create the array:

```
names = ["Michael", "John", "Agnes"]
```

or first create an empty array and then add elements (to the end):

```
names []
names.push ("Michael", "John", "Agnes")
```

If you want to access an element of an array, write (in this example) `names[1]` to get "John". Always remember that an array starts at index zero!

As in other programming languages, Ruby has a large set of useful functions to accomplish a whole lot of operations on arrays, such as sorting and reversing (see Appendix B for a handy reference).

> **TIP**
> In addition to classic arrays, Ruby can store key-value pairs of information in a special kind of array, a *hash*.
> ```
> grades = Hash["Mike" => 88, "Lucie" => 99]
> ```

Some String Peculiarities

If you use single quotes (as in `'Hello'`) to define a string, the text will be output as is. If you use double quotes (as in `"Hello"`) to define a string, any inline variable (as in `#{myvar}`) or command (such as the newline command `\n`) within the string will be interpreted. Also, if your text contains quotes themselves, you must escape them with a leading backslash (`\`). Here is an example that illustrates this:

```
author = 'someone'
puts 'This is #{author}\'s text.\nWho wrote it?'
```

will output `This is #{author}'s text.\nWho wrote it?`.
If you use double quotes instead:

```
author = 'someone'
puts "This is #{author}\'s text.\nWho wrote it?"
```

this will be the result:

```
This is someone's text.
Who wrote it?
```

As you can see, the newline was interpreted as such, and the `author` variable was inserted into the string. Other useful escape strings are `\t` for inserting a tab and `\\` for getting a single backslash.

If you want to use a formatted string, use the `format` or `sprintf` function, as in:

```
sprintf("%s: %d", "Value", 123)
```

This outputs `Value: 123`. As shown here, you can easily assign variables to placeholders this way. This is very useful if you want to write a formatted string to a file.

Reusing Stuff: Declaring and Using Methods

As always, the more you do with what you already have, the better. Therefore, if you reuse the same functionality more than once in your script, it makes sense to "package" it into a method. Ruby does this by simply using the `def` keyword:

```
def my_function( salutation, name )
    puts "Hello, #{salutation} #{name}"
    return name.length
end

len = my_function( "Mr.", "Bond" )
puts "Your name is #{len} characters long"
```

As you can see, you can assign attributes (such as *name*) to a method, let it do things, and even return values.

With Ruby being an object-oriented language, the most elegant (and language-appropriate) way to reuse code is to write a class that defines methods and variables and then use it by declaring a new object instance based on this class. Because the main focus of this chapter is to create geometry and to get you started quickly in Ruby, the discussion of classes is intentionally omitted here.

Controlling Things: *IF/THEN/ELSE*

You may want to do something in your code after checking something else. You can do this easily with the following lines:

```
length = 10
if length < 10
    puts "Short"
elsif length > 10
    puts "Long"
else
    puts "Exactly 10"
end
```

Modify this snippet to meet your needs. For example, you don't need the `elsif` or `else` parts if all you are checking for is `length < 10`. Also, the complete list of comparative operators is `<`, `>`, `==`, `<=`, `>=`, and `!=` for "not equal." You can combine comparisons using `&&` for "and" and `||` for "or" as in `length == 10 && color == 'blue'`.

There are other ways to use the `if` statement, too. Here are some examples:

```
# used as a statement modifier
puts 'Exactly 10' if length == 10

# used as a one-liner
if length == 10: puts 'Exactly 10' end

# the 'ternary operator' version for assignment
label = length == 10 ? 'Exactly 10': 'Not 10'
```

You can always use the exclamation mark to negate a comparison, as in `!(length == 10)`.

TIP

Beyond `IF`, other control structures are `UNLESS`, which works similarly to `IF` and uses the same structure, and `CASE`, which applies code based on variable switches.

Repeating Things: *FOR, WHILE,* and *More*

Whenever you need to repeat code in a loop, Ruby actually has various ways to let you do this. Let's look at some of them. First is the classic `for` loop:

```
for i in 1..10
    print i
end
```

As you can see, this uses a range (`1..10`) to describe how often this code should repeat. Another version is the `WHILE` statement:

```
num = 1
while num < 10 do
```

```
        print num
        num += 1
    end
```

You can also use the elegant each method, as in:

```
(0..10).each { |i|
    print i
}
```

In this form, i is assigned to each element. Although in our case this simply becomes a numeric index, we will use this extensively in SketchUp coding later to iterate through objects.

Finally, the integer object also has a times method that you can employ like this. Any (multiline) code in the curly brackets will be executed 10 times in this case.

```
10.times { |i|
    print i
}
```

Making It Work: Some More Ruby Syntax Details

You've already seen that Ruby does not require you to tell it when a line ends (many other programming languages need a semicolon there). There are also more language-specific things you need to know:

- A one-line comment starts with a #. Anything after the #, until the end of the line, is ignored by Ruby.
- A multiline comment starts with =begin and ends with =end.
- Parentheses are optional in method calls (to enclose the arguments), though it might be a good idea to add them for readability.
- You can often make things easier in repetitive Ruby code by using ranges. A range comes in a form like this: 1..5, which includes all integer numbers from 1 to 5. A good example is (1..5).to_a, which creates an array like this: [1, 2, 3, 4, 5]. Other valid ranges are: 0.1..0.9 and 'a'..'m'.
- There are two ways to create code blocks: One uses curly brackets, { at the beginning and } at the end; the other uses do at the beginning and end at the end. In many cases, you can use either one to enclose code (e.g., for an each statement).

What Else Is There?

Of course, there is more! Particularly when you need to define your own classes or use some specialized Ruby classes and extensions, there is more to discover. But—as I've said before—this is a pragmatic introduction and we'll limit language functions to only what is absolutely necessary to complete our tasks. There are several useful links at the end of this section that will help you delve deeper into Ruby. We will also cover file operations in some of the upcoming examples.

What's in SketchUp's Ruby API?

SketchUp's Ruby API is an extension to plain Ruby (covered previously) and includes objects and methods that are useful in SketchUp. Some of these allow you to interact with the SketchUp application or the currently open model. Others allow you to add or modify geometry (*entities*). There are also methods to attach *observers* to anything in the software. This is useful if you need your code to spring into action when the user changes something. Look through Appendix C to get an understanding of how extensive this API actually is.

The full API documentation can be viewed at http://www.sketchup.com/developers/sketchup-ruby-api, where you can also find numerous code examples and revision notes. The links in the next section give you even more resources for finding documentation, code samples, and discussion forums.

You can use any of the SketchUp API's objects and methods in your code whenever you like. As long as your Ruby code runs inside SketchUp, there is no need to include or define any external files. As demonstrated, when you added a triangle to the model, one line is enough to get things started. Let's quickly look at this code again and take it apart:

```
Sketchup.active_model.entities.add_face [0,0,0],[0,10,0],[0,10,10]
```

Here you are accessing the currently open model (the `active_model`) through the `Sketchup` object. If you want to add any geometry in there, you can't simply add it to the model; you need to add it to the `entities` collection in the model. This makes sense, of course, because everything in a model is somehow organized into collections (there are also `layer`, `material`, `styles`, `tools`, etc., collections). Once you get hold of the entities collection, you can add a face using the `add_face` method.

The `add_face` method, in turn, accepts 3D points as arguments; because this face is a triangle, you need to supply three points. These points, in turn, are sufficiently defined by an `x,y,z` coordinate, which you are supplying as a three-number array (`[0,0,0]` is the point definition for the origin, of course). This is a triplet coordinate array, which corresponds to the location based on the x (red axis), y (green axis), and z (blue axis) coordinate components, respectively.

TIP

When you look deeper into Ruby, you will learn that what I call an *object* is often called a *class*. I do this to (hopefully) reduce confusion. Technically, methods and the like are defined in a class in Ruby, which then is instantiated as an object when you use it.

When you start up the Ruby Code Editor in SketchUp (installed using the extension, as described earlier in this chapter), you see that a few shortcuts are already preprogrammed:

```
mod = Sketchup.active_model  # Open model
ent = mod.entities  # All entities in model
sel = mod.selection  # Current selection
```

This makes it easy to work with some of the basic collections. With these three lines at the beginning of our code, you can now simply add a fourth line to accomplish what you did before:

```
ent.add_face [0,0,0],[0,10,0],[0,10,10]
```

If you have selected any objects in your current model, you could simply access the first selected object using sel[0], for example, to move or copy it.

Instead of going through the list of available objects and methods, the next sections show you an overview diagram and explore some of the functionality using code examples. To serve you as a reference, the complete API object and methods listing is included in Appendix C.

Object Reference Diagram

The makers of SketchUp have produced a useful diagram, shown in **Figure 7.7**, that explains visually the object (or class) hierarchy. Please note that the following are not included in this diagram:

Core Ruby Classes: Array, Length, Numeric, String

UI Classes: Command, InputPoint, PickHelper, Menu, Toolbar, WebDialog

Geom Classes: BoundingBox, LatLong, Point3d, PolygonMesh, Transformation, Vector3d, Vertex

App Level Classes: Animation, Color, Extension, Importer, Options Manager, Options Provider, Set, TextureWriter, UVHelper

Observers: OptionsProviderObserver.

Length Units in SketchUp

Because SketchUp works with actual dimensions for lengths, locations, and so on, it is important to understand how to use them in Ruby Scripts, too.

Many examples in this book use plain numbers such as [10,10,10]. Because SketchUp's default unit is the inch (independent of which local version you are using), these numbers default to inches. Therefore, "10" automatically means "10 inches" in the software.

If you are using a combination of feet and inches or are working with a different unit system altogether (e.g., using meters in the metric or SI system), you must enter units differently. One method is to give SketchUp the length, including its unit, as a string. Fortunately, there is a built-in method (of the Length object) to_l, which attempts to convert any length to SketchUp's internal default unit. Here are some examples:

```
new_length = "1m".to_l
=> 39.3700787401575

new_length = "2'6".to_l
=> 30.0
```

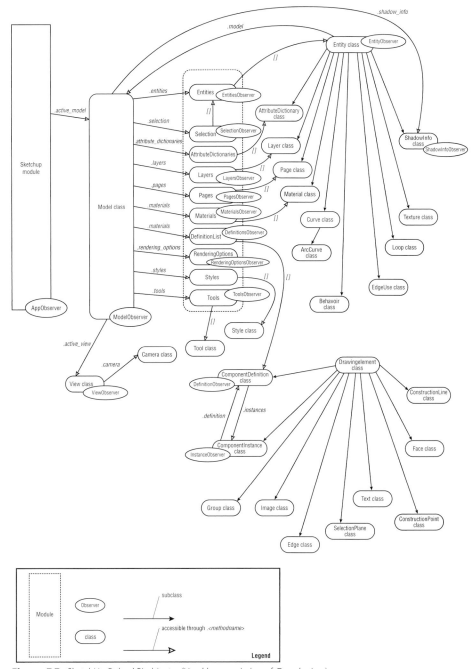

Figure 7.7: SketchUp Ruby API objects *(Used by permission of Google, Inc.)*

Alternatively, you can use some of the methods of the `Numeric` object. The following is a complete list of all of its methods:

```
Numeric (Parent: Object)

.cm .degrees .feet .inch .km
.m .mile .mm .radians .to_cm .to_feet
.to_inch .to_km .to_l .to_m .to_mile
.to_mm .to_yard .yard
```

Examples of this approach are as follows:

```
2.cm + 4.inch
=> 4.78740157480315

24.to_feet
=> 2.0
```

Links to Further Reading

The following list features books and websites that you can use as further reference for both the language Ruby and SketchUp's Ruby API. Keep this list handy as a reference.

For Ruby:

- Jason D. Clinton, *Ruby Phrasebook* (Boston: Pearson Education, 2009).
- Michael Fitzgerald, *Ruby Pocket Reference* (Sebastopol, CA: O'Reilly Media, 2007).
- www.ruby-lang.org—The main website for the Ruby language.
- http://tryruby.org—A well-made interactive site that lets you learn and try out Ruby interactively.
- http://ruby-doc.org—The main documentation for Ruby objects and methods (as of this writing, the Ruby version in SketchUp is 2.0.0). This site also features some introductory texts.
- http://en.wikibooks.org/wiki/Ruby_Programming—An online book on Ruby programming.
- www.techotopia.com/index.php/Ruby_Essentials—Another online book.
- www.zenspider.com/Languages/Ruby/QuickRef.html—A cheat sheet for Ruby.

For SketchUp's API:

- Matthew Scarpino, *Automatic SketchUp: Creating 3D Models in Ruby* (Walnut Creek, CA: Eclipse Engineering, 2010).
- http://www.sketchup.com/developers/sketchup-ruby-api—The official documentation of the SketchUp API.
- http://forums.sketchup.com/c/developers—Trimble's forum for SketchUp developers.
- http://sketchucation.com/forums/viewforum.php?f=180—A forum for Ruby API developers on SketchUcation.

Creating Geometry with Ruby

Creating geometry is easy to do with the API. In essence, you add a new entity (a geometry object) to the collection of entities in the current model. To do this, you can use any of the methods of the `Entities` object. For example, `add_line` adds a line based on two points in 3D space. Here is a list of most methods and properties of the `Entities` collection:

```
Entities (Parent: Object)

.[] .add_3d_text .add_arc .add_circle
.add_cline .add_cpoint .add_curve
.add_edges .add_face
.add_faces_from_mesh .add_group
.add_image .add_instance .add_line
.add_ngon .add_observer .add_text
.at .clear! .count .each .erase_entities
.fill_from_mesh .intersect_with .length
.model .parent .remove_observer
.transform_by_vectors
.transform_entities
```

In addition to these methods, you can also create a "raw" mesh directly by using the `PolygonMesh` object. Its methods and properties are as follows:

```
PolygonMesh (Parent: Object)

.add_point .add_polygon .count_points
.count_polygons .new .normal_at
.point_at .point_index .points
.polygon_at .polygon_points_at .polygons
.set_point .transform! .uv_at .uvs
```

To be able to add any of these objects to your model, you must first retrieve the `Entities` collection in the current (active) model. Because you are using the Ruby Code Editor, you can simply use *ent* as a shortcut variable for this collection. Just make sure you leave the three top lines of code in there and add yours below them. This is the default code:

```
mod = Sketchup.active_model  # Open model
ent = mod.entities  # All entities in model
sel = mod.selection  # Current selection
```

Once you have this, simply add to the collection whatever you need.

```
new_line = ent.add_line ([0,0,0],[10,10,10])
```

As you can see here, you are again giving SketchUp 3D points as coordinate arrays. Technically, you have given SketchUp `Point3d` objects here. While the shorthand version shown here works well, the longer version would have been:

```
pt1 = Geom::Point3d.new(0,0,0)
pt2 = Geom::Point3d.new(10,10,10)
new_line = ent.add_line (pt1, pt2)
```

This works similarly to when you need to use a vector. As you may have expected, there is also a `Vector3d` object in SketchUp. You can create it in an analogous fashion. Either use the direct triplet entry (which this time represents a direction rather than a 3D point) or create a `Vector3d` object using its `new` method:

```
vec1 = [x,y,z]
vec1 = Geom::Vector3d.new(x,y,z)
```

But enough of the theory for now! Let's take a look at some examples that show how you can create geometric objects using scripting.

TIP

Instead of typing the following script examples painstakingly into the editor, go to this book's companion website **http://sketchupfordesign.com** and download them all as a ZIP archive of Ruby files (from the Chapter 7 page).

Lots of Boxes

To get started, let's create a 3D grid of regularly spaced boxes. In the following code snippet, you'll define a number of boxes per axis *n*, a box spacing *s*, and a box width *w*. You'll then do three loops: one for multiples along the x-axis (the red axis), one for multiples along the y-axis (the green axis), and a third for the z-axis (the blue axis). You will also use the `pushpull` method of the `Face` object to extrude the faces into boxes.

Paste the following code into the Ruby Code Editor in SketchUp and click on Run Code:

```
mod = Sketchup.active_model   # Open model
ent = mod.entities   # All entities in model
sel = mod.selection   # Current selection

n = 5   # Number of boxes
s = 100   # Spacing
w = 20   # Box width


# Iterate in all three dimensions
(0..n-1).each {  |i|
```

```
(0..n-1).each {  |j|
    (0..n-1).each {  |k|

        # add a face first
        face = ent.add_face [i*s,j*s,k*s],
                            [i*s,j*s+w,k*s],
                            [i*s+w,j*s+w,k*s],
                            [i*s+w,j*s,k*s]
        # then pushpull it to get a box
        face.pushpull -w

    }
  }
}
```

The result will look like **Figure 7.8**.

As this demonstrates, creating extruded geometry is very easy. First, you needed to create a face. This was done using the `add_face` method. As always, the face was simply added to the `Entities` collection.

Instead of just adding it, though, you assigned it at the same time to the variable *face*. This gave us a way to apply the `pushpull` method to the face and extrude it by a given amount *w*.

You might have noticed that *w* is entered as a negative number (there is a minus sign in front of it). This is because whenever you create a face in SketchUp, the white side of the face (the front) points downward. A positive *w* would have extruded it downward as well. Because you want to extrude it upward, *w* must be negative (or you would have needed to first flip the face's orientation using its `reverse!` method).

Of course, you have to be careful with this script. As you can imagine, changing a single number (*n*) significantly impacts the amount of geometry created. After all, each cube consists of 18 elements: 6 faces and 12 edges.

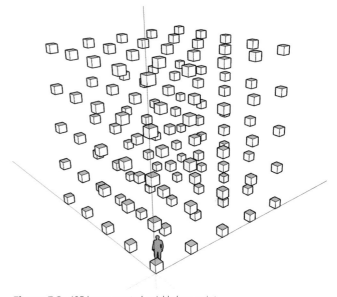

Figure 7.8: 125 boxes created quickly by a script

This gets the job done, but it is not very efficient. You are creating geometry for each of the many similar boxes. Ultimately, all these faces, edges, and vertices need to be stored in the SketchUp file that you save to your hard disk. One of the following sections shows you how to improve on this by using components and transformations.

Lots of Boxes with Color

Let's create a slight variation of the preceding example. This time, you'll put each of the boxes into a group and add color to them all!

Paste the following code into the Ruby Code Editor in SketchUp and click on Run Code:

```
mod = Sketchup.active_model  # Open model
ent = mod.entities  # All entities in model
sel = mod.selection  # Current selection

n = 6  # Number of boxes in each direction
s = 100  # Spacing
w = 50  # Box width

# Iterate in all three dimensions
(0..n-1).each { |i|
    (0..n-1).each { |j|
        (0..n-1).each { |k|

            # Create a group for each box
            group = ent.add_group
            # Add the face to the group's entities
            face = group.entities.add_face [i*s,j*s,k*s],
                                           [i*s,j*s+w,k*s],
                                           [i*s+w,j*s+w,k*s],
                                           [i*s+w,j*s,k*s]
            # Add a material (an RGB color)
            face.back_material = [(255/(n-1)*i).round,
                                  (255/(n-1)*j).round,
                                  (255/(n-1)*k).round]
            # Now extrude the box
            face.pushpull -w

        }
    }
}
```

This should at least significantly improve the visuals of the previous example. **Figure 7.9** shows what you will see.

What did we do differently this time? We didn't just add the faces to the Entities collection as before; this time, we first added a group to that collection using the add_group method. Because we assigned a variable to the group (*group*), we were able to add geometry to the Entities collection of that group. That is all you need to create grouped geometry using Ruby.

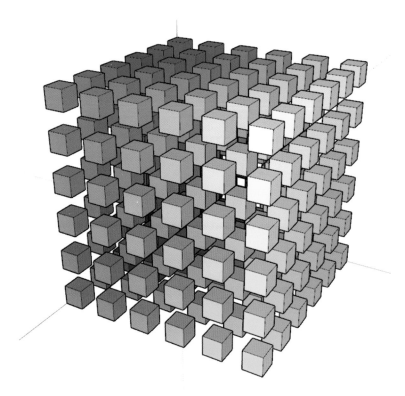

Figure 7.9: Boxes colored in the full spectrum

The other trick we used was to add a material to the face *before* we extruded it. This added the material to the entire box by way of extrusion.

As you can see, adding a color (a "material") to a face is very easy, too. You just need to use one of the two related methods of the face object: `material` for the front side and `back_material` for the reverse side. As before, the reverse side (the blue side) is pointing in the direction of the extrusion, so you need to apply the material to that side.

Materials can be applied as a reference to an existing material in SketchUp (check for those in the Materials window), as a color name, or—as in this case—as a color defined by RGB (red, green, blue) values. The following are all valid material assignments (assuming that `mat1` is a material that was previously defined in your code):

```
face.material = mat1
face.material = "red"
face.material = 0xff0000
face.material = "#ff0000"
face.material = Sketchup::Color.new(255, 0, 0)
face.material = [1.0, 0.0, 0.0]
face.material = [255, 0, 0]
face.material = 255
```

One thing you will notice when you create and use a lot of different colors is that SketchUp will have to add all of them to the already defined materials, which might take some time. You can always review the result of your creation in the Materials window under In Model by clicking on the house symbol (see **Figure 7.10**).

Whenever you define colors using RGB values, keep in mind that the maximum value for each of them is 255. Here are some sample colors:

```
[0,0,0]       # black
[255,0,0]     # red
[255,255,0]   # yellow
[125,125,125] # a medium gray
```

Figure 7.10: The newly created materials

Creating a Small City

Let's try something similar now: Create boxes with a random height—and let's call it a city. As you can see in the following code, you are just producing a 2D grid of boxes. This time, however, you are using feet as the dimension. Instead of giving all of the boxes the same height, you are now using Ruby's rand method to randomize their height (between 100 and 200 feet, as you can see in **Figure 7.11**).

```
mod = Sketchup.active_model   # Open model
ent = mod.entities   # All entities in model
sel = mod.selection   # Current selection
```

```
n = 10  # number of buildings
s = 100.feet  # spacing
w = 60.feet  # base width

# Iterate over ground (x and y)
(0..n-1).each { |i|
    (0..n-1).each { |j|

        # add a face first
        face = ent.add_face [i*s,j*s,0],[i*s,j*s+w,0],
                            [i*s+w,j*s+w,0],[i*s+w,j*s,0]

        # then pushpull it to get a box
        height = 100.feet + rand(100).feet
        face.pushpull -height

    }
}
```

Figure 7.11: A small city with buildings of random heights

Figure 7.11 shows how to use dimensions other than inches in a script and how to employ the built-in random-number generator to add variation to your creations. Giving anything generated by a computer at least some randomness usually adds quite a bit of realism. We will use this later with transformations as well.

Randomizing Extrusions

Instead of applying randomized extrusions to newly created geometry, this example applies them to already existing geometry, which allows us to learn about using selections.

First, create some geometry in your model; you need to have several faces at your disposal. For this example, I used one of SketchUp's preinstalled sphere components as well as a square face with intersecting lines (see **Figure 7.12**). Make sure the front (the white side of each face) points outward and upward; use the Reverse Faces right-click tool if you need to correct any. Then select everything. Paste the following (very short) snippet into the Ruby Code Editor in SketchUp and click on Run Code:

```ruby
mod = Sketchup.active_model  # Open model
ent = mod.entities  # All entities in model
sel = mod.selection  # Current selection

# Iterate through selection
sel.each do |e|

    # First check if this is a face
    if e.typename == "Face"

        # Then extrude it
        e.pushpull rand(100)

    end

end
```

This time, you are not adding anything to the Entities collection. Instead, you are using what you have selected by employing *sel*. As shown in **Figure 7.12**, the faces extruded randomly.

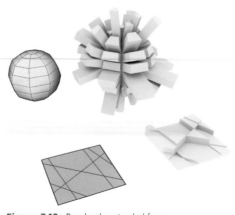

Figure 7.12: Randomly extruded faces

As is evident in the code, sometimes it makes sense to check the type of entity you have selected before you do anything to it (thereby preventing errors). This is done using the `typename` method, and some possible entity types are *Face*, *Edge*, *ConstructionPoint*, *ComponentInstance*, and *Group*. Alternatively, you can use this query: `e.is_a? Sketchup::Face`.

Using Formulas for Patterned Panels

Scripting geometry becomes especially effective (and beautiful) when you use a nonlinear formula to define size, position, color, and so forth. The next piece of code creates a rectangular grid of circles on the x-y plane (the ground) where the circle size is determined in two directions by a sine function.

Paste the following code into the Ruby Code Editor in SketchUp and click on Run Code:

```
mod = Sketchup.active_model   # Open model
ent = mod.entities   # All entities in model
sel = mod.selection   # Current selection

width = 36   # Width of panel
n = 10   # Number of circles in each direction
s = width / (n+1).to_f   # Spacing of circles

# add the square base for the panel
ent.add_face [0,0,0],[width,0,0],[width,width,0],[0,width,0]

# Iterate in the panel plane
(0..n-1).each { |i|
    (0..n-1).each { |j|

        # add the circles
        radius = Math::sin(i/(n-1).to_f*1*Math::PI)*s/5.0+
                Math::sin(j/(n-1).to_f*1*Math::PI)*s/5.0
        ent.add_circle [s+i*s,s+j*s,0], [0,0,1], radius

    }
}
```

After running the script, what you see on the x-y plane should look like **Figure 7.13**.

You can now use this geometry as the basis for further modeling. In this case, I used SketchUp's standard Push/Pull tool to extrude the patterned panel (there is no need to do everything using code!). When the circles were placed on top of the square face, their faces were automatically separated from the underlying face. This allowed me in turn to use a single push/pull operation to finish the panel. The rendering looks like **Figure 7.14**.

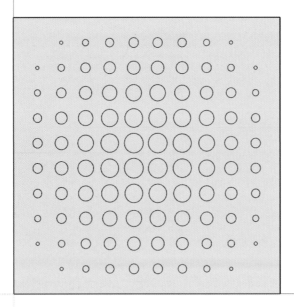

Figure 7.13: Panel layout with sinusoidal pattern

Figure 7.14: Rendered panels

You can get creative with this little bit of code if you replace some of the `sin` functions with `cos` or any other mathematical formula. You can also experiment with some of the factors that end up determining circle diameter (the last parameter in the `add_circle` method) or the expression between the brackets in the sine function.

One thing that may stump you when doing calculations in Ruby is Ruby's reluctance to give a floating-point value after dividing two integers. This is the reason you see `to_f` in a few places in the code. This little snippet converts any number to a *float*, a real number. Alternatively, you could initialize the variables with an extra digit, as in `width = 36.0`.

Plotting Data from Text Files

When you create geometry, the parameters might need to come from a source outside of SketchUp. This would be the case if you had an Excel spreadsheet with x-, y-, z-coordinates (as would be available from a LIDAR laser scan or from a land surveyor). You might also have other software (structural or other building analysis software) export parameters that you could use to create geometry. In any case, let's assume for this example that you had point coordinates stored in a text file in the following format:

```
81.82821,16.42147,205.31
83.07821,16.33147,204.91
83.57821,10.31147,204.87
...
```

As you can see, each point is printed on a single line in the `x,y,z` format. Units are feet in this case, but you can ignore them for now (which defaults the units to inches, of course).

Let's explore how to import and plot them in your SketchUp model. First, you have to read from the text file line-by-line and then plot each data point to SketchUp. To do this, you will add construction points (little tick marks that you usually create using the Tape Measure tool) with the `add_cpoint` method.

First, paste the point data listed previously, or any similarly formatted data, into a text file (its naming isn't crucial). Then paste the following code snippet into the Ruby Code Editor and click Run:

```ruby
mod = Sketchup.active_model   # Open model
ent = mod.entities   # All entities in model
sel = mod.selection   # Current selection

# Starts at line zero, modify if you have a header line
startline = 0

# Use the openpanel to get the file name
filename = UI.openpanel 'Select Data File'

# Iterate through all lines in the file and plot the cpoints
if filename != nil
    file = File.open(filename)
    file.each { |line|
```

```
      if file.lineno >= startline
          pointXYZ = line.strip.split(",")
          ent.add_cpoint [pointXYZ[0].to_f,
                          pointXYZ[1].to_f,
                          pointXYZ[2].to_f]
      end
   }
   file.close
end
```

This code first asks you to provide the filename by showing you the openpanel dialog. It then opens the file and iterates through each line. Once it reads each line, it applies two methods to the line object: First, it uses strip to remove any white spaces around your data. Then it uses split(",") to split each line at the commas into an array of elements. As you can see, you can conveniently supply the character that is used to make the split (a comma, in this case). Finally, the x,y,z data is used to add construction points to the Entities collection (and, therefore, your model).

This little example demonstrated a few new things. You learned how to work with the openpanel (as you might have guessed, there is also a savepanel in SketchUp) and then use the supplied file reference. You also learned how to work with external files and the very useful split method.

Figure 7.15 shows the result of importing a large file consisting of point coordinates using the method described here. The raw data in this case came from a LIDAR flyover of a historic church.

Figure 7.15: Construction points from an imported file

Working with Text Files

As the preceding example shows, it is quite easy to work with text files. The common approach to reading from a file is this:

```
filename = 'data.txt'
f = File.open(filename)
f.each { |line|
    # Do something with the line here
}
f.close
```

Alternatively, you could replace the middle three lines of this code with `content = f.readlines`, which reads the entire file as an array into the `content` variable. You would then use `content.each` to iterate through the lines.

To write to a file, use this syntax:

```
filename = 'data.txt'
f = File.new(filename,'w')
f.puts 'Hello world!'
f.close
```

As you might have guessed, the `'w'` at the end of the second line prepares the file for writing. Another useful switch is `'a'`, which appends anything you write to the file at its end (instead of overwriting any existing content).

Saving Vertices to a Text File

In this example, let's reverse the process of the last one. Assume you have created a very complex shape in SketchUp and now need to export edge coordinates (vertices) to a text file, so that you can use them in different software (in Excel, for example). The following code takes your current selection of objects and writes a text file with x,y,z data for each unique vertex.

Create some geometry (that has edges) in SketchUp, select it (make sure it is not grouped), paste the following code snippet into the Ruby Code Editor, and click Run:

```
mod = Sketchup.active_model   # Open model
ent = mod.entities   # All entities in model
sel = mod.selection   # Current selection

# Empty array for vertices
verts = []
```

```
# Iterate over the selection and store vertices
sel.each do |e|

    # Only consider edges
    if e.typename == "Edge"
        # Add vertices to array
        verts.push e.vertices
    end

end


# Remove any sub-arrays (if necessary)
verts.flatten!
# Remove duplicates in array
verts.uniq!

# Ask for export file
filename = UI.openpanel 'Text file for vertex coordinates'

# Write vertices to file
if filename
    f = File.open(filename, 'w')
    # Write x,y,z coordinates in default units (inches)
    verts.each { |v|
        f.print v.position.x.to_inch,',',v.position.y.to_inch,',',
                v.position.z.to_inch,"\n"
    }
    f.close
end
```

As you can see, you are again using the Selection collection of objects. In a first step, you iterate over this selection using sel.each. As in the earlier example, you check that we are dealing with an edge and then add its (two) vertices to the verts array using the push method.

Obviously, some of those vertices will be duplicates. Consider that two edges of a square meeting at one point will write this point twice to the collection. To fix this, you use the Ruby array method uniq!, which removes duplicates from the array.

Finally, you print all of the x-, y-, z-coordinates to a new text file, which the user can select through an openpanel. This is done by first getting the position of each vertex, then getting its x,y,z value, and, finally, converting these values to SketchUp's default units using the to_inch method (otherwise, they will be stored in your localized unit system—e.g., as 8'4"). You can now check that everything worked correctly by using the code in the "Plotting Data from Text Files" section to read the points back into SketchUp. (See **Figure 7.16**.)

Figure 7.16: Saving vertex locations for a shell

Transformations Change Things Up

What you know in SketchUp as the Move, Rotate, and Scale tools are technically just different implementations of a *transformation*. Therefore, you actually won't find a move or rotate method in SketchUp's Ruby API. While this might be less obvious or convenient, using transformations to create copies of objects and/or move them is not too hard with Ruby.

A transformation is based on its equivalently named object. The following snippet lists all of the available methods.

```
Transformation (Parent: Object)

.* .axes .clone .identity?
.interpolate .inverse .invert!
.new .origin .rotation .scaling
.set! .to_a .translation
.xaxis .yaxis .zaxis
```

Although this (and the online documentation) might appear a bit confusing, let's look at just a subset of the available features. This provides enough functionality for what we want to do. The relevant methods are these:

```
# Point Transformation—use for placing objects
t1 = Geom::Transformation.new( point )

# Translation Transformation—use for moving
t2 = Geom::Transformation.translation( vector )

# Rotation Transformation—use for rotating
t3 = Geom::Transformation.rotation( center, axis, angle )
```

```
# Scaling Transformation—use for scaling
t4 = Geom::Transformation.scaling( center, scale )
t4 = Geom::Transformation.scaling( center, xscale, yscale, zscale )
```

As you can see, they all use perfectly understandable parameters. If you want to move something from location A to location B, then the vector between those points (expressed as "go *m* units in the x direction, *n* units in the y direction, and *o* units in the z direction") is enough information to get it there. And if you want to rotate something, SketchUp needs to know *about which point* you want it to rotate, *about which axis* you want it to rotate, and *by how many degrees* it should turn. Finally, the scaling translation accepts either a uniform scale or different scale factors in each coordinate direction.

In order to use these transformations, you need to add them as parameters to appropriate methods. There are various approaches to this: Use `transform_entities` on the model's `Entities` collection as a universal approach. You can also directly apply a transformation to groups or components, especially when you place an instance of a component (the transformation describes the insertion point in that case).

Let's look at this in action in a short code snippet. Select an object in your model (if you select multiple, only the first gets used). Then paste the following code into the Ruby Code Editor and click Run Code:

```
mod = Sketchup.active_model   # Open model
ent = mod.entities   # All entities in model
sel = mod.selection   # Current selection

# Get the center of the selected object
center = sel[0].bounds.center

# Define all possible translations
t1 = Geom::Transformation.new([100,0,0])
t2 = Geom::Transformation.translation([100,0,0])
t3 = Geom::Transformation.rotation(center, [1,0,0], 45.degrees)
t4 = Geom::Transformation.scaling(center, 2)

# Choose one of them — for now
t = t2

# Transform first object in selection
ent.transform_entities(t, sel[0])
```

You can test the main transformations simply by modifying the t = t2 statement. Feel free to experiment with the code a bit to test it out.

If you want to apply more than one transformation, then replace this line with something like t = t2 * t3 * t4 (i.e., multiply the ones you want to apply). This combines t2, t3, and t4 into a single transformation.

The following examples apply these principles in various ways.

Lots of Boxes Using Components

This is essentially the same example that you did earlier. In SketchUp, however, the approach that takes the least computational effort and smallest amount of space on the hard disk is usually to create one geometry item (the box, in this case), convert it to a component, and then just insert component instances. Instead of saving a whole lot of geometry, only insertion points and scales are then being stored. This results in smaller file sizes and models that handle much better (during zooming, orbiting, etc.).

The following code does this by creating a grouped box, converting it into a component, and then copying (placing) it multiple times using transformations.

```ruby
mod = Sketchup.active_model  # Open model
ent = mod.entities  # All entities in model
sel = mod.selection  # Current selection

s = 100  # Spacing
w = 10  # Box width
n = 10  # Number of boxes

# First create a component of a box
group = ent.add_group
face = group.entities.add_face [0,0,0],[w,0,0],[w,w,0],[0,w,0]
face.pushpull -w
comp = group.to_component

# Iterate in all three dimensions
(0..n).each { |i|
  (0..n).each { |j|
    (0..n).each { |k|

      # Now place copies at final locations using transformation
      transformation = Geom::Transformation.new([i*s,j*s,k*s])
      ent.add_instance(comp.definition, transformation)

    }
  }
}
```

As you can see, this code creates a grid of boxes similar to **Figure 7.8**. In contrast to what you did before, this time you created *one* box that has the appropriate geometry. Then you changed it into a component using the `group.to_component` method. It is only after this that you loop through the locations, define an insertion point using a transformation, and add a component instance (as `comp.definition`) using the `add_instance` method at that insertion point.

Building a Curved Wall

Let's expand a bit on the previous code. In this snippet, you'll take a preexisting component—a 1' × 1' × 2' block in the example used here—and place it multiple times while rotating it. The rotation is again guided by a combination of sine and cosine in the horizontal and vertical directions.

To use this code, you must first have a component instance in your model (the block you see in **Figure 7.17** is the one used here; place it anywhere you like). Before you run the code, make sure you select only the component—otherwise, nothing will happen.

```
mod = Sketchup.active_model  # Open model
ent = mod.entities  # All entities in model
sel = mod.selection  # Current selection

s = 28  # x-spacing
t = 12  # z-spacing
h = 20  # number in x
v = 20  # number in z
max_deg = 90  # Max "opening" angle

# Make sure selection is a component
if (sel[0].typename == 'ComponentInstance')
    v.times { |j|
        h.times { |i|

            # Place a brick at the specified location
            t1 = Geom::Transformation.translation([i*s,0,j*t])
            instance = ent.add_instance(sel[0].definition, t1)

            # Calculate angle and rotate the brick around vertical axis
            angle = (Math::sin((i*180/h).degrees)+
                    Math::sin((j*360/v).degrees))*max_deg/2
            t2 = Geom::Transformation.rotation instance.bounds.center,
                [0,0,1], angle.degrees
            instance.transform! t2

        }
    }
end
```

There are a few more parameters in this code than you had before (brick spacing in both directions, number of bricks, and opening angle), but this gives you the flexibility to experiment with them and generate variations in the results.

In the code, you first check that the selected item is actually a ComponentInstance. Next, you iterate through each horizontal and vertical brick placement. In this iteration, you use a `translation` to place the brick and then you apply a rotation to the new component instance. This allows you to rotate the brick "in place."

Figure 7.18 shows a rendering of a generated wall.

Figure 7.17: Single selected brick and generated wall

Figure 7.18: Rendering of generated wall

Placing Components on Faces

In this example, you'll take a component (a simple circle) and copy it onto the center of each selected face of some existing geometry. To make the code work, prepare the component first: Create a circle and turn it into a component using SketchUp's standard tools. Edit the component so that the circle is centered on the component's coordinate system, as shown here.

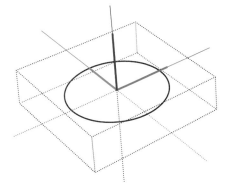

Create any shape you like that has faces. In this example, I created a shell using the Extrude Edges by Edges tool from the Extrusion Tools plugin (see Chapter 4). **Figure 7.19** shows both the single component and all ungrouped faces selected and ready for the code to do its magic.

> **TIP**
>
> Whenever you work with components in Ruby, it is very important to have the component's axes (the ones that you see when you edit or double-click the component) in the correct location. Copies will be placed using a component's origin. Double-check their placement if your results don't look as expected.

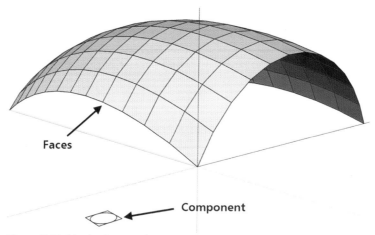

Faces

Component

Figure 7.19 Selection for example

```
mod = Sketchup.active_model  # Open model
ent = mod.entities  # All entities in model
sel = mod.selection  # Current selection

# Get the single component's definition first
comp = nil
sel.each { |e|
    if e.typename == "ComponentInstance"
        comp = e.definition
    end
}

# Iterate through all ungrouped faces
sel.each { |e|
    if e.typename == "Face"

        # Place a copy at the center of the bounding box
        center = e.bounds.center
        t = Geom::Transformation.new center, e.normal
        new = ent.add_instance comp, t

        # Now scale objects by some criteria (z-height in this case)
        new.transform! Geom::Transformation.scaling center,
          center.z/100

        # Explode it so that we can remove the face afterwards
        new.explode

    end
}
```

When you run this code, it first looks through your selection and isolates the one `ComponentInstance` (the circle). Then it iterates through each face and places a new instance at the center of the face. It does this by finding the center point, using the `bounds.center` method of the Entity object (which gives the center of the bounding box). The new instance is then placed with its orientation (its normal vector) aligned with the face's normal vector (which describes the direction perpendicular to the face).

A scaling transformation is applied to the circle, which varies the circle's scale by how far away from the ground it is. This results in small circles (openings) at the base of the shell, and the largest ones at the apex. As a last step, the component instance is exploded, which lets us remove the circle's faces manually, leaving nice circular openings in the shell. The result is shown in **Figure 7.20**.

Figure 7.20: Rendered view of canopy after removal of circle faces

Feel free to experiment with different components using this code. You can even place ones that have thickness (e.g., a cylinder) using this method.

Randomizing Everything

In the following code, you revisit the use of random numbers and combine this with what you learned about transformations. Specifically, you take the selected objects (all must be component instances) and apply a random rotation as well as random scaling to each. Before you run this code, add some components to your model—trees or other shrubbery make great examples. Just make sure you are not using face-me components.

```
mod = Sketchup.active_model  # Open model
ent = mod.entities  # All entities in model
```

```
sel = mod.selection  # Current selection

max_rotation_angle = 90  # Only rotate max. 90 degrees
size_var = 0.5  # Size variations. Keep below 1

# Iterate through selection
sel.each { |e|

    # Apply only to component instances
    if e.typename == "ComponentInstance"

        # Get the center of the selected object
        center = e.bounds.center
        # Als get the base center for scaling
        base = center.clone
        z_height = (e.bounds.max.z - e.bounds.min.z)
        base.z = base.z - z_height/2

        # Transform this object
        t1 = Geom::Transformation.rotation(center , [0,0,1],
            (rand * max_rotation_angle).degrees)
        t2 = Geom::Transformation.scaling base,
            1 - size_var/2 + rand*size_var
        # Combine transformations
        t = t1 * t2

        e.transform! t

    end

}
```

As you can see in **Figure 7.21**, this little snippet can add quite a bit of realism, especially to natural objects like trees.

To create this effect, the code first takes the entire Selection collection and iterates through each element using sel.each. It then checks that the current element is a ComponentInstance. You could apply this to all kinds of entities; however, transform! is a method that works only for the ComponentInstance object. You would have to modify the transformation slightly for other objects.

Next, the code finds the center of the bounding box of the component as well as the center of its base. To find the base center, you needed to calculate the height of the box and then subtract half the height from the z value.

Finally, you define two transformations, one for rotation and one for scaling, and combine them by multiplication. As you can see in the code, two variables allow you to modify the maximum rotation angle as well as the maximum size variation (as a ratio). Experiment with these values until you get the results you are after.

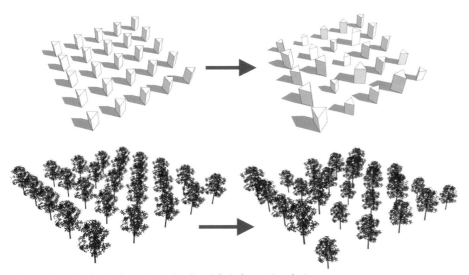

Figure 7.21: Randomized rotation and scaling (left: before; right: after)

Attracted to Attractors

The following examples show how you can modify geometry based on proximity to some other object (or any relationship you can think of, such as "height from ground"). This often yields very interesting designs and lets you express relationships visually in your designs.

At the minimum, what is required to make these examples work is (1) some geometry that you intend to modify and (2) one or more objects that act as attractors, on which the modification is based. A good example of the first is a facade panel with a color or shape you intend to modify. It doesn't have to be a face, though—you could instead use a group or a component instance.

The attractor can be any object. For convenience, I like using either component instances (the default figure in SketchUp's template for example) or groups or construction points, but it is up to you to decide what works best in your case. Just modify the code examples slightly to make them work if you deviate from the examples.

Coloring Faces by Proximity

This code takes several faces and one or more component instances and then colors the faces according to their proximity to the centers of the component instances (the *attractors*). A face that is close to an attractor gets a blue color, one that is far away turns yellow, and any faces in between receive colors from a graduated spectrum.

This example uses a facade made up of several 4' × 8' glass panels. These are simply faces (rectangles) copied edge to edge. You leave them all ungrouped so that the code can identify them as faces. In addition, you need to place one or more copies of the default

SketchUp "person" in various locations and with differing distances to the facade (the closest is the one on the left side). Before running the code, select all of the faces and the people components. **Figure 7.22** shows the raw setup with the facade panels and only one attractor. It also illustrates the result of running the code on this setup.

Figure 7.22: Single-attractor-based coloring of facade panels

Paste this code into the Ruby Code Editor, select the necessary objects in your SketchUp model, and then click on Run:

```ruby
mod = Sketchup.active_model  # Open model
ent = mod.entities  # All entities in model
sel = mod.selection  # Current selection

# Array with attractor center points
attractors = []

# Adjust this value to play with the scaling
max_val = 500

# Get all ComponentInstances as attractor points
sel.each { |e|
    if e.typename == 'ComponentInstance'
        attractors.push e.bounds.center
    end
}

# Iterate through objects and scale based on distance
if attractors.length > 0

    # Do this for each face
    sel.each { |e|
        if e.typename == "Face"
```

```
            # Get the center of the face
            center = e.bounds.center

            # Calculate minimum distance between face and
            # all attractors
            dist = 1000000   # Start with a large number

            # Find the smallest distance
            attractors.each { |apoint|
                dist_calc = apoint.distance center
              dist = dist_calc if dist_calc < dist
            }

            # Adjust color of face between blue and yellow
            e.material = [(dist/max_val*255).round,
                          (dist/max_val*255).round,
                          (255-dist/max_val*255).round]


        end
      }

  end
```

This results in a very colorful and interesting facade pattern. **Figure 7.23** shows how this would look in a rendering of a building.

Figure 7.23: Rendering of an entire building with attractor-based facade pattern

Similar to what you did with the previous code, you start this one by finding the component instances and adding their center points to the `attractors` array. After a check that the attractors are actually in the selection (`attractors.length > 0`), you proceed to iterate through the entire selection again—this time, considering only the faces. For each face, you then calculate the distances between the center of the face and each attractor and keep the shortest distance as the basis for the coloring. Finally, you apply materials (colors) to the front faces (making sure they are in the correct orientation this time) by specifying red, green, and blue values.

This code can be modified in many ways to generate different results. At the very least, you can modify `max_val`, which affects the magnitude of the attractors' influence on the coloring. You could also modify the color assignment by using less dramatic color combinations.

Scaling Objects by Proximity

Figure 7.24: 4′ × 4′ Wall panel component

Instead of coloring faces according to their proximity to an attractor, you could instead modify their geometry, for example, by scaling them. In this example, you take a wall that is made up of 4′ × 4′ slightly bulging wall panels and let the attractors adjust the panels' thickness.

The panels for this example are created from four edge lines using the Soap Skin & Bubble extension. The component axis is placed at the center of the back of the component definition, where the panels would be attached to a wall. (See **Figure 7.24**.)

This code is very similar to the previous code, the difference being that you now use groups as attractors (two small boxes) and component instances as the objects you modify. The only major change in the code is at the end, where you apply the scaling transformation. See **Figure 7.25** for the resulting paneled wall.

Paste this code into the Ruby Code Editor, select the necessary objects in your SketchUp model, and then click on Run:

```
mod = Sketchup.active_model  # Open model
ent = mod.entities  # All entities in model
sel = mod.selection  # Current selection

# Array with attractor center points
attractors = []

# Adjust this value to adjust the proximity influence
max_val = 200

# Get all attractor points from groups in selection
sel.each { |e|
```

```
        if e.typename == 'Group'
            attractors.push e.bounds.center
        end
}


# Iterate through components and scale based on distance
if attractors.length > 0

        # Do this for each group
        sel.each { |e|
            if e.typename == "ComponentInstance"

                # Get the center of the group
                center = e.bounds.center
                # Set the y-value to zero so that we
                # scale "outward"
                center.y=0

                # Calculate minimum distance between face and
                # all attractors
                dist = 1000000  # Start with a large number

                # Find the smallest distance
                attractors.each { |apoint|
                    dist_calc = apoint.distance center
                    dist = dist_calc if dist_calc < dist
                }

                # Calculate scale
                scale = (dist/max_val)**2
                t = Geom::Transformation.scaling center, 1, scale, 1
                e.transform! t

            end
        }

end
```

As you can see in the last few lines of code, this scaling transformation uses the syntax that allows for different scale factors in each dimension. Because the panels are oriented with the y direction (the components' green axis) perpendicular to the wall, all other scale factors remain as 1.

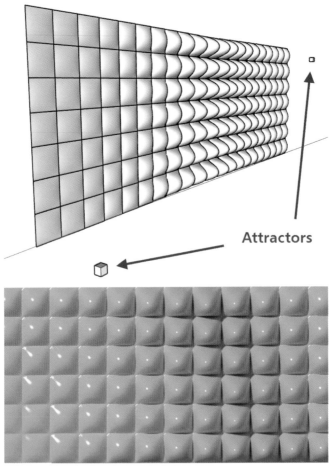

Figure 7.25: Modified panels and the two attractor boxes

Solar-Responsive Design

This script does not use attractors per se. It is, however, an example of how you could use a direction (expressed as a vector) to drive your design. To make your design more responsive to lighting, we'll use the "south" direction in your model to modify the shape of components that you place on a curved surface.

To accomplish this, we'll reuse the code from the "Placing Components on Faces" script from earlier. All you need to do this time is modify the section that transforms the copied `ComponentInstance`.

You can try this if you have various faces in your selection as well as one component. The example shown in **Figure 7.26** uses a curved surface that was subdivided into many faces and the same circle component as was used with the earlier code. Once you have these, select them, copy the following code into the Ruby Code Editor, and click on Run.

```
mod = Sketchup.active_model   # Open model
ent = mod.entities   # All entities in model
sel = mod.selection   # Current selection

# Get the one component's definition
comp = nil
sel.each { |e|
    if e.typename == "ComponentInstance"
        comp = e.definition
    end
}

# Iterate through all ungrouped faces
sel.each { |e|
    if e.typename == "Face"

        # Place a copy at the center of the bounding box
        center = e.bounds.center
        t = Geom::Transformation.new center, e.normal
        new = ent.add_instance comp, t

        # Now scale objects by south orientation
        scale = 1-[(e.normal.angle_between [0,-1,0]),0.2].max
        new.transform! Geom::Transformation.scaling center, scale,
                                                    scale, scale*2

        # Explode it so that we can remove the face afterwards
        new.explode

    end
}
```

As you can see in **Figure 7.26**, this code places scaled circles (due to unequal scaling, they actually become ellipses) onto each of the selected faces. If the face's orientation points south, the circles become enlarged, yet the farther the face deviates from this direction, the smaller the circle becomes.

In the preceding code, you can see that we kept the first part as before: You loop through the entities in the selection to find the one ComponentInstance. Next, you again iterate through all the faces and place copies of the circle at their centers (oriented with the face normal). Finally, you scale them based on orientation. To do this, you need to calculate the angle between the face normal and the south orientation. This is conveniently done using the angle_between method, which operates on the face normal and checks it against a unit vector in the south direction ([0,-1,0]). This yields the angle in radians, but since this number is between 0 and 1, it is perfect for us to use as a scale factor. To ensure that the circles don't get too small, pick as a scale factor the maximum value of either the angle or 0.2 using the max method ([angle, 0.2].max), which looks for the largest value in an array. Finally, apply the transformation with a doubled value in the z direction, which creates the ellipses.

Figure 7.26: Solar-oriented opening placement

What Else Is Possible with This?

As the preceding examples demonstrated, you can create interesting and intriguing geometry using scripting in SketchUp. The combination of manual modeling and Ruby scripting is a very efficient and effective approach to get results fast. If this was your introduction to computational geometry, then feel free to explore further. Start by modifying the code examples and see where that takes you. It is also a good idea to browse the Ruby API documentation for methods that could be of value for your design tasks. Here are some ideas:

- Insert images using the Image object.
- Influence the current view using the Camera object.
- Geo-locate your model and add geometry using the LatLong methods.
- Interact with data from web services using Ruby's 'net/http' methods. See this tutorial for an example that loads images from Flickr into SketchUp: http://sketchupfordesign.com/news/whats-new-in-sketchup-2014-better-ruby-for-example.
- Modify the layers in your model using the methods of the Layers collection.
- Add view tabs to your model using the Pages collection's methods.
- Add an attribute (a text-based parameter) to an object (e.g., a component) and read it out to a text file. Relevant methods are model.set_attribute and model.get_attribute.

- Add a menu item to SketchUp and assign your code to it. Relevant methods are `menu.add_item` and `menu.add_submenu`.

- Create a `WebDialog` and display some HTML pages in it. You can even make Ruby interact with a WebDialog's content or JavaScript.

If you decide that Ruby scripting is for you, you might want to look at some of the web links mentioned previously and even explore extension development. If you used Ruby code to create a solution to a problem, then it likely will be useful to someone else, too. Packaging code as an extension requires only a few more lines of code (see Appendix D for this) and is a great way to share your work.

Some Pitfalls and Things to Watch Out For

So SketchUp crashed after you clicked Run in the Code Editor? Here are some things to watch out for:

- **Save both your Ruby code and your SketchUp model early and often!** This will prevent headaches later. It's especially important to save just before you decide to run the code.

- **Errors are okay!** Part of scripting anything is generating (and then fixing) errors. You may observe your code not doing anything at some point. If you are lucky, it will give you an error that sounds meaningful. But often it won't.

  Try running your code again with SketchUp's Ruby Console open. Often, that reveals more information. If that doesn't help, comment out code parts that might be problematic. If the code runs fine without those parts, you are one step closer to finding the problem. A useful method to stop code execution and display a variable's value for testing is inserting `UI.messagebox var` at the desired location.

- **Your code can create geometry at an alarming pace!** If you are writing loops to create geometry, test them with only a few elements first. You can easily grind SketchUp (or even your computer) to a complete halt. Usually, *killing* (closing) SketchUp and restarting it gets you back to where you were before (as long as you saved everything, of course).

- **Be careful if your code creates overlapping geometry!** As always in SketchUp, when ungrouped geometry overlaps, SketchUp tries to attach faces or resolve intersections. This can take some time if there are a lot of intersections.

Your Turn!

The following tasks allow you to practice the topics in this chapter:

1. **Design a panel.**
   Create a panel design of your own. Use a 4′ × 4′ panel and populate it with a scripted pattern of boxes, circles, or lines. Create an interesting and aesthetically pleasing pattern.

---

2. Create panels for CNC manufacturing.
Create a panel design that is to be manufactured using a CNC router. Assume a drill bit size and modify your code so that all minimum circle diameters conform to this size.

3. Create a parametric brick wall.
Create a brick wall where bricks are offset from course to course (the way they actually would be built). Use the script sample from earlier in this chapter as a basis. Do this first for a straight wall. Then create a curved wall based on parameters of your choosing.

4. Design a solar façade.
Create a solar-responsive design for a facade, a wall, or a screen. Place shading elements on wall panels and size them according to solar orientation.

Appendix A
SketchUp Quick Reference Cards

SketchUp Pro Quick Reference Card | Windows

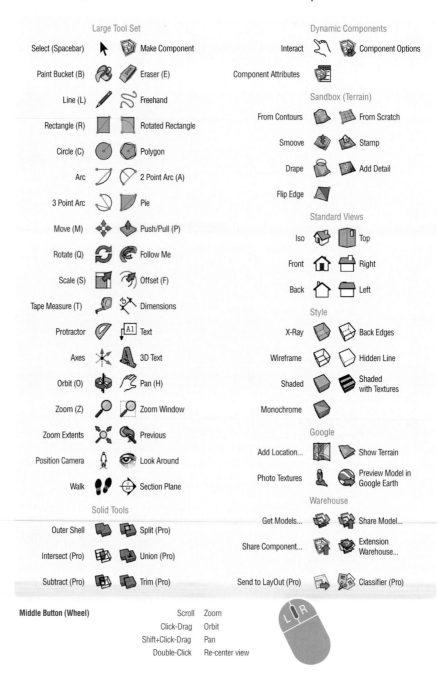

Large Tool Set

Select (Spacebar)		Make Component
Paint Bucket (B)		Eraser (E)
Line (L)		Freehand
Rectangle (R)		Rotated Rectangle
Circle (C)		Polygon
Arc		2 Point Arc (A)
3 Point Arc		Pie
Move (M)		Push/Pull (P)
Rotate (Q)		Follow Me
Scale (S)		Offset (F)
Tape Measure (T)		Dimensions
Protractor		Text
Axes		3D Text
Orbit (O)		Pan (H)
Zoom (Z)		Zoom Window
Zoom Extents		Previous
Position Camera		Look Around
Walk		Section Plane

Solid Tools

Outer Shell		Split (Pro)
Intersect (Pro)		Union (Pro)
Subtract (Pro)		Trim (Pro)

Dynamic Components

Interact		Component Options
Component Attributes		

Sandbox (Terrain)

From Contours		From Scratch
Smoove		Stamp
Drape		Add Detail
Flip Edge		

Standard Views

Iso		Top
Front		Right
Back		Left

Style

X-Ray		Back Edges
Wireframe		Hidden Line
Shaded		Shaded with Textures
Monochrome		

Google

Add Location...		Show Terrain
Photo Textures		Preview Model in Google Earth

Warehouse

Get Models...		Share Model...
Share Component...		Extension Warehouse...
Send to LayOut (Pro)		Classifier (Pro)

Middle Button (Wheel)

Scroll	Zoom
Click-Drag	Orbit
Shift+Click-Drag	Pan
Double-Click	Re-center view

Tool	Operation	Instructions
2 Point Arc (A)	Bulge	specify bulge amount by typing a number and Enter
	Radius	specify radius by typing a number, the R key, and Enter
	Segments	specify number of segments by typing a number, the S key, and Enter
Circle (C)	Shift	lock in current plane
	Radius	specify radius by typing a number and Enter
	Segments	specify number of segments by typing a number, the S key, and Enter
Eraser (E)	Ctrl	soften/smooth (use on edges to make adjacent faces appear curved)
	Shift	hide
	Ctrl+Shift	unsoften/unsmooth
Follow Me	Alt	use face perimeter as extrusion path
	Better Way	first Select path, then choose the Follow Me tool, then click on the face to extrude
Line (L)	Shift	lock in current inference direction
	Arrows	up or down arrow to lock in blue direction; right to lock in red; left to lock in green
	Length	specify length by typing a number and Enter
Look Around	Eye Height	specify eye height by typing a number and Enter
Move (M)	Ctrl	move a copy
	Shift	hold down to lock in current inference direction
	Alt	auto-fold (allow move even if it means adding extra edges and faces)
	Arrows	up or down arrow to lock in blue direction; right to lock in red; left to lock in green
	Distance	specify move distance by typing a number and Enter
	External Copy Array	n copies in a row: move first copy, type a number, the X key, and Enter
	Internal Copy Array	n copies in between: move first copy, type a number, the / key, and Enter
Offset (F)	Double-Click	apply last offset amount to this face
	Distance	specify an offset distance by typing a number and Enter
Orbit (O)	Ctrl	hold down to disable "gravity-weighted" orbiting
	Shift	hold down to activate Pan tool
Paint Bucket (B)	Ctrl	paint all matching adjacent faces
	Shift	paint all matching faces in the model
	Ctrl+Shift	paint all matching faces on the same object
	Alt	hold down to sample material
Push/Pull (P)	Ctrl	push/pull a copy of the face (leaving the original face in place)
	Double-Click	apply last push/pull amount to this face
	Distance	specify a push/pull amount by typing a number and Enter
Rectangle (R)	Dimensions	specify dimensions by typing length, width, and Enter, e.g., 20,40
Rotated Rectangle	Shift	lock in current direction/plane
	Alt	lock drawing plane for first edge (after first click)
	Angle, Dimensions	click to place first two corners, then type angle, width, and Enter, e.g., 90,20
Rotate (Q)	Ctrl	rotate a copy
	Angle	specify an angle by typing a number and Enter
	Slope	specify an angle as a slope by typing a rise, a colon (:), a run, and Enter, e.g., 3:12
Scale (S)	Ctrl	hold down to scale about center
	Shift	hold down to scale uniformly (don't distort)
	Amount	specify a scale factor by typing a number and Enter, e.g., 1.5 = 150%
	Length	specify a scale length by typing a number, a unit type, and Enter, e.g., 10m
Select (Spacebar)	Ctrl	add to selection
	Shift	add/subtract from selection
	Ctrl+Shift	subtract from selection
Tape Measure (T)	Ctrl	create a new Guide
	Arrows	up or down arrow to lock in blue direction; right to lock in red; left to lock in green
	Resize	resize model: measure a distance, type intended size, and Enter
Zoom (Z)	Shift	hold down and click-drag mouse to change Field of View

© 2014 Trimble

(Used by permission of Trimble Navigation Ltd.)

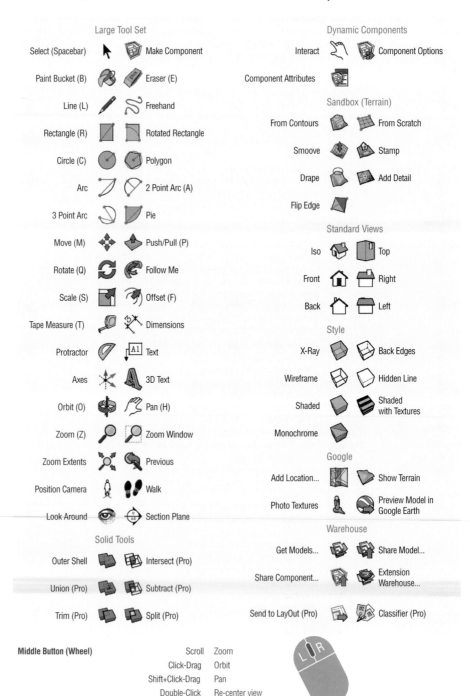

SketchUp Pro Quick Reference Card | Mac OS X

Tool	Operation	Instructions
2 Point Arc (A)	Bulge	specify bulge amount by typing a number and Enter
	Radius	specify radius by typing a number, the R key, and Enter
	Segments	specify number of segments by typing a number, the S key, and Enter
Circle (C)	Shift	lock in current plane
	Radius	specify radius by typing a number and Enter
	Segments	specify number of segments by typing a number, the S key, and Enter
Eraser (E)	Ctrl	soften/smooth (use on edges to make adjacent faces appear curved)
	Shift	hide
	Ctrl+Shift	unsoften/unsmooth
Follow Me	Alt	use face perimeter as extrusion path
	Better Way	first Select path, then choose the Follow Me tool, then click on the face to extrude
Line (L)	Shift	lock in current inference direction
	Arrows	up or down arrow to lock in blue direction; right to lock in red; left to lock in green
	Length	specify length by typing a number and Enter
Look Around	Eye Height	specify eye height by typing a number and Enter
Move (M)	Ctrl	move a copy
	Shift	hold down to lock in current inference direction
	Alt	auto-fold (allow move even if it means adding extra edges and faces)
	Arrows	up or down arrow to lock in blue direction; right to lock in red; left to lock in green
	Distance	specify move distance by typing a number and Enter
	External Copy Array	n copies in a row: move first copy, type a number, the X key, and Enter
	Internal Copy Array	n copies in between: move first copy, type a number, the / key, and Enter
Offset (F)	Double-Click	apply last offset amount to this face
	Distance	specify an offset distance by typing a number and Enter
Orbit (O)	Ctrl	hold down to disable "gravity-weighted" orbiting
	Shift	hold down to activate Pan tool
Paint Bucket (B)	Ctrl	paint all matching adjacent faces
	Shift	paint all matching faces in the model
	Ctrl+Shift	paint all matching faces on the same object
	Alt	hold down to sample material
Push/Pull (P)	Ctrl	push/pull a copy of the face (leaving the original face in place)
	Double-Click	apply last push/pull amount to this face
	Distance	specify a push/pull amount by typing a number and Enter
Rectangle (R)	Dimensions	specify dimensions by typing length, width, and Enter, e.g., 20,40
Rotated Rectangle	Shift	lock in current direction/plane
	Alt	lock drawing plane for first edge (after first click)
	Angle, Dimensions	click to place first two corners, then type angle, width, and Enter, e.g., 90,20
Rotate (Q)	Ctrl	rotate a copy
	Angle	specify an angle by typing a number and Enter
	Slope	specify an angle as a slope by typing a rise, a colon (:), a run, and Enter, e.g., 3:12
Scale (S)	Ctrl	hold down to scale about center
	Shift	hold down to scale uniformly (don't distort)
	Amount	specify a scale factor by typing a number and Enter, e.g., 1.5 = 150%
	Length	specify a scale length by typing a number, a unit type, and Enter, e.g., 10m
Select (Spacebar)	Ctrl	add to selection
	Shift	add/subtract from selection
	Ctrl+Shift	subtract from selection
Tape Measure (T)	Ctrl	create a new Guide
	Arrows	up or down arrow to lock in blue direction; right to lock in red; left to lock in green
	Resize	resize model: measure a distance, type intended size, and Enter
Zoom (Z)	Shift	hold down and click-drag mouse to change Field of View

© 2014 Trimble

(Used by permission of Trimble Navigation Ltd.)

Appendix B
Ruby Class and Method Reference

The following is a selection of the most commonly used Ruby core classes and methods as included with the current version of SketchUp (2015 using Ruby version 2.0.0). *Please note:* Some contain SketchUp-specific methods. Double-colons (::) indicate class methods, and the pound sign (#) indicates instance methods.

```
Array (Parent: Object)
::[] ::try_convert #& #* #+ #- #<< #<=> #== #[] #[]= #assoc #at
#bsearch #clear #collect #collect! #combination #compact #compact!
#concat #count #cross #cycle #delete #delete_at #delete_if #distance
#distance_to_line #distance_to_plane #dot #drop #drop_while #each
#each_index #empty? #eql? #fetch #fill #find_index #first #flatten
#flatten! #frozen? #hash #include? #index #insert #inspect #join
#keep_if #last #length #map #map! #normalize #normalize! #offset
#offset! #on_line? #on_plane? #pack #permutation #pop #product
#project_to_line #project_to_plane #push #rassoc #reject #reject!
#repeated_combination #repeated_permutation #replace #reverse
#reverse! #reverse_each #rindex #rotate #rotate! #sample #select
#select! #shift #shuffle #shuffle! #size #slice #slice! #sort
#sort! #sort_by! #take #take_while #to_a #to_ary #to_s #transform
#transform! #transpose #uniq #uniq! #unshift #values_at #vector_to
#x #x= #y #y= #z #z= #zip #|
```

```
File (Parent: IO)
::absolute_path ::atime ::basename ::blockdev? ::chardev? ::chmod
::chown ::ctime ::delete ::directory? ::dirname ::executable?
::executable_real? ::exist? ::exists? ::expand_path ::extname ::file?
::fnmatch ::fnmatch? ::ftype ::grpowned? ::identical? ::join ::lchmod
::lchown ::link ::lstat ::mtime ::owned? ::path ::pipe? ::readable?
::readable_real? ::readlink ::realdirpath ::realpath ::rename
::setgid? ::setuid? ::size ::size? ::socket? ::split ::stat ::sticky?
::symlink ::symlink? ::truncate ::umask ::unlink ::utime ::world_
readable? ::world_writable? ::writable? ::writable_real? ::zero?
#atime #chmod #chown #ctime #flock #lstat #mtime #path #size
#to_path #truncate
```

Hash (Parent: Object)
::[] ::try_convert #== #[] #[]= #assoc #clear #compare_by_identity
#compare_by_identity? #default #default= #default_proc #default_
proc= #delete #delete_if #each #each_key #each_pair #each_value
#empty? #eql? #fetch #flatten #has_key? #has_value? #hash #include?
#index #inspect #invert #keep_if #key #key? #keys #length #member?
#merge #merge! #rassoc #rehash #reject #reject! #replace #select
#select! #shift #size #store #to_a #to_h #to_hash #to_s #update
#value? #values #values_at

IO (Parent: Object)
::binread ::binwrite ::copy_stream ::for_fd ::foreach ::new ::open
::pipe ::popen ::read ::readlines ::select ::sysopen ::try_convert
::write #<< #advise #autoclose= #autoclose? #binmode #binmode?
#bytes #chars #close #close_on_exec= #close_on_exec? #close_read
#close_write #closed? #codepoints #each #each_byte #each_char
#each_codepoint #each_line #eof #eof? #external_encoding #fcntl
#fdatasync #fileno #flush #fsync #getbyte #getc #gets #inspect
#internal_encoding #ioctl #isatty #lineno #lineno= #lines #pid #pos
#pos= #print #printf #putc #puts #read #read_nonblock #readbyte
#readchar #readline #readlines #readpartial #reopen #rewind #seek
#set_encoding #stat #sync #sync= #sysread #sysseek #syswrite #tell
#to_i #to_io #tty? #ungetbyte #ungetc #write #write_nonblock

Math
::acos ::acosh ::asin ::asinh ::atan ::atan2 ::atanh ::cbrt ::cos
::cosh ::erf ::erfc ::exp ::frexp ::gamma ::hypot ::ldexp ::lgamma
::log ::log10 ::log2 ::sin ::sinh ::sqrt ::tan ::tanh

Numeric (Parent: Object)
#% #+@ #-@ #<=> #abs #abs2 #angle #arg #ceil #cm #coerce #conj
#conjugate #degrees #denominator #div #divmod #eql? #fdiv #feet
#floor #i #imag #imaginary #inch #integer? #km #m #magnitude #mile
#mm #modulo #nonzero? #numerator #phase #polar #quo #radians #real
#real? #rect #rectangular #remainder #round #singleton_method_added
#step #to_c #to_cm #to_feet #to_inch #to_int #to_km #to_l #to_m
#to_mile #to_mm #to_yard #truncate #yard #zero?

String (Parent: Object)
::try_convert #% #* #+ #<< #<=> #== #=== #=~ #[] #[]= #ascii_only?
#b #bytes #bytesize #byteslice #capitalize #capitalize! #casecmp
#center #chars #chomp #chomp! #chop #chop! #chr #clear #codepoints
#concat #count #crypt #delete #delete! #downcase #downcase! #dump

```
#each_byte #each_char #each_codepoint #each_line #empty? #encode
#encode! #encoding #end_with? #eql? #force_encoding #getbyte
#gsub #gsub! #hash #hex #include? #index #insert #inspect #intern
#length #lines #ljust #lstrip #lstrip! #match #next #next! #oct
#ord #partition #prepend #replace #reverse #reverse! #rindex #rjust
#rpartition #rstrip #rstrip! #scan #setbyte #size #slice #slice!
#split #squeeze #squeeze! #start_with? #strip #strip! #sub #sub!
#succ #succ! #sum #swapcase #swapcase! #to_c #to_f #to_i #to_l
#to_r #to_s #to_str #to_sym #tr #tr! #tr_s #tr_s! #unpack #upcase
#upcase! #upto #valid_encoding?
```

```
Time (Parent: Object)
::at ::gm ::httpdate ::iso8601 ::local ::mktime ::now ::parse
::rfc2822 ::rfc822 ::strptime ::utc ::xmlschema ::zone_offset #+
#- #<=> #asctime #ctime #day #dst? #eql? #friday? #getgm #getlocal
#getutc #gmt? #gmt_offset #gmtime #gmtoff #hash #hour #httpdate
#inspect #isdst #iso8601 #localtime #mday #min #mon #monday? #month
#nsec #rfc2822 #rfc822 #round #saturday? #sec #strftime #subsec
#succ #sunday? #thursday? #to_a #to_date #to_datetime #to_f #to_i
#to_r #to_s #to_time #tuesday? #tv_nsec #tv_sec #tv_usec #usec
#utc #utc? #utc_offset #wday #wednesday? #xmlschema #yday #year
#zone
```

Appendix C
SketchUp API Class and Method Reference

This is a complete listing of all API classes and methods (except those core Ruby classes included in Appendix B) as they were included in the version of SketchUp that was current as of this writing (2015).

```
Animation (Parent: Object)
.nextFrame .pause .resume .stop


AppObserver (Parent: Object)
.onNewModel .onOpenModel .onQuit


ArcCurve (Parent: Curve)
.center .end_angle .normal .plane .radius .start_angle .xaxis .yaxis


AttributeDictionaries (Parent: Entity)
.[] .delete .each .length .size


AttributeDictionary (Parent: Entity)
.[] .[]= .delete_key .each .each_key .each_pair .keys .length .name
.size .values


Behavior (Parent: Entity)
.always_face_camera= .always_face_camera? .cuts_opening= .cuts_
opening? .is2d= .is2d? .no_scale_mask= .no_scale_mask? .shadows_
face_sun= .shadows_face_sun? .snapto .snapto=


BoundingBox (Parent: Object)
.add .center .clear .contains? .corner .depth .diagonal .empty?
.height .intersect .max .min .valid? .width
```

```
Camera (Parent: Object)
.aspect_ratio .aspect_ratio= .center_2d .description .description=
.direction .eye .focal_length .focal_length= .fov .fov= .fov_
is_height? .height .height= .image_width .image_width= .is_2d?
.perspective= .perspective? .scale_2d .set .target .up .xaxis .yaxis
.zaxis
```

```
Classification Schema(Parent: Object)
.<=> .name .namespace
```

```
Classifications (Parent: Object)
.[] .each .keys .length .load_schema .size .unload_schema
```

```
Color (Parent: Object)
.alpha .alpha= .blend .blue .blue= .green .green= .red .red= .to_a
.to_i .to_s
```

```
Command (Parent: Object)
.large_icon .large_icon= .menu_text .menu_text= .set_validation_proc
.small_icon .small_icon= .status_bar_text .status_bar_text= .tooltip
.tooltip=
```

```
ComponentDefinition (Parent: Drawingelement)
.<=> .== .add_classification .add_observer .behavior .count_instances
.description .description= .entities .get_classification_value
.group? .guid .hidden? .image? .insertion_point .insertion_point=
.instances .internal? .invalidate_bounds .merge .name .name= .path
.refresh_thumbnail .remove_classification .remove_observer .save_as
.save_thumbnail .set_classification_value
```

```
ComponentInstance (Parent: Drawingelement)
.add_observer .copy .definition .definition= .description
.equals? .explode .glued_to .glued_to= .guid .intersect .locked=
.locked? .make_unique .manifold? .move! .name .name= .outer_shell
.remove_observer .show_differences .split .subtract .transform!
.transformation .transformation= .trim .union .volume
```

```
Console (Parent: Object)
.<< .clear .flush .hide .show .sync .visible? .write
```

```
ConstructionLine (Parent: Drawingelement)
.direction .direction= .end .end= .position .position= .reverse!
.start .start= .stipple .stipple=
```

ConstructionPoint (Parent: Drawingelement)
.position

Curve (Parent: Entity)
.count_edges .each_edge .edges .first_edge .is_polygon? .last_edge
.length .move_vertices .vertices

DefinitionList (Parent: Entity)
.[] .add .add_observer .at .each .length .load .load_from_url
.purge_unused .remove_observer .size .unique_name

DefinitionObserver (Parent: EntityObserver)
.onComponentInstanceAdded .onComponentInstanceRemoved

DefinitionsObserver (Parent: Object)
.onComponentAdded .onComponentPropertiesChanged .onComponentRemoved
.onComponentTypeChanged

Dimension (Parent: Drawingelement)
.add_observer .aligned_text_position .aligned_text_position= .arrow_
type .arrow_type= .has_aligned_text= .has_aligned_text? .plane
.remove_observer .text .text= .text_position .text_position=

DimensionLinear (Parent: Dimension)
.end .end= .offset_vector .offset_vector= .start .start=

DimensionObserver (Parent: Object)
.onTextChanged

DimensionRadial (Parent: Dimension)
.arc_curve .arc_curve= .leader_break_point .leader_break_point=
.leader_points

Drawingelement (Parent: Entity)
.bounds .casts_shadows= .casts_shadows? .erase! .hidden= .hidden?
.last_scaling_factors .layer .layer= .local_transformation .material
.material= .receives_shadows= .receives_shadows? .scaled_size .set_
last_size .unscaled_size .visible= .visible?

```
Edge (Parent: Drawingelement)
.all_connected .common_face .curve .end .explode_curve .faces .find_
faces .length .line .other_vertex .reversed_in? .smooth= .smooth?
.soft= .soft? .split .start .used_by? .vertices
```

```
EdgeUse (Parent: Entity)
.edge .end_vertex_normal .face .loop .next .partners .previous
.reversed? .start_vertex_normal
```

```
Entities (Parent: Object)
.[] .active_section_plane .active_section_plane= .add_3d_text
.add_arc .add_circle .add_cline .add_cpoint .add_curve .add_
dimension_linear .add_dimension_radial .add_edges .add_face .add_
faces_from_mesh .add_group .add_image .add_instance .add_line
.add_ngon .add_observer .add_section_plane .add_text .at .clear!
.each .erase_entities .fill_from_mesh .intersect_with .length
.model .parent .remove_observer .size .transform_by_vectors
.transform_entities
```

```
EntitiesObserver (Parent: Object)
.onElementAdded .onElementModified .onElementRemoved
.onEraseEntities
```

```
Entity (Parent: Object)
.add_observer .attribute_dictionaries .attribute_dictionary .delete_
attribute .deleted? .entityID .get_attribute .inspect .model .parent
.remove_observer .set_attribute .to_s .typename .valid?
```

```
EntityObserver (Parent: Object)
.onChangeEntity .onEraseEntity
```

```
ExtensionsManager (Parent: Object)
.[] .each .keys .length .size
```

```
Face (Parent: Drawingelement)
.all_connected .area .back_material .back_material= .classify_point
.edges .face_flip .followme .get_UVHelper .get_glued_instances .get_
texture_projection .loops .mesh .normal .orient_connected_faces
.orient_connected_faces_LOFT .orient_connected_lathed_faces .outer_
loop .plane .position_material .pushpull .reverse! .set_texture_
projection .vertices
```

```
Geom (Parent: N/A)
.closest_points .fit_plane_to_points .intersect_line_line
.intersect_line_plane .intersect_plane_plane .linear_combination
.point_in_polygon_2D
```

```
Group (Parent: Drawingelement)
.add_observer .copy .definition .description .description=
.entities .equals? .explode .guid .intersect .local_bounds .locked=
.locked? .make_unique .manifold? .move! .name .name= .outer_shell
.remove_observer .show_differences .split .subtract .to_component
.transform! .transformation .transformation= .trim .union .volume
```

```
HLR (Parent: Entity)
.calculate .cleanup .num_faces
```

```
Image (Parent: Drawingelement)
.explode .height .height= .normal .origin .origin= .path .pixelheight
.pixelwidth .size= .transform! .transformation .transformation=
.width .width= .zrotation
```

```
Importer (Parent: Object)
.description .do_options .file_extension .id .load_file .show_
summary .supports_options?
```

```
InputPoint (Parent: Object)
.== .clear .copy! .degrees_of_freedom .depth .display? .draw .edge
.face .pick .position .tooltip .transformation .valid? .vertex
```

```
InstanceObserver (Parent: EntityObserver)
.onClose .onOpen
```

```
LatLong (Parent: Object)
.latitude .longitude .to_a .to_s .to_utm
```

```
Layer (Parent: Entity)
.<=> .== .color .color= .name .name= .page_behavior .page_behavior=
.visible= .visible?
```

```
Layers (Parent: Entity)
.[] .add .add_observer .at .each .length .purge_unused .remove
.remove_observer .size .unique_name
```

```
LayersObserver (Parent: Object)
.onCurrentLayerChanged .onLayerAdded .onLayerChanged
.onLayerRemoved .onRemoveAllLayers
```

```
Length (Parent: Object)
.* .** .+ .- ./ .< .<= .== .=== .> .>= .between? .finite? .hash
.infinite? .inspect .is_a? .kind_of? .nan? .rationalize .to_f .to_i
.to_r .to_s
```

```
Loop (Parent: Entity)
.convex? .edges .edgeuses .face .outer? .vertices
```

```
Material (Parent: Entity)
.<=> .== .alpha .alpha= .color .color= .colorize_deltas .colorize_type
.colorize_type= .display_name .materialType .name .name= .texture
.texture= .use_alpha? .write_thumbnail
```

```
Materials (Parent: Entity)
.[] .add .add_observer .at .current .current= .each .length .purge_
unused .remove .remove_observer .size
```

```
MaterialsObserver (Parent: Object)
.onMaterialAdd .onMaterialChange .onMaterialRefChange
.onMaterialRemove .onMaterialSetCurrent .onMaterialUndoRedo
```

```
Menu (Parent: Object)
.add_item .add_separator .add_submenu .set_validation_proc
```

```
Model (Parent: Object)
.abort_operation .active_entities .active_layer .active_layer=
.active_path .active_view .add_note .add_observer .attribute_
dictionaries .attribute_dictionary .behavior .bounds .classifications
.close .close_active .commit_operation .definitions .delete_attribute
.description .description= .edit_transform .entities .entityID
.export .find_entity_by_id .georeferenced? .get_attribute .get_
datum .get_product_family .guid .import .latlong_to_point .layer
.layers .list_datums .materials .merge .mipmapping= .mipmapping?
.model_attribute_dictionaries .modified? .name .name= .number_faces
.options .pages .path .place_component .point_to_latlong .point_to_
utm .raytest .remove_observer .rendering_options .save .save_copy
.save_thumbnail .select_tool .selection .set_attribute .set_datum
.shadow_info .skpdoc .start_operation .styles .tags .tags= .title
.tools .typename .utm_to_point .valid?
```

```
ModelObserver (Parent: Object)
.onActivePathChanged .onAfterComponentSaveAs
.onBeforeComponentSaveAs .onDeleteModel .onEraseAll .onExplode
.onPlaceComponent .onPostSaveModel .onPreSaveModel .onSaveModel
.onTransactionAbort .onTransactionCommit .onTransactionEmpty
.onTransactionRedo .onTransactionStart .onTransactionUndo
```

```
OptionsManager (Parent: Object)
.[] .each .keys .length .size
```

```
OptionsProvider (Parent: Object)
.[] .[]= .add_observer .each .each_key .each_pair .each_value .has_
key? .key? .keys .length .name .remove_observer .size
```

```
OptionsProviderObserver (Parent: Object)
.onOptionsProviderChanged
```

```
Page (Parent: Entity)
.camera .delay_time .delay_time= .description .description= .hidden_
entities .label .layers .name .name= .rendering_options .set_
visibility .shadow_info .style .transition_time .transition_time=
.update .use_axes= .use_axes? .use_camera= .use_camera? .use_
hidden= .use_hidden? .use_hidden_layers= .use_hidden_layers? .use_
rendering_options= .use_rendering_options? .use_section_planes=
.use_section_planes? .use_shadow_info= .use_shadow_info? .use_
style= .use_style?
```

```
Pages (Parent: Entity)
.[] .add .add_matchphoto_page .add_observer .each .erase .length
.parent .remove_observer .selected_page .selected_page= .show_
frame_at .size .slideshow_time
```

```
PagesObserver (Parent: EntitiesObserver)
.onContentsModified .onElementAdded .onElementRemoved
```

```
PickHelper (Parent: Object)
.all_picked .best_picked .count .depth_at .do_pick .element_at
.init .leaf_at .path_at .pick_segment .picked_edge .picked_element
.picked_face .test_point .transformation_at .view
```

```
Point3d (Parent: Object)
.+ .- .< .== .[] .[]= .clone .distance .distance_to_line .distance_
to_plane .inspect .offset .offset! .on_line? .on_plane? .project_
to_line .project_to_plane .set! .to_a .to_s .transform .transform!
.vector_to .x .x= .y .y= .z .z=
```

```
PolygonMesh (Parent: Object)
.add_point .add_polygon .count_points .count_polygons .normal_
at .point_at .point_index .points .polygon_at .polygon_points_at
.polygons .set_point .set_uv .transform! .uv_at .uvs
```

```
RenderingOptions (Parent: Entity)
.[] .[]= .add_observer .each .each_key .each_pair .keys .length
.remove_observer .size
```

```
RenderingOptionsObserver (Parent: Object)
.onRenderingOptionsChanged
```

```
SectionPlane (Parent: Drawing element)
.activate .active? .get_plane .set_plane
```

```
Selection (Parent: Object)
.[] .add .add_observer .at .clear .contains? .each .empty? .first
.include? .is_curve? .is_surface? .length .model .nitems .remove
.remove_observer .shift .single_object? .size .toggle
```

```
SelectionObserver (Parent: Object)
.onSelectedCleared .onSelectionAdded .onSelectionBulkChange
.onSelectionRemoved
```

```
Set (Parent: Object)
.clear .contains? .delete .each .empty? .include? .insert .length
.size .to_a
```

```
ShadowInfo (Parent: Entity)
.[] .[]= .add_observer .each .each_key .each_pair .keys .length
.remove_observer .size
```

```
ShadowInfoObserver (Parent: Object)
.onShadowInfoChanged
```

Sketchup (Parent: N/A)
.active_model .add_observer .app_name .break_edges= .break_edges?
.create_texture_writer .display_name_from_action .extensions
.face_shadows_drawing_method .face_shadows_drawing_method=
.face_shadows_drawing_method_default .file_new .find_support_
file .find_support_files .fix_shadow_strings= .fix_shadow_strings?
.format_angle .format_area .format_degrees .format_length .full_
detail_render_delay_max .full_detail_render_delay_max= .full_detail_
render_delay_min .full_detail_render_delay_min= .get_datfile_info
.get_i18n_datfile_info .get_locale .get_resource_path .get_
shortcuts .install_from_archive .is_64bit? .is_online .is_pro? .is_
valid_filename? .load .max_draw_time .max_draw_time= .open_file
.os_language .parse_length .platform .plugins_disabled= .plugins_
disabled? .quit .read_default .register_extension .register_importer
.remove_observer .require .required_camera_lod .required_camera_
lod= .required_tool_lod .required_tool_lod= .save_thumbnail .send_
action .set_status_text .status_text= .temp_dir .template .template=
.template_dir .undo .use_lod= .use_lod? .vcb_label= .vcb_value=
.version .version_number .write_default

SketchupExtension (Parent: Object)
.check .copyright .copyright= .creator .creator= .description
.description= .load_on_start? .loaded? .name .name= .new
.registered?
.uncheck .version .version=

Style (Parent: Object)
.description .description= .name .name=

Styles (Parent: Object)
.[] .active_style .active_style_changed .add_style .each .length
.parent .purge_unused .selected_style .selected_style= .size
.update_selected_style

Text (Parent: Drawing element)
.arrow_type .arrow_type= .display_leader= .display_leader? .has_
leader? .leader_type .leader_type= .line_weight .line_weight= .point
.point= .set_text .text .text= .vector .vector=

Texture (Parent: Entity)
.average_color .filename .height .image_height .image_width .size=
.valid? .width

```
TextureWriter (Parent: Object)
.count .filename .handle .length .load .write .write_all
```

```
Tool (Parent: Object)
.activate .deactivate .draw .enableVCB? .getExtents
.getInstructorContentDirectory .getMenu .onCancel .onKeyDown
.onKeyUp
.onLButtonDoubleClick .onLButtonDown .onLButtonUp
.onMButtonDoubleClick
.onMButtonDown .onMButtonUp .onMouseEnter .onMouseLeave
.onMouseMove
.onRButtonDoubleClick .onRButtonDown .onRButtonUp .onReturn
.onSetCursor
.onUserText .resume .suspend
```

```
Toolbar (Parent: Object)
.add_item .add_separator .each .get_last_state .hide .length .name
.restore .show .size .visible?
```

```
Tools (Parent: Object)
.active_tool_id .active_tool_name .add_observer .model .pop_tool
.push_tool .remove_observer
```

```
ToolsObserver (Parent: Object)
.onActiveToolChanged .onToolStateChanged
```

```
Transformation (Parent: Object)
.* .clone .identity? .inverse .invert! .origin .rotx .roty .rotz .set!
.to_a .xaxis .xscale .yaxis .yscale .zaxis .zscale
```

```
UI (Parent: N/A)
.add_context_menu_handler .beep .create_cursor .inputbox
.inspector_names .menu .messagebox .model_info_pages .openURL
.openpanel .play_sound .preferences_pages .refresh_inspectors
.savepanel .select_directory .set_cursor .set_toolbar_visible .show_
inspector .show_model_info .show_preferences .start_timer .stop_
timer .toolbar .toolbar_names .toolbar_visible?
```

```
UTM (Parent: Object)
.to_a .to_latlong .to_s .x .y .zone_letter .zone_number
```

```
UVHelper (Parent: Object)
.get_back_UVQ .get_front_UVQ
```

```
Vector3d (Parent: Object)
.% .* .+ .- .< .== .[] .[]= .angle_between .axes .clone .cross
.dot .inspect .length .length= .normalize .normalize! .parallel?
.perpendicular? .reverse .reverse! .samedirection? .set! .to_a .to_s
.transform .transform! .unitvector? .valid? .x .x= .y .y= .z .z=
```

```
Vertex (Parent: Entity)
.common_edge .curve_interior? .edges .faces .loops .position
.used_by?
```

```
View (Parent: Object)
.add_observer .animation= .average_refresh_time .camera .camera=
.center .corner .draw .draw2d .draw_line .draw_lines .draw_points
.draw_polyline .draw_text .drawing_color= .dynamic= .field_of_
view .field_of_view= .guess_target .inference_locked? .inputpoint
.invalidate .last_refresh_time .line_stipple= .line_width= .lock_
inference .model .pick_helper .pickray .pixels_to_model .refresh
.remove_observer .screen_coords .set_color_from_line .show_frame
.tooltip= .vpheight .vpwidth .write_image .zoom .zoom_extents
```

```
ViewObserver (Parent: Object)
.onViewChanged
```

```
WebDialog (Parent: Object)
.add_action_callback .allow_actions_from_host .bring_to_front
.close .execute_script .get_default_dialog_color .get_element_value
.last_height .last_height= .last_width .last_width= .max_height
.max_height= .max_width .max_width= .min_height .min_height= .min_
width .min_width= .navigation_buttons_enabled= .navigation_buttons_
enabled? .post_url .screen_scale_factor .set_background_color
.set_file .set_full_security .set_html .set_on_close .set_position
.set_size .set_url .show .show_modal .visible? .write_image
```

Appendix D
Creating Your Own Extensions

The following is a basic template to get you started writing your own extensions for SketchUp. Even if you don't want to publish your extension, it might be useful sometimes to install a script you created in SketchUp using this convenient method (e.g., to have it available as a menu item).

RBZ Extension File Structure

The RBZ file format has been available in SketchUp since Maintenance Release 2 of Version 8. Packaging an extension this way allows users to easily install it from SketchUp's Preferences dialog or via the Extension Warehouse (after an approval process).

To enable use of the RBZ-installer functionality, all files that make up an extension must be packaged in one single compressed file (note that the RBZ file format is simply a renamed ZIP file). The following is a minimal, sample file structure. You can add as many other files and folders as necessary for your extension. The entire content of the compressed file (including the folder structure) is copied into SketchUp's Plugins folder on installation (as explained in Chapter 4), and the extension is made available immediately.

```
my_extension_v1.0.0.rbz (compressed file)
  |
  |- my_extension.rb (loader file)
  |
  |- my_extension (directory)
       |
       |- my_extension_file.rb (extension files)
       |- ...
```

Extension Template Structure

It is a good idea to (1) use SketchUp's extension system (so that extensions can be turned on and off by the user) and (2) wrap your extension in its own unique Ruby Module (to prevent conflicts between installed extensions). Following is some sample code to get you started. Replace my with your company name or initials to identify you as the author and keep things clean. In the filenames, extension is a unique name for your extension.

Contents of `/my_extension.rb` (in the main directory):

```
=begin
Copyright 2015, Author
All Rights Reserved
THIS SOFTWARE IS PROVIDED "AS IS" AND WITHOUT ANY EXPRESS OR IMPLIED
WARRANTIES, INCLUDING, WITHOUT LIMITATION, THE IMPLIED WARRANTIES OF
MERCHANTABILITY AND FITNESS FOR A PARTICULAR PURPOSE.
License: AuthorsLicenseStatement
Author: AuthorName
Organization: AuthorAffiliationOrOrganizationIfAny
Name: ScriptName
Version: ScriptVersion
SU Version: MinimumSketchUpVersion
Date: Date
Description: ScriptDescription
Usage: ScriptUsageInstructions
History:
 1.000 YYYY-MM-DD Description of changes
=end

require "sketchup.rb"
require "extensions.rb"

# Load extension
my_extension_loader = SketchupExtension.new "My Extension",
                      "my_extension/my_extension_file.rb"
my_extension_loader.copyright   = "Copyright 2015 by Me"
my_extension_loader.creator     = "Me, myself and I"
my_extension_loader.version     = "1.0.0"
my_extension_loader.description = "Description of this extension."
Sketchup.register_extension my_extension_loader, true
```

Contents of `/my_extension/my_extension_file.rb` (in subfolder):

```
require "sketchup.rb"
# Main code (start module name with capital letter)
module My_extension
  def self.my_method
    # do something...
  end
  def self.my_second_method
    # do something else...
```

```
End
# Create menu items
unless file_loaded?(__FILE__)
  menu = UI.menu("Plugins").add_submenu("My Extension")
  menu.add_item("My Tool 1") { self.my_method }
  menu.add_item("My Tool 2") { self.my_second_method }
  file_loaded(__FILE__)
end
end
```

TIP

If you prefer not to have your extension's source code visible, you can use SketchUp's Scrambler to encrypt Ruby files. You can download it from here:

www.sketchup.com/intl/en/developer/docs/utilities

Appendix E
Dynamic Component Function Reference

The following list includes all of the Dynamic Component functions available in the current SketchUp release (2015):

Predefined Attributes:

```
X, Y, Z, LenX, LenY, LenZ, RotX, RotY, RotZ, Hidden, Copies, Copy, Name,
Summary, Description, Creator, ItemCode, ImageURL, DialogWidth,
DialogHeight, onClick, Material
```

Math Functions:

```
ABS(number), CEILING(number, significance), DEGREES(number), EVEN(number),
EXP(number), FLOOR(number, significance), INT(number), ISEVEN(number),
ISODD(number), LN(number), LOG10(number), ODD(number), PI(),
RADIANS(number), RAND(), RANDBETWEEN(bottom, top), ROUND(number, count),
SIGN(number), SQRT(number)
```

SketchUp Functions:

```
CHOOSE(index,value1,value2, ...valueN), CURRENT("attributeName"), EDGES(),
FACEAREA("materialName"), FACES(), LARGEST(value1,value2,...valueN), LAT(),
LNG(), NEAREST(originalValue, value1, value2, ...valueN),
OPTIONINDEX("attributeName"), OPTIONLABEL("attributeName"),
SMALLEST(value1,value2,...valueN), SUNANGLE(), SUNELEVATION()
```

Text Functions:

```
CHAR(number), CODE(text), CONCATENATE(text1, text2, ...textN),
DOLLAR(value, decimals), EXACT(text1, text2), FIND(findText, text,
position), LEFT(text, number), LEN(text), LOWER(text), MID(text, start,
number), PROPER(text), REPLACE(text, position, length, new), REPT(text,
number), RIGHT(text, number), SUBSTITUTE(text, searchText, newText,
occurrence), TRIM(text), UPPER(text), VALUE(text)
```

Trigonometric Functions:

```
ACOS(number), ACOSH(number), ASIN(number), ASINH(number), ATAN(number),
ATANH(number), COS(number), COSH(number), SIN(number), SINH(number),
TAN(number), TANH(number)
```

Logical Functions:

```
AND(logicalValue1, logicalValue2, ...logicalValueN), FALSE(), IF(test,
thenValue, elseValue), NOT(logicalValue), OR(logicalValue1, logicalValue2,
...logicalValueN), TRUE()
```

OnClick Functions:

```
ALERT("message"), ANIMATE(attribute, state1, state2, ... stateN),
ANIMATESLOW(attribute, state1, state2, ... stateN), ANIMATEFAST(attribute,
state1, state2, ... stateN), ANIMATECUSTOM("attribute", time, easein,
easeout, state1, ...stateN), GOTOSCENE("sceneName," time, easein, easeout),
REDRAW(), SET("attribute", state1, state2, ...stateN)
```

Supported Operators:

```
+ (add), - (subtract), * (multiply), / (divide), < (less than), > (greater
than), <= (less than or equal to), >= (greater than or equal to), =
(equal), () (parentheses), <> (not equal to)
```

Appendix F
Creating a Simple Custom XML Schema

While you most commonly will use a predefined schema such as IFC in your models, some-times it might make sense to create your own schema definition to add another organiza-tional layer into your SketchUp model via its Classifier tools. As discussed in Chapter 3, such a schema—compiled in an XSD or SKC file—can easily be loaded into a SketchUp model and even multiple schemas can be used in the same model.

As an example, paste the following into a text file and save it as my_schema.xsd. Then import it into a SketchUp model using the Classifications tab on the Model Info window and apply it to components using the methods shown in Chapter 3.

```xml
<?xml version="1.0" encoding="utf-8"?>
<xs:schema elementFormDefault="qualified"
xmlns:xs="http://www.w3.org/2001/XMLSchema">
  <xs:element name="Furniture">
    <xs:complexType>
      <xs:sequence>
        <xs:element name="Manufacturer" type="xs:string" />
        <xs:element name="Cost" type="xs:string" />
        <xs:element name="Type" minOccurs="0">
          <xs:simpleType>
            <xs:restriction base="xs:string">
              <xs:enumeration value="Table" />
              <xs:enumeration value="Chair" />
              <xs:enumeration value="Shelving" />
            </xs:restriction>
          </xs:simpleType>
        </xs:element>
      </xs:sequence>
    </xs:complexType>
  </xs:element>
  <xs:element name="Lighting">
  </xs:element>
</xs:schema>
```

This schema allows you to apply two possible classifications to components: *Furniture* and *Lighting*. The *Furniture* class also has properties such as *Cost*—modify as needed. Also check your database software (if you use any) or the web for automatic ways to generate these kinds of XSD schema files.

Index

woodworking, 289
workspace, 15, 19
Wudworx Tools, 139

X

XML, 187
XML schema, custom, 389

XSD, 389

Z

z-fighting, 315
ZIP, 107, 384
Zoom tool, 25
Zorro2, 152